LAROUSSE

FRENCH GRAMMAR

LA

D0412226

Réalisé par/Produced by

LAROUSSE

ANNE-MARIE BRUN

CATHERINE JULIA

ROKHSAREH ASHORI

HUGH O'DONNELL

WENDY LEE

CALLUM BRINES

RUTH NOBLE

LAURENCE LARROCHE

© Larousse, 1995

ISBN 2-03-406005-9

Larousse, Paris

Distributeur au Canada/Sales : Les Éditions Françaises Inc., Boucherville, Québec

ISBN 2-03-430980-4

Diffusion/Sales Larousse plc, London

Printed in France

INTRODUCTION

The **French Grammar** is designed to be the ideal revision aid, thanks to its attractive presentation and handy size. It is aimed at all students of French, whether they are studying at home, secondary school or college.

The hundreds of examples it contains are written in up-to-date, everyday French. In addition, certain design features have been introduced to help you with your studies: *notes* throughout the text explain points of interest to the foreign learner; *pronunciation* difficulties are highlighted and clarified; and special features invite you to *compare* and contrast specific points which may seem initially confusing for the student.

At the end of the book you will find three sections designed for quick reference: a guide to the relationship between spelling and pronunciation, a glossary of technical terms, and a full index. Each chapter begins with a breakdown of all the topics covered within that chapter. Both main headings (e.g. **1. The definite article**) and sub-headings (**1.1 Forms of the definite article**) are numbered for ease of reference. Cross-references which do not mention another chapter (e.g. *see* **3.** or **3.1**) direct you to points of interest or explanations within the same chapter. If another chapter is mentioned by name (e.g. VERBS, **8.4**), you will need to turn to that other chapter to explore your topic further.

CONTENTS

NOUNS

1. Gender
un homme ▲ un village ▲ le Jura
une femme ▲ une ville ▲ la Seine

2. Making a Noun Feminine
un ami → une amie ▲ un acteur → une actrice
un enfant → une enfant

3. Making a Noun Plural
une maison → des maisons ▲ un prix → des prix
un animal → des animaux

A noun is a word which refers to an object, a person, an organization, an animal, an activity or an idea of some kind. Examples of nouns in English are **television, cousin, government, sheep, football, success** and so on. Most nouns can appear in both the singular and the plural.

1. Gender

In English, only nouns referring to living creatures are masculine or feminine. All other nouns referring to objects, institutions, ideas and so on – for example **house, school, justice** – are neuter. In French, however, all nouns are either masculine or feminine. This means that nouns relating to objects, institutions, ideas and so on are also either masculine or feminine. Although all *nouns* are either masculine or feminine in French, there is a small number of neuter *pronouns* (see PRONOUNS, **6.**1).

In French, nouns referring to living creatures usually take the gender corresponding to the sex of the person or animal they are referring to. However, although all inanimate nouns (objects, ideas and the like) are either masculine or feminine, there are no fixed rules for their gender. If you are uncertain, you should look them up in a dictionary.

■ The following nouns are mostly masculine:
– nouns referring to men or male animals:

un homme ▲ un petit garçon ▲ un chien ▲ un chat

NOUNS

There are exceptions, however (*see* **2**.2).
– nouns ending in:

-age	un village ▲ un voyage ▲ un maquillage
	<u>BUT</u> la page ▲ la cage ▲ la nage ▲ la rage
-eau	un bateau ▲ un château
	<u>BUT</u> la peau
-eu	un feu ▲ un cheveu
-ou	le cou ▲ un hibou
-i	un pari ▲ un souci
-ier	un papier ▲ le charcutier
-illon	un grillon ▲ un portillon
-in	un sapin ▲ un requin
	<u>BUT</u> la fin
-isme	le journalisme ▲ le libéralisme
-ment	le lancement ▲ un filament
-oir	le dortoir ▲ le couloir
-on	un dindon ▲ un champion
	<u>BUT</u> la façon

– names of days, seasons and points of the compass:

un dimanche ▲ le printemps ▲ le sud

– names of languages, letters of the alphabet, trees, weights, measurements, metals, numbers and colours:

le latin ▲ le a ▲ un chêne ▲ un kilo ▲ un mètre ▲ du fer ▲ le deux ▲ le bleu
<u>BUT</u> **la vigne ▲ une livre** (a pound)

– nouns ending in a consonant, for example:

un bec ▲ le bord ▲ un bourg ▲ du sel ▲ un prénom ▲ un panier ▲ un prêt ▲ le gaz ▲ un emprunt ▲ du velours ▲ le froid
<u>BUT</u> **la mer**

– names of mountains and rivers:

le Jura ▲ le Caucase ▲ l'Annapurna
le Rhône ▲ le Rhin ▲ le Tibre
<u>BUT</u> **la Seine ▲ la Tamise ▲ la Loire**

> NOTE: French speakers do not consider the names of towns to be
> either masculine or feminine. To avoid a problem a phrase is used
> instead:
>
> **La ville de Nice est belle.**

– compound nouns consisting of a verb and a noun, even when the noun
element is feminine:

un ouvre-bouteille ▲ un tire-bouchon ▲ un aide-mémoire

■ The following nouns are mostly feminine:
– nouns referring to women or female animals:

la reine ▲ une fille ▲ une lionne ▲ une chatte

There are exceptions, however (*see* **2.**2).
– nouns ending in:

-e (unpronounced)	**une fosse ▲ une selle ▲ une couverture ▲**
	la paille ▲ la soie
	<u>BUT</u> **le foie**
-oi	**la loi ▲ la foi ▲ la paroi**
	<u>BUT</u> **le roi ▲ l'effroi** (*m*)
-sion	**la passion ▲ la tension**
-tion	**la communication ▲ la nation**
-té	**la beauté ▲ la santé ▲ la qualité ▲ la liberté**
	<u>BUT</u> **un été**
-gion	**la région ▲ la contagion**
-aison	**la maison ▲ la saison ▲ la raison**
-ance	**la confiance ▲ l'avance** (*f*)
-anse	**la danse ▲ la panse**
-ence	**la cadence ▲ l'impudence** (*f*) **▲ la patience**
	<u>BUT</u> **le silence**
-ense	**la dépense ▲ la défense**

– names of religious festivals and of branches of learning:

la Toussaint ▲ la Saint-Valentin
la littérature ▲ la philosophie ▲ la psychologie
<u>BUT</u> **le droit**

■ Some nouns change their meaning when they change gender. For
example:

un livre **de géographie** ▲ *une livre* **de cerises** (book/pound)
un manche **à balai** ▲ *une manche* **de chemise** (handle/sleeve)
un mode **d'emploi** ▲ *la mode* **parisienne** (method/fashion)
un moule **à tarte** ▲ *une moule* **crue** (baking tin/mussel)
un mousse **travailleur** ▲ *la mousse* **d'un arbre** (cabin boy/moss)
un physique **de déesse** ▲ *la physique* **nucléaire** (physique/physics)
un poste **de vendeur** ▲ **aller à** *la poste* (job/post office)
un petit tour ▲ *la tour* **de Pise** (walk/tower)
un vase **de porcelaine** ▲ *la vase* **de l'étang** (vase/mud)
le voile **des religieuses** ▲ *la voile* **du bateau** (veil/sail)

> NOTE: **Après-midi** can be either masculine or feminine.

2. Making a noun feminine

2.1 The usual rules

■ In most cases, the feminine is indicated by an -e at the end of the noun.

The addition of an **-e** at the end of a word can affect pronunciation:

* The feminine and masculine forms are pronounced in the same way if the masculine form already ends in a vowel:

-é → -ée	un employé [ãplwaje]	→	une employée [ãplwaje]
-i → -ie	un ami [ami]	→	une amie [ami]
-u → -ue	un inconnu [ɛ̃kɔny]	→	une inconnue [ɛ̃kɔny]

* However, if the masculine form ends in a consonant, adding -e changes the pronunciation of the ending of the feminine form:

-d → -de	un marchand [marʃɑ̃]	→	une marchande [marʃɑ̃d]
-t → -te	un candidat [kɑ̃dida]	→	une candidate [kɑ̃didat]
-an → -ane	un gitan [ʒitɑ̃]	→	une gitane [ʒitan]
-ais → -aise	un Français [frɑ̃sɛ]	→	une Française [frɑ̃sɛz]
-ain → -aine	un Mexicain [mɛksikɛ̃]	→	une Mexicaine [mɛksikɛn]
-in → -ine	un cousin [kuzɛ̃]	→	une cousine [kuzin]

2.2 More complex changes

Making a noun feminine can result in a more substantial change to the end of the word.

■ An accent can be added:

-er	→	**-ère**	un boucher	→	une bouchère
-ier	→	**-ière**	un infirmier	→	une infirmière

■ The final consonant can be doubled:

-an	→	**-anne**	un paysan	→	une paysanne
-en	→	**-enne**	un Européen	→	une Européenne
-ien	→	**-ienne**	un chien	→	une chienne
-on	→	**-onne**	un lion	→	une lionne
-t	→	**-tte**	un sot	→	une sotte

■ The ending of the word can be changed more dramatically:

-e	→	**-esse**	un maître	→	une maîtresse
-eau	→	**-elle**	un jumeau	→	une jumelle
-eur	→	**-euse**	un chanteur	→	une chanteuse
-f	→	**-ve**	un veuf	→	une veuve
-teur	→	**-trice**	un acteur	→	une actrice
-x	→	**-se**	un époux	→	une épouse

■ Some masculine nouns already ending in -e do not change in the feminine. Gender is then indicated by the article, the possessive or demonstrative adjective etc. (*see* DETERMINERS). For example:

un/une adulte ▲ un/une acolyte ▲ un/une adversaire ▲ un/une artiste ▲ un/une athlète ▲ le/la chimiste ▲ mon/ma collègue ▲ quel/quelle concierge ▲ cet/cette élève

Remember:

un/une enfant

■ Some nouns are always used with a masculine article, whether they refer to a man or a woman. For example:

un amateur ▲ un architecte ▲ un auteur ▲ un assassin ▲ un chirurgien ▲ un défenseur ▲ un écrivain ▲ un guide ▲ un ingénieur ▲ un juge ▲ un magistrat ▲ un mannequin ▲ un médecin ▲ un professeur ▲ un sculpteur ▲ un témoin

Others, mainly names of animals, are always used with a feminine article:

une grenouille ▲ une souris ▲ une girafe ▲ une victime

> *NOTE*: By using the adjectives **mâle** and **femelle** it is always possible to specify whether you are referring to a male or female animal:
>
> **une souris mâle**

■ In certain cases the masculine and feminine, though based on the same noun, in fact have very different endings. For example:

un compagnon	→	une compagne
un neveu	→	une nièce
un héros	→	une héroïne
un roi	→	une reine
un serviteur	→	une servante
un loup	→	une louve
un copain	→	une copine
un fils	→	une fille

■ Alternatively, as in English, they can be based on quite different nouns. For example:

un homme	→	une femme (man → woman)
un monsieur	→	une dame (gentleman → lady)
un cheval	→	une jument (horse → mare)

3. Making a noun plural

3.1 The usual rules

■ In most cases, the plural of nouns is indicated by adding an -s at the end of the singular form:

une maison	→	des maisons
une pièce	→	des pièces
un lit	→	des lits

> * The **-s** of the plural is not pronounced.
> * The words **œuf, bœuf, os** *do* change their pronunciation in the plural:
>
> | | | |
> |---|---|---|
> | un œuf [œf] | → | des œufs [ø] |
> | un bœuf [bœf] | → | des bœufs [bø] |
> | un os [ɔs] | → | des os [o] |

■ The article, possessive or demonstrative adjective etc. (*see* DETERMINERS) indicates whether the noun is singular or plural. This can be useful if the singular and plural forms of the noun are identical.

3.2 Irregular plurals

■ Nouns ending in -s, -x, -z do not change in the plural:

un fils	→	des fils
un prix	→	des prix
un nez	→	des nez

■ Nouns ending in -eau, -au, -eu form their plural in -eaux, -aux, -eux:

un cadeau	→	des cad*eaux*
un tuyau	→	des tuy*aux*
un cheveu	→	des chev*eux*
<u>BUT</u>		
un pneu	→	des pneus
un bleu	→	des bleus
un landau	→	des landaus

■ Seven words ending in -ou have their plural in -oux:

bijou	→	bij*oux*
caillou	→	caill*oux*
chou	→	ch*oux*
genou	→	gen*oux*
hibou	→	hib*oux*
joujou	→	jouj*oux*
pou	→	p*oux*

The others simply add -s:

fou	→	fous
trou	→	trous
voyou	→	voyous

■ Most nouns ending in -ail form their plural with -aux. For example:

bail	→	b*aux*
corail	→	cor*aux*
émail	→	ém*aux*
soupirail	→	soupir*aux*
vitrail	→	vitr*aux*

However, a few form their plural with -ails. For example:

dé**tail**	→	dé**tails**
por**tail**	→	por**tails**

■ Most nouns ending in -al form their plural with -aux. For example:

anim**al**	→	anim**aux**
chev**al**	→	chev**aux**
journ**al**	→	journ**aux**
hôpit**al**	→	hôpit**aux**

However, a few form their plural with -als. For example:

b**al**	→	b**als**
carnav**al**	→	carnav**als**

3.3 Special cases

■ Some nouns have a somewhat unique plural. For example:

œil	→	yeux
ciel	→	cieux
monsieur	→	messieurs
madame	→	mesdames
mademoiselle	→	mesdemoiselles
bonhomme	→	bonshommes

■ Some nouns exist only in the plural. For example:

annales ▲ environs ▲ frais

■ Some nouns have a different meaning in the singular and plural. For example:

un ciseau de menuisier ▲ *des ciseaux* d'écolier (chisel/scissors)
une lunette astronomique ▲ *des lunettes* de soleil (telescope/glasses)
c'est *un comble* ! ▲ une chambre dans *les combles* (limit/attic)

■ In most cases, family names do not take an -s in the plural:

Nous dînons chez les *Durand* ce soir.

However, family names *do* take an -s when they relate to:
– famous families:

les Bourbons

– paintings or books:

Les deux Renoirs volés à Orsay ont été retrouvés hier.

■ Nouns relating to nationalities take an -s in the plural:

les Espagnols
les Belges

3.4 The plural of compound nouns

The plural of compound nouns depends mostly on the nature of the different words which go together to make them up: nouns and adjectives which are part of a compound noun can take an -s, whereas adverbs, verbs and prepositions usually remain unchanged:

NOUN + NOUN	PL + PL	**des bateaux-mouches ▲ des portes-fenêtres**
ADJECTIVE + ADJECTIVE	PL + PL	**des sourds-muets**
NOUN + ADJECTIVE	PL + PL	**des coffres-forts ▲ des arcs-boutants**
NOUN + PREPOSITION + NOUN	PL + SG	**des chefs-d'œuvre ▲ des arcs-en-ciel**
ADVERB + NOUN	SG + PL	**des haut-parleurs ▲ des non-lieux**
VERB + NOUN	SG + PL	**des tire-bouchons ▲ des ouvre-boîtes**

The plural of compound nouns should usually be checked in a dictionary.

3.5 The plural of foreign words in French

■ Latin words usually take an -s in the plural:

un média	→	des médias
un maximum	→	des maximums
un forum	→	des forums
BUT		
un errat*um*	→	des errat*a*
un stimul*us*	→	des stimul*i*
un post-script*um*	→	des post-script*um*
un curricul*um* vitae	→	des curricul*um* vitae

■ Most words of Italian origin take an -s. For example:

des scénarios ▲ des imprésarios ▲ des allégros ▲ des adagios

The names of pasta can either stay the same in the plural or take an -s:

des spaghetti <u>OR</u> **des spaghettis**

However, some musical terms do not:

des crescendo ▲ des andante

■ English words are more complex:

– Words ending in -ch or -sh add -s or -es in the plural. The pronunciation remains unchanged:

un sandwi*ch*	→	**des sandwi*ch*es**
un sket*ch*	→	**des sket*ch*es**
un fla*sh*	→	**des fla*sh*es**
un mat*ch*	→	**des mat*ch*es**

– Words ending in -y usually simply add an -s instead of changing to -ies:

un dand*y*	→	**des dand*y*s**
<u>BUT</u>		
un whisk*y*	→	**des whisk*ies*** <u>OR</u> **des whisk*y*s**
un hobb*y*	→	**des hobb*ies*** <u>OR</u> **des hobb*y*s**

– The plural of words ending in -man is usually formed in French by adding an -s:

un bar*man*	→	**des bar*man*s**

– Compound nouns of English origin form their plural by adding an -s at the very end:

des best-sellers ▲ des cow-boys ▲ des snack-bars

3.6 Some differences between French and English

■ Some words which are plural in English are singular in French. They mostly relate to items of clothing:

trousers	→	**un pantalon**
shorts	→	**un short**
underpants	→	**un slip**

■ On the other hand, some which are singular in English are plural in French:

furniture	→	**des meubles**
hair	→	**des cheveux**
advice	→	**des conseils**
information	→	**des renseignements**
business	→	**les affaires**

DETERMINERS

1. **The Definite Article**
   le, la, l', les *(the)*

2. **The Indefinite Article**
   un, une, des *(a ▲ some)*

3. **The Partitive Article**
   du, de la, de l', des *(some)*

4. **Possessive Adjectives**
   mon, ma, mes ▲ ton, ta, tes etc. *(my ▲ your etc.)*

5. **Demonstrative Adjectives**
   ce, cette, cet, ces *(this ▲ that etc.)*

6. **Interrogative Adjectives**
   quel ?, quelle ?, quels ?, quelles ? *(which? ▲ what?)*

7. **Indefinite Adjectives**
   quelques ▲ plusieurs ▲ chaque etc. *(some ▲ several ▲ each etc.)*

8. **Numerals**
   un ▲ deux ▲ trois etc. *(one ▲ two ▲ three etc.)*

9. **Cases where the Noun may be used without an Article**

It is quite common in English to use nouns without **the** or **a** in front of them. For example, we can say **music helps you relax, exercise is good for you, I prefer coffee to tea,** and so on. In French, it is very unusual to find nouns without the equivalent of **the** or **a** or some other similar word in front of them. As explained in section 9 of this chapter, this is only possible with certain prepositions and when nouns appear in a list. Normally nouns must have an article, numeral or a particular type of adjective in front of them. The technical name for these usually fairly short words is *determiners*. What they are and how they are used are explained in more detail in this chapter. Determiners (but not numerals) also indicate the gender of the noun in French, as well as showing whether it is singular or plural.

1. The definite article

The definite article in English is the; it remains unchanged whether the noun it precedes is masculine, feminine or neuter, and whether it is singular or plural. In French there are several forms of the definite article, depending on whether the noun is masculine or feminine, singular or plural. It is important to use the form of the definite article which corresponds to the noun in question (masculine singular if the noun is masculine singular, feminine plural if the noun is feminine plural, and so on). It is also important to note that French uses the definite article in a number of situations where it is not used in English.

1.1 Forms of the definite article

	singular		*plural*
	masculine	feminine	
standard	**le**	**la**	**les**
elided	**l'**	**l'**	**–**
with à	**au**	**à la**	**aux**
with de	**du**	**de la**	**des**

Je vais *au* **marché/***à la* **plage/***aux* **États-Unis.**
Je reviens *du* **marché/***de la* **plage/***des* **États-Unis.**

■ Before both masculine and feminine singular nouns beginning with a vowel or a mute **h** (*see* GUIDE TO SPELLING AND PRONUNCIATION) the definite article changes to **l'**:

    *l'***avion** ▲ *l'***homme** ▲ *l'***harmonie**

<u>BUT</u> it does not change if the **h** is aspirate (*see* GUIDE TO SPELLING AND PRONUNCIATION):

    le hérisson ▲ *la* **hache** ▲ *le* **hareng**

■ The definite article **le** combines with the preposition **à** to form **au**, while **les** combines with the same preposition to form **aux**:

    Elle est partie *au* **cinéma.**
    Le footballeur a parlé *aux* **journalistes.**

■ Likewise, the definite article **le** combines with the preposition **de** to form **du**, while **les** combines with the same preposition to form **des**:

    Elle revient *du* **cinéma.**
    Il aime bien parler *des* **vacances.**

16

1.2 Uses of the definite article

■ The following uses of the definite article in French are the same as in English:

– with official titles given to only one person:

le pape ▲ *le* président de la République ▲ *le* Premier ministre

– with well-known objects of which there is only one:

le soleil ▲ *le* monde ▲ *la* tour Eiffel ▲ *la* tour de Pise

– with the names of rivers, mountain ranges and oceans:

la Loire ▲ *le* Danube ▲ *les* Vosges ▲ *le* Pacifique

– with a noun referring to an object which is clearly identified, or which has already been mentioned:

Apporte-moi *le* livre qui est sur *la* table.
Où sont *les* clés ?
Est-ce que vous aurez besoin de *la* voiture ce soir ?
Passe-moi *le* sel, s'il te plaît.

■ The following uses of the definite article in French are different from the way it is used in English, and should be studied with care. The definite article is used:

– with first names or surnames, if the name is preceded by an adjective:

le petit Jean-Pierre
le vieux M. Duval

– with abstract nouns (i.e. nouns relating to ideas, concepts and the like rather than concrete objects – *see also* **2**.2):

la beauté ▲ *la* vieillesse ▲ *le* courage

– with concrete nouns used in a general sense:

Les **fruits sont bons pour la santé.** (i.e. all fruit)
Elle n'aime pas *le* fromage. (i.e. any cheese)
J'aime jouer *au* football. (i.e. football in general, not a specific match)

– with nouns relating to a part of the body (*see* **4**.2)

– with the names of countries and continents:

la France ▲ *le* Portugal ▲ *l'*Asie ▲ *l'*Europe

<u>BUT</u> the definite article is omitted when feminine countries and continents

are preceded by the preposition **en**:

> **Il habite en France.**
> **Nous avons voyagé partout en Europe.**

– with the names of French *départements* (administrative divisions) and of mountain peaks:

> *le* **Lot** ▲ *le* **mont Blanc**

– with the names of languages:

> **Il parle *le* russe.**
> **J'aime *l'*italien.**

<u>BUT</u> the article is not always used in the following expression:

> **Vous parlez très bien français.**

Nor is it used when the language is preceded by the preposition **en**:

> **Le livre était écrit en anglais.**

– with the names of academic subjects:

> **J'aime *les* maths, mais je déteste *la* géographie.**

<u>BUT</u> the definite article is not used if the subject is preceded by the preposition **en**:

> **Marie est très forte en mathématiques.**

– with dates (note that in this case French simply uses the definite article on its own, where in English we would use the preposition **on**):

> **Nous sommes partis *le 24 octobre*.** (on 24 October)

– with the names of the seasons:

> *le* **printemps** ▲ *l'*été ▲ *l'*automne ▲ *l'*hiver

<u>BUT</u> the article is not used after the preposition **en**:

> **Il est parti en vacances *en été*, et il est revenu *en automne*.**

> *NOTE*: **En** is used with **été**, **automne** and **hiver**, but **au** must be used with **printemps**.

– with the names of religious festivals:

> **Ils reviendront pour *la Pentecôte*.**

NOTE:

* **Pâques** never takes an article:

    À Pâques, nous partons en vacances dans le sud.

* **Noël** is normally used without an article:

    J'ai eu des tas de cadeaux à Noël.

COMPARE

* Note the difference between:

    Je vais au théâtre *samedi*. (= this Saturday)
    Elle va à la piscine *le samedi*. (= on Saturdays)
    Nous avons rendez-vous *le 10 janvier*. (= this year)
    Ils se sont rencontrés *un 10 janvier*. (= some time in the past)

* Whereas English uses **a** or **an** in expressions of price or rate, French uses the definite article:

    Ils coûtent vingt francs *le kilo*. (twenty francs a kilo)
    Il roulait à cent kilomètres à *l'heure*. (one hundred kilometres an hour)

2. The indefinite article

The indefinite article in English is a (or an if the word begins with a vowel) in the singular. There is no plural indefinite article in English. In other words, the plural of a book (I bought a book) is simply books (I bought books), though it is also possible to use the word some in such cases (I bought some books), or any in negative sentences (I didn't buy any books). In French, there are forms of the indefinite article for both the singular *and* plural. The plural indefinite article cannot be left out in the same way that some can be omitted in English.

2.1 Forms of the indefinite article

	singular	*plural*
masculine	**un**	**des**
feminine	**une**	**des**

un ananas ▲ *une* pomme ▲ *des* fruits ▲ *des* fraises

■ In a negative sentence (i.e. one containing ne … pas, ne … jamais or something similar – *see* MAKING VERBS NEGATIVE) the indefinite articles un, une and des change to de (d' before a vowel or a mute h):

Ils ont *une* voiture.	→	Ils n'ont pas *de* voiture.
Il y a *des* verres propres.	→	Il n'y a plus *de* verres propres.
Il y a *des* assiettes propres.	→	Il n'y a pas *d'*assiettes propres.

> NOTE: If the negative is simply used to correct a mistaken impression, the indefinite article remains unchanged:
>
> **Il n'a pas acheté *des* pommes, il a acheté des oranges.**
> **Nous n'avons pas envoyé *une* lettre, nous avons envoyé un télégramme.**

■ The plural article des changes to de when an adjective is used *before* a plural noun:

Ils ont *de* grands enfants.

However, des remains unchanged if the adjective is placed *after* the noun:

Ils ont *des* enfants bien élevés.

COMPARE

* When ADJECTIVE + NOUN together make up a particular type of set phrase called a *compound noun,* whose meaning is different from that of each of its elements used separately, the indefinite article **des** remains unchanged:

Il a dit *des gros mots*. (bad language)
Il reste encore *des petits-fours*. (cakes)

* If, however, ADJECTIVE + NOUN do not make up a compound noun, in other words if each element keeps its original meaning, then **des** does change to **de**:

Ils ont *de* gros ennuis.
Il a *de* petits yeux.

2.2 Uses of the indefinite article

■ As in English, the indefinite article is used with a noun which relates to someone or something which is not clearly identified, or which is being mentioned for the first time:

Ils viennent de s'acheter *un* appartement. (They have just bought themselves a flat.)
Il y a *des* soldes en ce moment. (There are sales on at the moment.)
Il y a eu *un* appel pour vous. (There was a call for you.)

■ Unlike English, French requires the indefinite article to be used with abstract nouns if they are described by an adjective:

Il s'est montré d'*un* courage incroyable.
Elle a fait preuve d'*une* patience remarquable.

3. The partitive article

There is no real partitive article in English, though the adjectives **some** or **any** come close to expressing the same idea. In the singular, the partitive article is used in French to express a quantity or amount of, for example, water, bread, butter or anything else which is normally thought of in terms of amounts rather than numbers. (For example, while it would be quite normal to speak of **five films**, it would be very unusual to speak of **five waters**!) These nouns are termed *uncountable*. In the plural, the partitive article is used with all kinds of noun.

The partitive article in French does not say whether the amount involved is small or large. If you want to indicate this, you must use a phrase such as **beaucoup de** or **un peu de**. Unless you indicate the actual amount in this way, the partitive article must *always* be used when referring to quantity or amount in French.

3.1 Forms of the partitive article

	singular		*plural*
	masculine	feminine	
standard	**du**	**de la**	**des**
elided	**de l'**	**de l'**	**–**

Je voudrais *du* lait/*de la* viande/*de l'* eau/*des* bonbons.

■ Before both masculine and feminine singular nouns beginning with a vowel or mute h, de l' is used:

Il a bu *de l'*eau.

■ The partitive article changes to de in a negative sentence:

'Voulez-vous *du* café ?' 'Non merci, je ne prendrai pas *de* café.'
'Voulez-vous *de la* confiture ?' 'Non, je ne veux pas *de* confiture.'
'Il a bu *de l'*eau ?' 'Non, il n'a pas bu *d'*eau, il a bu *du* vin.'

3.2 Uses of the partitive article

■ The partitive article is used to indicate an indefinite quantity or amount:

Il est allé acheter *du* pain.
Il y a *de l'*eau partout dans la salle de bain.
Voulez-vous encore *des* épinards ? (Would you like some more spinach?)

4. Possessive adjectives

As the name suggests, possessive adjectives are used to express possession. We use them to distinguish my money from your money or their money and so on. In English it is the identity of the person(s) possessing the thing(s) in question that is important in choosing which possessive adjective to use. In French, however, the gender of the thing(s) possessed, and whether it is/they are singular or plural, are also important.

4.1 Forms of the possessive adjectives

	singular		*plural*	
	masculine	feminine		
(je)	**mon**	**ma**	**mes**	(my)
(tu)	**ton**	**ta**	**tes**	(your)
(il/elle/on)	**son**	**sa**	**ses**	(his/her/its/one's)
(nous)	**notre**	**notre**	**nos**	(our)
(vous)	**votre**	**votre**	**vos**	(your)
(ils/elles)	**leur**	**leur**	**leurs**	(their)

C'est *mon* vélo.
J'aime bien *ta* nouvelle robe.

Ses enfants s'appellent Nicolas et Marie.
Leur maison est la plus grande du quartier.

■ The form of the possessive adjective must have the same gender as the object which is owned, and must also be singular or plural, depending on whether the object owned is singular or plural:

Il a oublié *sa* montre.
Les enfants ont mis *leurs* chaussures.
N'oubliez pas *votre* maillot.
N'oubliez pas *vos* chaussures.

■ When they are used in front of feminine nouns which begin with a vowel or a mute h (*see* GUIDE TO SPELLING AND PRONUNCIATION), the possessive adjectives ma, ta and sa change to mon, ton and son:

mon histoire ▲ *ton* aventure ▲ *son* idée

4.2 Uses of the possessive adjectives

■ As in English, possessive adjectives are used in French to express ownership of things or relationships between people:

Où sont *mes* lunettes ?
Je vous présente *mon* mari.
C'est *mon* patron.

■ The idea of ownership can be made stronger by using the adjective **propre** (equivalent to English *own*) along with the possessive adjective, or by adding the phrase à + stressed OBJECT PRONOUN after the noun. The pronoun must obviously be the one which corresponds to the person who owns the thing in question (*see* PRONOUNS, **1.**):

Elle a *sa propre* opinion. (her *own* opinion)
Ce n'est pas *son* avis *à lui*. (*his* view)
C'était *son* idée *à elle*, pas la mienne. (*her* idea)

■ There is a difference between French and English when it comes to expressing ideas like they put on their swimming costumes. In English we say swimming costumes in the plural since there is more than one costume involved. In French, however, the noun is put into the singular, since each person puts on only *one* swimming costume:

Les enfants ont mis *leur* maillot.

Another example:

Ils ont tendu *leur* passeport au douanier. (They handed their passports to the customs officer.)

NOTE: In French it is the definite article which is used to refer to parts of the body, not the possessive adjective as in English:

Je me suis coupé *le* doigt.
Il a levé *la* main.
Ils ont levé *la* tête.
Ils se sont lavé *le* visage.
Il s'est cassé *la* jambe.

BUT the possessive adjective is used if the part of the body is the subject of the verb:

Ses yeux étaient grands ouverts.
Sa tête reposait sur le bras du fauteuil.

5. Demonstrative adjectives

The demonstrative adjectives in English are this and that in the singular, and these and those in the plural. They are used to point to or to single out one object or group of objects from all others of its kind.

5.1 Forms of the demonstrative adjectives

	singular	*plural*
masculine	ce	ces
feminine	cette	ces

ce village ▲ *cette* table ▲ *ces* haricots verts ▲ *ces* pommes

■ When used before a masculine noun which begins with a vowel or a mute h (*see* GUIDE TO SPELLING AND PRONUNCIATION), the adjective ce changes to cet:

cet enfant ▲ *cet* homme

5.2 Uses of the demonstrative adjectives

■ The demonstrative adjectives given above usually mean *this*, though they can also mean *that*, depending on how and when they are used and on any gestures which accompany them. As in English, they are used to:

– single out or point to someone or something which can be seen:

> *Ce* livre est à moi.
> Je voudrais *ce* gâteau s'il vous plaît.
> Combien coûte *ce* fauteuil ?

– single out a person or thing which has already been mentioned:

> Tu connais leur fille ? *Cette* petite est adorable.

– introduce a topic you are going to give more information about:

> Elle m'a donné *cette* adresse : 10, rue de Rivoli, 75001 Paris.

■ When it becomes important to distinguish between the notions of *this* and *that*, longer forms of the demonstrative adjectives can be used in French:

– ce ...-ci, cet ...-ci, cette ...-ci, ces ...-ci are used for things which are close in time or space, and are therefore the equivalent of *this* or *these*:

> Je préfère *ce* gâteau-*ci*.

– ce ...-là, cet ...-là, cette ...-là, ces ...-là are used for objects which are further away in time or space, and are therefore the equivalent of *that* or *those*:

> *Cette* montagne-*là* est le mont Blanc.
> En *ce* temps-*là*, on voyageait à cheval.

> NOTE: Even so, the distinction between ce ...-ci and ce ...-là is not always absolutely clear, and ce ...-là is often used to refer to things which are actually quite close. In such cases, things which are further away are referred to using ce ... là-bas (that one over there):
>
> Ce n'est pas *ce livre-là* qu'il me faut, passe-moi *cet autre là-bas*.

6. Interrogative adjectives

The interrogative adjectives are used in questions when we want an object or group of objects to be identified more clearly. The equivalent terms in

English are which or what, for example which person?, what car?

6.1 Forms of the interrogative adjective

	singular	*plural*
masculine	**quel**	**quels**
feminine	**quelle**	**quelles**

■ Like all other adjectives in French, interrogative adjectives must agree in gender and number with the noun they relate to:

> *Quel* **film as-tu vu ?**
> *Quelle* **heure est-il ?**

6.2 Uses of the interrogative adjective

■ The interrogative adjectives used in direct questions are also used in indirect questions (*see* DIFFERENT KINDS OF SENTENCE, **4.**):

> **Je me demande** *quelle* **heure il est.**

■ As in English, French interrogative adjectives can also be used in exclamations to express surprise, indignation, admiration and the like. Remember that the indefinite article is *not* used in French in such cases (*see* DIFFERENT KINDS OF SENTENCE, **3.**):

> *Quel* **idiot !** (What an idiot!)
> *Quelle* **surprise !** (What a surprise!)

7. Indefinite adjectives

7.1 Forms of the indefinite adjectives

There are many different kinds of indefinite adjective. Like all other adjectives in French, they agree in gender and number with the noun they describe. Sometimes this type of adjective is called a *determiner* or *quantifier*.

7.2 Uses of the indefinite adjectives

■ The indefinite adjectives are not preceded by a partitive article (*see* **3.**) in the plural.

■ Here are some indefinite adjectives consisting of one word which are used to identify people or things:

– Quelque (**mfpl** *quelques*)

In the singular, quelque means some ... or other. It is only used in the singular in rather formal French:

Il a été retardé par *quelque* **problème grave.** (He has been held up by some serious problem.)

In the plural it means a certain number of, a small number of, and translates into English as some:

Il a *quelques* **propositions à te faire.** (He has some suggestions to make to you.)

Il reste encore *quelques* **étudiants dans la salle.** (There are still some students in the room.)

– Plusieurs

Plusieurs has the same form for both masculine and feminine. It is used only in the plural, and means several:

Plusieurs **personnes sont venues ce soir.**

Il a fait *plusieurs* **essais avant de réussir.**

– Chaque

Chaque is always used in the singular, and has the same form for both masculine and feminine. It means each or every:

Il faut se laver les mains avant *chaque* **repas.**

Chaque **fois que je sors, il pleut.**

– Tout (f *toute,* mpl *tous,* fpl *toutes*)

When used without an article in the singular, tout means any or every. This usage is rather formal:

Pour *tout* **achat supérieur à cent francs, il vous sera offert un livre.**

Toute **personne désirant un renseignement peut se rendre au bureau information.**

When it is followed by a determiner, tout means all:

Il a perdu *tout* **son argent.**

Il a réuni *tous* **ses enfants autour de lui.**

When tout is used in the plural before a definite article, however, the best translation into English is often every, and the noun sounds more natural in the singular:

Il sort *tous* les jours à la même heure. (every day)

– Quelconque

Quelconque does not change its form for the feminine, and is usually used in the singular. When placed before the noun, **quelconque** means any … at all or any … whatsoever. When placed after the noun, it means some … or other. In both cases it is preceded by the indefinite article:

Appuyez sur une *quelconque* touche pour commencer. (Press any key to start.)

Il a dû sortir pour une raison *quelconque*. (He had to go out for some reason or other.)

- Tel (f *telle*, mpl *tels*, fpl *telles*)

Tel in the singular means such-and-such a:

Il aurait dû lui donner rendez-vous *tel* jour à *telle* heure.

Il est impossible d'utiliser *telle* méthode ou *telle* autre.

When used with the indefinite article, tel means such a:

Je ne travaillerais jamais avec un *tel* homme.

In this sense tel can be used in the plural. In such cases it is preceded by the indefinite article de:

Il est prudent d'éviter de *telles* personnes.

- Même (mfpl *mêmes*)

When it comes between the determiner and the noun, même means same:

On restera dans les *mêmes* locaux. (We'll stay in the same premises.)

C'est le *même* type de travail qu'il faut réaliser.

– Autre (mfpl *autres*)

Autre means other, and is placed between the indefinite article and the noun:

Je prendrais bien un *autre* verre.

Vous feriez mieux de revenir un *autre* jour.

Note that in the plural it is preceded by the indefinite article d':

en *d'autres* mots (in other words)

J'en ai vu *d'autres* ailleurs.

NOTE: The adjectives **certain**, **différent** and **divers** can also function as *indefinite* adjectives. When used in this way, they are not preceded by an indefinite article in the plural:

* *Certain* (f *certaine,* mpl *certains,* fpl *certaines*)

When **certain** is used on its own before the noun or together with the indefinite article **un**, it behaves like an indefinite adjective. When used with **un** in the singular, it means the same as **certain** in English. In the plural its meaning is usually **some**:

> Il y avait un *certain* nombre de personnes.
> *Certains* enfants marchent dès l'âge d'un an.

* *Différents* (fpl *différentes*)

Différents is always used in the plural when it is an indefinite adjective, and means **various**:

> *Différentes* personnes me l'ont demandé.
> Il y a *différentes* façons de vivre.

* *Divers* (fpl *diverses*)

Divers is always used in the plural and also means **various**:

> *Divers* moyens ont été employés.
> *Diverses* raisons l'ont poussé à partir.

■ Here are some indefinite adjectives consisting of more than one word which are also used to identify people or things:

– *N'importe quel* (f *n'importe quelle,* mpl *n'importe quels,* fpl *n'importe quelles*)

N'importe quel means **any … at all**, **any … whatsoever**, and is placed before the noun. The form of **quel** must agree in gender and number with the noun in question:

> **Prenez** *n'importe quelle* **assiette.** (Take any plate.)
> *N'importe quels* **locaux lui conviendraient.** (Any premises would suit him.)

– There are two indefinite adjectives which express the idea of **none** or **not … any**:

– *Aucun* (f *aucune*)

Aucun is always used in the singular, even when the English

translation is sometimes in the plural. **Ne** is always placed before the verb in a sentence containing **aucun**:

Il *n'*a pu prendre *aucune* décision. (any decisions)
***Aucune* décision *n'*a été prise.** (no decision)
Tu *n'*as plus *aucun* droit. (no right)

– *Nul* (f *nulle*)
Nul appears only in the singular, and is only used in formal French. Ne is always placed before the verb in the sentence:

Il *n'*avait *nulle* envie d'y aller.

8. Numerals

■ There are two kinds of number:
– cardinal numbers, which are used for counting: un, deux, trois …
– ordinal numbers, which are used for placing things in order: le premier, le deuxième, le troisième …

■ The cardinal numbers are:

0	zéro	21	vingt et un	110	cent dix
1	un	22	vingt-deux	120	cent vingt
2	deux	23	vingt-trois	121	cent vingt et un
3	trois	30	trente	200	deux cents
4	quatre	40	quarante	300	trois cents
5	cinq	50	cinquante	900	neuf cents
6	six	60	soixante	1 000	mille
7	sept	70	soixante-dix	1 001	mille un
8	huit	71	soixante et onze	1 002	mille deux
9	neuf	72	soixante-douze	1 100	mille cent,
10	dix	73	soixante-treize		onze cents
11	onze	80	quatre-vingts	1 200	mille deux cents
12	douze	81	quatre-vingt-un	1 900	mille neuf cents
13	treize	82	quatre-vingt-deux	2 000	deux mille
14	quatorze	90	quatre-vingt-dix	3 000	trois mille
15	quinze	91	quatre-vingt-onze	1 000 000	un million
16	seize	92	quatre-vingt-douze	2 000 000	deux millions
17	dix-sept	93	quatre-vingt-treize	1 000 000 000	un
18	dix-huit	100	cent	milliard	
19	dix-neuf	101	cent un		
20	vingt	102	cent deux		

NOTE:

* **Mille** never adds an **-s** in the plural.
* **Quatre-vingt** takes an **-s** when it comes at the end of a number:

  quatre-vingts ▲ deux cent quatre-vingts

Cent also adds an **-s** if it refers to two hundred or more and comes at the end of a number:

  cinq cents ▲ trois mille sept cents

However, when **cent** and **vingt** do not come at the end of the number, they do not add **-s** in the plural:

  trois cent vingt-cinq ▲ quatre-vingt-huit

* Both **million** and **milliard** are always followed by **de** if they are used with another noun. Unlike their English equivalents, they also add an **-s** when they are preceded by a plural number:

  Il y a deux millions _de_ chômeurs.
  Le coût total était de trois milliards _de_ francs.

■ As in English, cardinal numbers are placed _between_ the determiner (definite article, demonstrative or possessive adjective) and the noun they go with:

  Je voudrais _ces trois_ tartelettes.
  Ses deux enfants sont jumeaux.

■ However, contrary to English, cardinal numbers are placed _in front of_ an indefinite adjective or the adjectives **premiers** or **derniers**:

  les _trois premiers_
  les _deux derniers_
  Je voudrais _quatre autres_ croissants, s'il vous plaît.

■ Ordinal numbers are formed by adding -ième to the end of the cardinal number:

  deuxième ▲ sixième ▲ dixième

If the cardinal number ends in -e, this is dropped:

  onzième ▲ seizième

There are minor spelling changes in the case of **cinq** and **neuf**:

> **cinquième** ▲ **neuvième**

Note also that the French for first is **premier** (*f* **première**). Twenty-first, thirty-first etc., however, are translated as **vingt et unième**, **trente et unième** etc.

> *NOTE:* Remember that cardinal numbers are used in dates in French:
>
> > **le *dix* janvier** (the tenth of January)

■ Note the existence in French of approximate numbers, which are formed by adding -aine to the end of the precise number (deleting the final -e of the precise number if there is one):

> **une vingtaine** (about twenty)
> **une cinquantaine** (about fifty)
> **une centaine** (about one hundred)

These forms are followed by de if they are used with another noun:

> **une trentaine *d*'enfants**

Some of these approximate numbers have now acquired quite specific meanings:

> **une douzaine** (= a dozen)
> **une quinzaine** (= a fortnight)

■ Contrary to English, French uses a comma to mark the decimal part of a number:

> **6,5** (six virgule cinq)
> **12,9** (douze virgule neuf)
> **8,34** (huit virgule trente-quatre)
> **9,3468** (neuf virgule trois mille quatre cent soixante-huit)

9. Cases where the noun may be used without an article

■ In French no article is used in front of:
– nouns indicating profession when they follow a form of the verb être

which is not preceded by ce or c':

Il est professeur.
Elle est médecin.

NOTE:
* In the case of nouns relating to profession, an article *is* used if the noun is described in some way. The article used is the same as it would be in English:

   M. Laval était *un* très bon professeur.
   M. Laval est *le* professeur de français.

* Both the definite and the indefinite article are also used if the verb être is introduced by ce or c':

   Ce sont *des* professeurs.
   C'est *l'*avocat qui les a défendus.

– nouns used in a list:

   L'examen portait sur des matières scientifiques : mathématiques,
   physique, chimie, biologie.

– a noun used to provide additional information about another noun which appears immediately before it:

   M. Durand, ancien professeur ... (a former teacher)
   Paris, capitale de la France ... (the capital of France)

– abstract nouns which immediately follow the preposition **avec**, as long as they are not described in any way:

   Ils avançaient *avec* difficulté.

NOTE:
* The article is used after **avec** if the noun is described in some way:

   Il a réussi à le faire *avec un* grand effort.
   Il y est arrivé *avec une* grande aisance.

* The partitive article (*see* 3.) is also normally used when uncountable nouns (those which cannot be preceded by a numeral, e.g. **water, flour, furniture**) are used after **avec**:

   Ce plat se fait *avec du* lait.

– abstract and concrete nouns which immediately follow the preposition
sans, as long as they are not described in any way:

> **On peut entrer de ce côté-ci** *sans* **difficulté.**
> **Il est impossible d'y aller** *sans* **voiture.**

NOTE: If the noun after **sans** is described in some way, the article
must be used:

> **Il l'a fait** *sans l'*aide de personne.

– nouns immediately following the conjunction **comme**:

> **Il travaillait** *comme* **professeur.**
> **Je te parle** *comme* **ami.**

– nouns used in expressions of quantity, in expressions indicating what
something is made of, is full of or consists of, or what it is intended for:

> **beaucoup** *d'*argent
> **une table** *de* **bois**
> **un couteau** *en* **acier**
> **un verre** *de* **vin**
> **une leçon** *de* **géographie**
> **une tasse** *à* **thé**

– nouns used together with verbs in certain set phrases:

> **avoir froid** ▲ **avoir faim** ▲ **avoir confiance en** ▲ **avoir envie de** ▲ **avoir**
> **besoin de** ▲ **perdre courage** ▲ **tenir tête à** ▲ **reprendre haleine** ▲
> **rendre service à** ▲ **faire peur à**

ADJECTIVES

1. **Making an Adjective Feminine**
   bleu → bleue ▲ ancien → ancienne ▲ doux → douce

2. **Making an Adjective Plural**
   bleu → bleus ▲ beau → beaux ▲ amical → amicaux

3. **Agreement of Adjective and Noun**
   une journée pluvieuse ▲ de grands enfants

4. **The Position of the Adjective**
   une robe jaune ▲ un mauvais film ▲ un vieux livre relié

5. **The Comparative and Superlative of Adjectives**

   plus jeune que lui ▲ moins cher que l'avion ▲ aussi froid qu'hier
   le plus grand de la classe

Adjectives are used to describe nouns. The ending of the adjective changes according to whether the noun it is describing is masculine or feminine, and according to whether it is singular or plural.

   un petit garçon ▲ une petite fille
   des petits garçons ▲ des petites filles

1. Making an adjective feminine

1.1 The usual rules

■ In most cases, an adjective is made feminine by adding an -e at the end:

   un ciel bleu ▲ une mer bleue

■ If the masculine form of the adjective already ends in an -e, the masculine and feminine forms are the same. For example:

   agréable ▲ facile ▲ difficile ▲ jeune ▲ propre ▲ utile ▲ large ▲ honnête ▲ solide ▲ jaune ▲ aimable ▲ rouge

■ Some adjectives not ending in -e also have only one form for both masculine and feminine. For example:

un vêtement *chic* ▲ une allure *chic*
un comportement *snob* ▲ une attitude *snob*
un pull *angora* ▲ une écharpe *angora*
un tissu *marron* ▲ une étoffe *marron*

---

* Adding an -e does not change the pronunciation of the word in the following cases:

-al	→	-ale	un air jovial [ʒɔvjal] ▲ une attitude joviale [ʒɔvjal]
-é	→	-ée	un gamin futé [fyte] ▲ une idée futée [fyte]
-eul	→	-eule	un seul instant [sœl] ▲ une seule erreur [sœl]
-i	→	-ie	un joli chaton [ʒɔli] ▲ une jolie fille [ʒɔli]
-il	→	-ile	un parfum subtil [syptil] ▲ une stratégie subtile [syptil]
-ol	→	-ole	un châle espagnol [ɛspaɲɔl] ▲ une chanson espagnole [ɛspaɲɔl]
-r	→	-re	un matériau dur [dyr] ▲ une substance dure [dyr]
-u	→	-ue	un bébé tout nu [ny] ▲ une femme nue [ny]

* Adding an -e *does* change the pronunciation of the word in the following cases:

-ain	→	-aine	un geste humain [ymɛ̃] ▲ la race humaine [ymɛn]
-an	→	-ane	un plat catalan [katalɑ̃] ▲ la région catalane [katalan]
-ein	→	-eine	un verre plein [plɛ̃] ▲ une salle pleine [plɛn]
-in	→	-ine	un air coquin [kɔkɛ̃] ▲ une mine coquine [kɔkin]
-un	→	-une	un cheveu brun [brœ̃] ▲ une bière brune [bryn]
-d	→	-de	un vent chaud [ʃo] ▲ une nuit chaude [ʃod]
-s	→	-se	un manteau gris [gri] ▲ une souris grise [griz]
-t	→	-te	un parfum trop fort [fɔr] ▲ une voix forte [fɔrt]

1.2 More complex changes

Making an adjective feminine can result in a more substantial change to the end of the word.

■ An accent or diaeresis (¨) can be added:

-er	→	-ère	un vêtement léger ▲ une veste légère
-u	→	-uë	un son aigu ▲ une voix aiguë
			un discours ambigu ▲ une attitude ambiguë

■ The final consonant before the -e can be doubled.

---

* Sometimes doubling the consonant and adding an **-e** does not change the pronunciation:

-el → **-elle** un problème individuel [ɛ̃dividɥɛl] ▲ une
décision individuelle [ɛ̃dividɥɛl]

-eil → **-eille** un rouge vermeil [vɛrmɛj] ▲ une étoffe vermeille [vɛrmɛj]

-et → **-ette** un intérieur net [nɛt] ▲ une peau nette [nɛt]

-ul → **-ulle** un résultat nul [nyl] ▲ une note nulle [nyl]

* Sometimes the pronunciation does change as a result:

-en → **-enne** un pays européen [ørɔpeɛ̃] ▲ la monnaie
européenne [ørɔpeɛn]

-et → **-ette** mon frère cadet [kadɛ] ▲ ma sœur cadette [kadɛt]

-ien → **-ienne** un vêtement ancien [ɑ̃sjɛ̃] ▲ une maison
ancienne [ɑ̃sjɛn]

-on → **-onne** un marin breton [brɔtɔ̃] ▲ une galette
bretonne [brɔtɔn]

-ot → **-otte** un mobilier vieillot [vjejo] ▲ une décoration
vieillotte [vjejɔt]

-s → **-sse** un gros colis [gro] ▲ une grosse valise [gros]

NOTE: Some adjectives ending in **-et** in the masculine do not double their final consonant in the feminine; instead they end in **-ète**. For example:

comple*t*	→	comp**lète**
inquie*t*	→	inqu**iète**
concre*t*	→	conc**rète**
discre*t*	→	disc**rète**

■ The ending of the adjective is changed substantially:

-c	→	**-che**	un gilet blanc ▲ une robe blanche
-c	→	**-que**	un jardin public ▲ une annonce publique
-eau	→	**-elle**	un frère jumeau ▲ une sœur jumelle

-eur	→	-euse	un air moqueur ▲ une remarque moqueuse
-eux	→	-euse	un événement heureux ▲ une heureuse nouvelle
-f	→	-ve	un appartement neuf ▲ une voiture neuve
-g	→	-gue	un manteau long ▲ une jupe longue
-ou	→	-olle	un objet mou ▲ une substance molle
-teur	→	-teuse	un discours flatteur ▲ des paroles flatteuses
-teur	→	-trice	un air dominateur ▲ une mère dominatrice
-x	→	-se	un mari jaloux ▲ une femme jalouse
-x	→	-sse	des cheveux roux ▲ une perruque rousse
-x	→	-ce	un visage doux ▲ une peau douce

NOTE:

un *gentil* sourire ▲ une *gentille* attention
un *vieux* manteau ▲ une *vieille* voiture
un port *grec* ▲ une ville *grecque*
un mal *bénin* ▲ une maladie *bénigne*

■ These ten adjectives ending in -eur have their feminine in -eure:

antérieur ▲ extérieur ▲ inférieur ▲ intérieur ▲ majeur ▲ meilleur ▲
mineur ▲ postérieur ▲ supérieur ▲ ultérieur

■ Some very common adjectives have more than one masculine form. The adjectives beau, fou, nouveau and vieux become bel, fol, nouvel and vieil when they come before a masculine noun beginning with a vowel or a mute h (*see* GUIDE TO SPELLING AND PRONUNCIATION):

un *bel* enfant
un *fol* espoir (= formal usage)
un *nouvel* habit
un *vieil* homme

2. Making an adjective plural

■ In most cases, an adjective is made plural by adding -s:

un pull bleu	→	des pulls bleus
une fillette coquine	→	des fillettes coquines
une dictée difficile	→	des dictées difficiles

■ Adjectives which already end with -x or -s in the singular do not change in the masculine plural:

un élève sérieu*x*	→	des élèves sérieu*x*
un mur épai*s*	→	des murs épai*s*

■ Adjectives which end in -eau in the singular have -eaux as their plural ending:

un b*eau* paysage	→	de b*eaux* paysages

■ Adjectives which end in -al take the ending -aux in the masculine plural:

un sourire amic*al*	→	des sourires amic*aux*
le personnage princip*al*	→	les personnages princip*aux*

There are, however, a few exceptions:

un coup fat*al*	→	des coups fat*als*

NOTE: Most adjectives of colour follow the usual rules for forming the plural:

des chemises **vertes/blanches/bleues/roses/mauves/violettes**

However, compound adjectives of colour (i.e. those consisting of more than one word) do not change either in the feminine or in the plural:

des habits *bleu marine/vert olive/gris clair*

Certain adjectives of colour which were originally nouns do not change either. For example:

de la peinture *ivoire* ▲ un ton *ivoire* ▲ des murs *ivoire*

The same goes for **citron**, **crème** and **marron**.

3. Agreement of adjective and noun

■ When we say that the adjective agrees in number and gender with the noun(s) it describes, we mean that if the noun is masculine singular, then the adjective must also be masculine singular; if the noun is feminine plural, then the adjective must also be feminine plural, and so on:

La journée s'annonce *pluvieuse*.
Les enfants sont *grands* maintenant.

■ If an adjective describes more than one noun of the same gender, it is put into the plural of that gender:

Sa gentillesse et sa bonne volonté sont *évidentes*.

■ When an adjective describes more than one noun whose genders are different from each other, it is always put into the masculine plural:

> **La façade et le portail sont** *blancs*.
> **La façade et les volets sont** *blancs*.

4. The position of the adjective

An adjective can be used immediately beside a noun (**une maison blanche**), or it can be separated from the noun by a verb (**la maison est blanche**). When the adjective is used with the noun it is normally placed after it. None the less it can sometimes appear before the noun. The following are the most common rules:

■ The following adjectives are always placed after the noun:

– adjectives indicating shape, colour, nationality or religion:

> **un panneau** *triangulaire*
> **une robe** *jaune*
> **le gouvernement** *canadien*
> **une église** *catholique*

– adjectives which are in fact parts of verbs (present participle, past participle):

> **un intérieur** *soigné*
> **un enfant** *obéissant*

– adjectives which are followed by a phrase beginning with a preposition:

> **un exercice** *difficile* **à comprendre**
> **un visage** *rayonnant* **de joie**

■ Certain short and very common adjectives are mostly placed before the noun, for example:

> **bon** ▲ **beau** ▲ **dernier** ▲ **gros** ▲ **jeune** ▲ **joli** ▲ **long** ▲ **mauvais** ▲ **petit** ▲ **premier** ▲ **vieux** ▲ **haut** ▲ **nouveau** ▲ **vrai**

■ When a noun is described by two or more adjectives, these are placed before or after the noun according to the rules given above:

> **un** *vieux* **livre** *relié*
> **Il a une** *nouvelle* **voiture** *rouge*.

If both are placed after the noun they are joined by **et**:

> **des rues silencieuses** *et* **désertes**

> NOTE: Certain adjectives change their meaning depending on
> whether they are placed before or after the noun:
>
> **un meuble *ancien*** (= an old piece of furniture) ▲ **mon *ancien*
> appartement** (= my old flat, i.e. the one I used to have)
> **un homme *grand*** (= a tall man) ▲ **un *grand* homme** (= a great man)
> **une *seule* personne** (= a single person, i.e. just one person) ▲ **une
> personne *seule*** (= a person on his or her own)
> **un *pauvre* homme** (= an unfortunate man) ▲ **un homme *pauvre***
> (= a man who is not rich)
> **ce sont ses *propres* paroles** (= his very words) ▲ **des draps *propres***
> (= clean sheets)

■ An adjective can also be linked to a noun by a verb (être, devenir,
paraître, sembler, demeurer, passer pour, avoir l'air).

La journée est ensoleillée.
Elle devient gentille.
Il semble inquiet.
Ça me paraît évident.

5. The comparative and superlative of adjectives

5.1 Forming the comparative of superiority, inferiority and equality

■ The comparative of superiority (i.e. something is bigger, heavier, more
interesting etc. than something else) is formed as follows:

plus + ADJECTIVE + **que**

Elle est beaucoup *plus jeune que* lui.
C'était *plus intéressant que* la dernière fois.

■ The comparative of inferiority (i.e. something is less expensive, less
exciting etc. than something else) is formed as follows:

moins + ADJECTIVE + **que**

C'est *moins cher que* l'avion.
Il est *moins disponible qu'*elle.

■ The comparative of equality (i.e. something is as good, as awful etc. as something else) is formed as follows:

> **aussi** + ADJECTIVE + **que**
> Il fait *aussi froid qu'*hier.
> Elle est *aussi grande que* lui.

5.2 Forming the superlative

■ The superlative (i.e. biggest, oldest, most beautiful etc.) is formed as follows:

> **le/la/les plus** + ADJECTIVE
> Il a toujours été *le plus grand* de la classe.

NOTE:

* If the superlative comes immediately after the noun, the definite article is repeated both before the noun and before the adjective:

> Ce sont les résultats *les plus encourageants* depuis longtemps.
> Elle est l'élève *la plus intelligente* de la classe.

Sometimes the definite article can be replaced by another determiner:

> C'est *son* livre le plus passionnant.

* The idea of **in** in English (**in the class** in the example above) is expressed by **de** in French (**de la classe**):

> C'est l'homme le plus riche *du* monde (the richest man in the world)

* The verb in a clause following a superlative is put into the subjunctive (*see* VERBS, **8**.4):

> C'est *la plus belle* ville que je connaisse.

5.3 Irregular forms of the comparative and superlative

■ Four adjectives have an irregular comparative and superlative:

adjective	*comparative*	*superlative*
bon	**meilleur**	**le meilleur/la meilleure/les meilleur(e)s**

bien	mieux	le mieux etc.
mauvais	pire	le pire etc.
petit	moindre	le moindre etc.

NOTE: The adjectives **mauvais** and **petit** have a regular form when they relate to concrete objects, and an irregular form when they relate to more abstract notions and ideas:

C'est son plus mauvais film. (= concrete)
Ils craignaient le pire. (= abstract)
C'est la plus petite pointure qui nous reste. (= concrete)
C'est le moindre de ses défauts. (= abstract)

5.4 Differences between French and English

In English we sometimes use **most**, not to express a superlative, but to express the idea of **very** or **extremely**, as in a **most interesting idea** or a **most useful suggestion**. In cases such as these, **most** is translated into French as **très** or **extrêmement**:

une idée *très* intéressante
une solution *extrêmement* originale

PRONOUNS

1. **Subject and Object Pronouns**
   je, tu, il etc. *(I, you, he/it etc.)*
   me, te, le etc. *(me, you, him/it etc.)*
   moi, toi, lui etc. *(me, you, him/it etc.)*

2. **Reflexive Pronouns**
   me, te etc. *(myself, yourself etc.)*

3. **The Adverbial Pronouns *en* and *y***
   (of/about/from it OR them ▲ there)

4. **The Order of Pronouns**

5. **Possessive Pronouns**
   le mien, le tien etc. *(mine, yours etc.)*

6. **Demonstrative Pronouns**
   celui, cela *(this one, that etc.)*

7. **Relative Pronouns**
   qui ▲ que etc. *(who ▲ which ▲ that etc.)*

8. **Interrogative Pronouns and Adverbs**
   qui ? ▲ que ? ▲ quoi ? etc. *(who? ▲ what? etc.)*

9. **Indefinite Pronouns**
   quelqu'un ▲ personne etc. *(someone ▲ no-one etc.)*

10. **The Pronoun *on***
    (one, you)

Pronouns stand for nouns. All languages use pronouns to avoid having to repeat a noun once it has been introduced. For example, it would be very awkward to have to say **I saw John in the cinema yesterday. I waved to John and John waved back.** To avoid having to repeat **John** we say instead **I saw John in the cinema yesterday. I waved to him and he waved back.** The pronouns **he** and **him** stand for the noun **John**. Likewise, **I bought the book and read the book** is very clumsy compared with **I bought the book and read it**.

1. Subject and object pronouns

1.1 Forms of the subject and object pronouns

	subject unstressed	stressed	direct object unstressed	indirect object unstressed	direct & indirect object stressed
singular					
1st person	je, j'	moi	me, m'	me, m'	moi
2nd person	tu	toi	te, t'	te, t'	toi
3rd person m.	il	lui	le, l'	lui	lui
3rd person f.	elle	elle	la, l'	lui	elle
plural					
1st person	nous	nous	nous	nous	nous
2nd person	vous	vous	vous	vous	vous
3rd person m.	ils	eux	les	leur	eux
3rd person f.	elles	elles	les	leur	elles

■ Before a vowel or a mute h (*see* GUIDE TO SPELLING AND PRONUNCIATION), je becomes j'; me becomes m'; te becomes t'; and le and la become l'.

> *J'*habite Paris.
> Il ne *t'*a rien dit ?

1.2 Uses of the unstressed subject pronouns

■ The pronouns je, tu, il, elle, nous, vous, ils and elles are always used as the subject of the verb (*see* BUILDING SENTENCES, **1.**)

■ When the subject pronouns are placed in front of the verb, there is usually nothing between them and the verb. The only exceptions to this rule are the object pronouns (*see* **1.4** and **1.5**), the adverbial pronouns y and en (*see* **3.**), and the negative word ne (*see* MAKING VERBS NEGATIVE), which *do* come between the subject pronoun and the verb:

> *Je ne les* connais pas très bien.

■ When used with compound tenses (*see* VERBS, **2.**), subject pronouns are placed before the auxiliary verbs avoir and être:

> *Tu* les as invités hier.
> *Il* se l'est acheté.

■ When subject pronouns are placed after the verb in a question, they come *immediately* after the verb:

Qu'en penses-*tu* ?

When used in compound tenses in a question, the subject pronoun comes between the auxiliary verb and the past participle:

Où l'as-*tu* mis ?

> *NOTE:* In questions, the pronoun is joined to the verb by a hyphen. If the verb is third person singular and ends in a vowel, a -t- is placed between the verb and the subject pronoun; this -t- is not added if the verb already ends in a -t or a -d:
>
> **Qu'en *pense-t-elle* ?** <u>BUT</u> **Qu'en *dit-elle* ?**
> **Quand *viendra-t-elle* ?** <u>BUT</u> **Quand *vient-elle* ?**

■ The subject pronouns are as follows:
– Je, like I in English, refers to the person speaking:

Je viens tout de suite.

– Nous is we. Remember that any adjectives used to describe nous must be plural:

Nous sommes persuadés de son innocence.

> *NOTE:* In written texts or formal speeches, **nous** can be used to refer to the person speaking or writing:
>
> **Nous examinerons cette question dans notre dernier chapitre.**

– Tu means you, but can only be used when one person is being addressed. Vous can be used to address either one person or more than one person:

Tu peux venir à seize heures si tu veux.
Qui as-tu rencontré ?
Vous êtes très aimable. (= one person, therefore takes a singular adjective)
Vous êtes très aimables. (= more than one person, therefore takes a plural adjective)

COMPARE

Vous is used to address one person as a mark of respect. It is not easy to give hard-and-fast rules for this polite use. **Vous** implies a certain formality in the relationship between the person speaking and the person spoken to, and is generally used when speaking to strangers, people in a position of authority, or people spoken to in official situations. **Tu** is always used when speaking to friends, relatives, young children and animals:

Comment allez-*vous* ?
Je *vous* prie d'agréer l'expression de mes sentiments les meilleurs.
(the equivalent of **Yours faithfully** or **Yours sincerely** in a formal letter)

– Remember that, since French has no neuter nouns, the third person singular and plural pronouns il, elle, ils and elles stand not only for *people* under discussion or already mentioned, but also for *things*. In the singular, therefore, they translate it as well as he and she:

Paul est parti hier, *il* ne reviendra pas avant seize heures aujourd'hui. (he)
Je n'ai pas aimé *ce film*. *Il* n'est pas intéressant. (it)
Où est *la confiture* ? *Elle* est dans le placard de gauche. (it)

NOTE:
* **Ils** can stand for several masculine nouns or for a mixture of masculine and feminine nouns:

Je les aime bien, elle et son mari ; *ils* sont très accueillants.

* **Il** is also the form used as the subject of impersonal verbs in French. Impersonal verbs in English always have **it** (or sometimes **there**) as their subject, though it would normally be impossible to say what this **it** actually refers to: for example, **it is raining, it snows here every winter**. Impersonal verbs frequently relate to the weather or other natural conditions:

Il pleut souvent ici.
Il est déjà neuf heures.

There are many other impersonal expressions in French, all of which always have **il** as their subject (*see* VERBS, 7.).

1.3 Uses of the stressed subject pronouns

■ The stressed subject pronouns are used:
– after c'est, ce sont, and in the expressions c'est/ce sont … qui and c'est/ce sont … que:

> **Qui est-ce ? C'est *moi*.**
> **C'est *lui* qui me l'a dit.**
> **Ce n'est pas *vous* qui êtes en cause.**

– to emphasize the subject of a verb:

> ***Moi*, je vais passer Noël en famille.** (As for me, …)
> **Ma famille, *elle*, part dans les Vosges.** (As for my family, …)

– in answers, and in sentences which have no verb:

> **'Qui vient au cinéma ?' '*Moi*.' 'Et *toi* ?'**

– in comparisons:

> **Il est plus grand que *moi*.**
> **Elle est plus intelligente que *lui*.**

– when the subject of a verb consists of more than one person or group of persons, at least one of which is mentioned individually. Note that in spoken language, when the stressed pronoun moi is used as part of the subject, the normal subject pronoun nous is also usually stated; this is different from English:

> **Mon frère et *moi*, *nous* allons voir un match de foot.**
> **Vous ne travaillez pas beaucoup, tes amis et *toi*.**

■ The stressed subject pronouns are also used with même, which expresses the idea of self. Même is always joined to the pronoun by a hyphen:

> **J'ai rédigé cette lettre *moi-même*.** (myself)
> **C'est *elle-même* qui me l'a dit.** (she herself)
> **Il est venu *lui-même*.** (himself)

1.4 Uses of the unstressed direct object pronouns

■ Me, te, le, la, nous, vous and les represent the direct object of the verb (*see* BUILDING SENTENCES, **2.**):

> **Il ne *me* voit pas**
> **Je ne *les* connais pas.**

■ Me, te, nous and vous always stand for people or animals:

> **Elle ne peut pas *nous* voir d'ici.**
> **Il *me* dépose tous les jours au même endroit.**

■ Le, la and les can stand for people, animals or things. Le and la can therefore be translated as it, as well as him and her:

Les enfants ont fait tous	→	**Ils *les* ont tous faits.** (them)
leurs exercices.		
Je connais *son mari*.	→	**Je *le* connais.** (him)
Où est *la voiture* ?	→	**Je ne *la* vois pas.** (it)

■ The pronoun le can stand for an adjective preceded by a verb such as être, sembler or paraître. In this case it is always le (or l') which is used, even if the person or thing described by the adjective is feminine or plural:

> **Elle me paraît très *fatiguée*; elle *l'*est très souvent ces temps-ci.**
> **J'étais *furieuse*, et je *le* suis toujours.**

Le can also stand for a noun in similar circumstances. Again, it is always the pronoun le which is used, even if the noun it is standing for is feminine:

> **Ma mère était *infirmière*, et elle *l'*est en effet toujours.**
> **On ne naît pas *femme*, on *le* devient.**

Le can also stand for an entire clause. Once more, it is always le which is used:

> **Je savais bien *que ça ne marcherait pas*.** → **Je *le* savais bien.**

In such cases, it is sometimes translated as so in English:

> **Je *l'*espère.** (I hope so.)

1.5 Uses of the unstressed indirect object pronouns

■ The pronouns me, te, lui, nous, vous and leur stand for the indirect object of the verb (*see* BUILDING SENTENCES, **2.**):

Ils ont rendu visite *à leurs parents*.	→	**Ils *leur* ont rendu visite.**
Il a donné un cadeau *à son frère*.	→	**Il *lui* a donné un cadeau.**

NOTE:

* The forms **lui** and **leur** stand for either masculine or feminine nouns:

    Elle téléphone *à un de ses amis.*   →   **Elle *lui* téléphone.**
    Elle téléphone *à ses amies.*   →   **Elle *leur* téléphone.**

* The forms **me, te, nous** and **vous** can stand for either a direct or an indirect object:

    Elle a mis mon frère et moi au → **Elle *nous* a mis au courant.**
    courant.
    Je les confie à toi et à Paul. → **Je *vous* les confie.**

1.6 Uses of the stressed direct and indirect object pronouns

■ The stressed object pronouns are moi, toi, lui, elle, nous, vous, eux and elles.

■ They are used to emphasize the object of the verb (*see* EMPHASIZING DIFFERENT PARTS OF THE SENTENCE, **1.**):

    On ne la voit pas souvent, *elle*.

■ They are used after a preposition:

    Ce livre est à *moi*.
    Elle doit repasser chez *elle*.

■ They are also used when the object of a verb consists of more than one person or group of persons, at least one of which is mentioned individually:

    Je vous ai vus hier, ton frère et *toi*.

2. Reflexive pronouns

The reflexive pronouns are used when the object of the verb is the same as the subject of the verb. In English they are myself, yourself and the like. Examples of their use in English are he admires himself or they hurt themselves and so on. It is important to bear in mind that the reflexive pronouns are used rather more frequently in French than in English.

Reflexive pronouns can also express the idea of 'each other' (*see* VERBS, **6.**).

2.1 Forms of the reflexive pronouns

		direct and indirect object
singular	*1st person*	**me, m'**
	2nd person	**te, t'**
	3rd person	**se, s'** (*stressed form* **soi**)
plural	*1st person*	**nous**
	2nd person	**vous**
	3rd person	**se, s'**

■ Before a vowel or a mute h (*see* GUIDE TO SPELLING AND PRONUNCIATION), the pronouns me, te and se change to m', t' and s':

Il *s'*ennuie beaucoup.
Je *m'*en vais.
Il *s'*est endormi.

■ The reflexive pronouns have the same form as the direct object pronouns (*see* 1.4), except in the third person singular and plural, where they take the form se.

■ When the reflexive pronoun is indirect, the verb can be followed by another direct object:

Il *s'*est acheté une voiture.

This direct object can itself be replaced by a pronoun, which is then placed after the reflexive pronoun:

Il *se l'*est achetée.

COMPARE

* When a verb has an indefinite subject such as **on** or **chacun**, **soi** is used after a preposition:

On se sent *chez soi* ici.
Chacun *pour soi*.

* If, however, the verb has a definite subject, either **lui** or **elle** is used as appropriate:

Elle se sent *chez elle* ici.

* In the plural, only the forms **eux** and **elles** are used after prepositions:

Ils se sentent chez *eux* ici.

2.2 Position of the reflexive pronouns

■ In statements and questions the reflexive pronouns are always placed before the verb. They can only be separated from the verb by a direct object pronoun or by the pronouns en and y (*see* **3.**):

> Elle *se* regarde dans un miroir.
> Je *me* le suis souvent dit.
> Il *s'*en est acheté plusieurs.
> Je ne *m'*y intéresse pas.
> Tu *t'*es amusé ?

■ In commands the stressed form of the reflexive pronoun is placed after the verb (*see* **4.1**):

> Regarde-*toi* !

3. The adverbial pronouns *en* and *y*

There is no real equivalent of the French pronoun en in English; it usually stands for the preposition de + Noun or Pronoun. Y often means there, though it can also stand for the prepositions à, dans or sur + Pronoun.

3.1 *En*

The pronoun en can stand for people, things or abstract nouns. It may replace:
– a noun preceded by de, du, de la, de l' or des. It can therefore include any of the three meanings of de – of, about or from – as well as all the meanings of the partitive article (*see* Determiners, **3.**):

– *of:* note that when it has this meaning en is seldom translated into English:

> As-tu acheté *des journaux* ? J'*en* ai acheté deux (= two of them)
> Il y avait trop *de travail*. Nous n'avons pu *en* finir qu'une partie. (= part of it)

– *about:*

> Je comprenais *la situation*, puisqu'il m'*en* avait déjà parlé. (= about it)

– *from:*

> Elle est revenue hier *de Rome*.   →   Elle *en* est revenue hier.
> (= from there)

– partitive:

> **Un peu** *de vin* **? J'***en* **ai déjà, merci.** (some)
> **J'ai** *des bonbons.* **Tu** *en* **veux ?** (some)

■ In fact, en must always be used in French where the object of the verb is an expression of quantity of any kind, including numbers:

> **Il n'y a plus** *de verres,* **j'***en* **ai encore cassé un.** (one)
> **'Tu as acheté** *des disques* **?' 'Oui, j'***en* **ai acheté plusieurs.'** (several)
> **Qui sont** *ces filles* **? Je n'***en* **connais aucune.** (not … any)

■ En also stands for a noun which is the object of a verb followed by de:

> **Je te remercie** *de ton aide.* **Oui, je t'***en* **remercie vraiment.**
> **'Tu te souviens** *de ce film* **?' 'Non, je ne m'***en* **souviens pas.'**

■ However, if the original noun referred to a person, de + the appropriate stressed PRONOUN is used instead of en:

> **'Tu te souviens** *de Jean-Pierre* **?' 'Oui, je me souviens** *de lui.***'**

> *NOTE:* En is used in certain set expressions such as **en vouloir à**, **s'en faire**, **s'en aller** and **en avoir pour:**
>
> > **Tu ne m'***en* **veux pas ?** (You don't hold it against me؟)
> > **Ne t'***en* **fais pas.** (Don't worry.)
> > **Je m'***en* **vais.** (I'm off.)
> > **J'***en* **ai pour deux minutes.** (I'll only be a couple of minutes.)

3.2 Y

The pronoun y can stand for:

– a noun referring to a place preceded by à, dans, en or sur. In such cases y means there:

> **Elle part en vacances** *à Bordeaux.* **Elle** *y* **a toute sa famille.**
> **Je vais** *à la piscine.* **Tu veux** *y* **aller avec moi ?**
> **Ils ont une ferme** *dans les Cévennes.* **Ils** *y* **passent toutes leurs vacances.**
> **Marie part** *en Savoie* **pour** *y* **faire du ski.**
> **Cherche** *sur le haut de l'étagère.* **J'***y* **ai mis les serviettes de table.**

– a noun which is the object of a verb followed by à:

> **Je ne voulais pas croire *à cette histoire* mais j'*y* crois maintenant.**
> **Cette glace paraît délicieuse. Je ne peux pas *y* résister.**

COMPARE

If the original noun relates to a person, **à** + the appropriate form of the stressed PRONOUN is used instead of **y**:

> **Tu penses *à ton amie* ? Oui, je pense *à elle*.**
> **Tu penses *à tes vacances* ? Oui, j'*y* pense.**

4. The order of pronouns

4.1 In affirmative commands

■ An affirmative command is when someone is told *to do* something. (A negative command is when they are told *not to do* something.) Pronouns in affirmative commands are always placed after the verb.

■ When there is only one pronoun, it is always linked to the verb by a hyphen. Note that the pronouns **me** and **te** never appear at the end of an affirmative command. In such cases they are always replaced by **moi** and **toi**:

> **Écoute-*moi*.**
> **Tiens-*toi* bien.**
> **Téléphone-*lui*.**

■ When there are two pronouns, they are combined as follows:

(A)				
VERB	+	le la les	+	moi toi lui nous vous leur

> **Envoie-*nous* les photos.** → **Envoie-*les-nous*.**
> **Montre *cet article à Paul*.** → **Montre-*le-lui*.**

(B)				
VERB	+	m' t' lui nous vous leur	+	en

Il reste des chocolats. Donne-*lui-en* un.
Il n'y a pas assez de roses rouges dans ce bouquet. Rajoutez-*nous-en* quelques-unes, s'il vous plaît.

> *NOTE*: In affirmative commands there is always a hyphen between the verb and the pronoun and between two pronouns, except when two pronouns are joined by an apostrophe:
>
> Je voudrais *des oranges*. Mettez *m'en* un bon kilo.

4.2 In all other cases

The possible combinations are as follows:

	(1)	(2)	(3)	(4)	
	me, m'				
	te, t'				
	se, s'	le, l'			
SUBJECT +	nous +	la, l' +	lui +	en +	VERB
	vous	les	leur	y	
	se, s'				

(1) + (2):

   Cette affiche, mon oncle *me l'*a offerte pour Noël.

(1) + (4):

   Puisque *tu* n'as pas *de règle*, je *t'en* prêterai une.
   Hervé joue dans *ce club de tennis* au moins une fois par semaine. Il *s'y* est inscrit l'an dernier.

(2) + (3):

   Claire aimait *mon collier*, alors je *le lui* ai donné.
   Les enfants ont oublié *leurs maillots de bain*, je *les leur* envoie par la poste.

(2) + (4):

   Alexandre n'est jamais allé *au zoo*. Son père a promis de *l'y* emmener.
   Les enfants ont l'habitude de *faire les courses*. Tu peux *les en* charger.

(3) + (4):

   Jeanne comprendra *ton problème*. Tu peux *lui en* parler.
   Le bébé veut encore *un biscuit*. Je peux *lui en* donner un ?

> *NOTE:* **Y** and **en** are never combined, except in the set phrase **il y en a**:
>
> **J'aurais bien voulu du café, mais je ne sais pas s'*il y en a*.**

5. Possessive pronouns

5.1 Forms of the possessive pronouns

		one object		*several objects*	
		masculine	feminine	masculine	feminine
singular	1st person	le mien	la mienne	les miens	les miennes
	2nd person	le tien	la tienne	les tiens	les tiennes
	3rd person	le sien	la sienne	les siens	les siennes
plural	1st person	le nôtre	la nôtre	les nôtres	les nôtres
	2nd person	le vôtre	la vôtre	les vôtres	les vôtres
	3rd person	le leur	la leur	les leurs	les leurs

■ The possessive pronouns in French are always preceded by the definite article. They are equivalent to mine, yours etc. in English.

■ The gender of the possessive pronoun is the same as the gender of the noun it stands for, in other words the thing or things owned. The gender of the person who owns this thing or these things is irrelevant:

'Jeanne a oublié son parapluie ici.' 'Tu es sûr que c'est *le sien* ?'

5.2 Uses of the possessive pronouns

Possessive pronouns can be used in the following ways:

– as the subject of the verb:

Nous avons les mêmes vélos, mais *le sien* est vert.
Il est parti en vacances avec ses enfants. *Les nôtres* sont en Espagne.

– as the object of a verb or preposition:

J'ai perdu mon plan de la ville. Il m'a prêté *le sien*.
Cette robe ressemble à *la tienne*.

– after the verb être:

Ce n'est pas son tour à lui, c'est *le mien*.

NOTE: The possessive pronouns can be used in set expressions such as **faire des siennes** and **y mettre du sien**:

> Tu as encore fait *des tiennes* ! (You've gone and done it again!)
> Essaie d'y mettre *du tien*. (Try to help out a bit.)

6. Demonstrative pronouns

The demonstrative pronouns stand for an object or a person who has already been identified. They can also stand for an idea. Their equivalents in English are this one, that one, these and those.

6.1 Forms of the demonstrative pronouns

	short form		*long forms*		*neuter (sg)*
	masculine	feminine	masculine	feminine	
singular	**celui**	**celle**	**celui-ci**	**celle-ci**	**cela, ceci**
			celui-là	**celle-là**	**ça, ce (c')**
plural	**ceux**	**celles**	**ceux-ci**	**celles-ci**	
			ceux-là	**celles-là**	

■ Before e, ce changes to c':

> *C'*est là.
> *C'*est très aimable à vous.
> *C'*est dommage.

NOTE: Adjectives used with neuter pronouns are always masculine, irrespective of the actual noun which the neuter pronoun stands for:

> *C'*est bon, cette viande.
> Je trouve ça idiot.

6.2 Uses of the demonstrative pronouns

■ The short forms of the demonstrative pronouns are always followed by:
– PREPOSITION + NOUN, in which case their translation is usually **that** or **those**:

> Sa réaction a été plus positive que *celle de son associé.* (that of his associate, *or simply* his associate's)

In fact this is the only way of translating English 's into French when the object owned does not follow the noun ending in 's:

Leurs parents sont plus riches que *ceux de Fabien.* (Their parents are richer than Fabien's.)

– a RELATIVE PRONOUN, in which case their translation is usually **the one(s)**:

C'est *celui dont* **je t'ai parlé.** (the one I spoke to you about)
Celle que **je préfère, c'est la bleue.** (the one I prefer)

■ The long forms of the demonstrative pronouns are used with -ci to indicate closeness, or -là to indicate distance. The forms with -ci are equivalent to **this one, these**; the forms with -là are equivalent to **that one, those**:

Passe-moi cette bouteille. Non, pas *celle-ci, celle-là.*

> NOTE:
> * The distinction between **celui-ci** and **celui-là** is not always entirely clear (*see* DETERMINERS, 5.2).
> * **Celui-là … celui-ci** can also express the idea of **the former … the latter**. The form used must agree with the noun which the pronoun replaces:
>
> **Jeanne et Paulette sont déjà parties :** *celle-là* **est allée au cinéma,** *celle-ci* **à la piscine.**

■ The neuter demonstrative pronoun **ceci** normally means **this**, while **cela** normally means **that**.

– They can be used to refer to something you are actually pointing to in a specific situation:

Que pensez-vous de *ceci* **?**

– They can also refer to something which has already been said, or which you are about to say:

Cela, **c'est une autre histoire.**
Je vais vous dire *ceci* **: ne croyez pas ce qu'il dit.**

- **Ça** is normally used instead of **cela** in everyday French. **Ça** can stand for an object, a clause or a group of words:

J'ai trouvé *ça* **au marché.**

J'ai fait des courses toute la journée, *ça* m'a fatiguée.
J'adore *ça*.
Ça ne dépend que de toi.

> NOTE: **Ça** is also used in set phrases:
>
> **Ça va ?** (How are things?)
> **Comment *ça* va ?** (How are things?)
> **Il ne manquait plus que *ça* !** (That's all we needed!)

– Ce and c' are used with the verb être to form the phrases **c'est** and **ce sont**. These are very common phrases, and are used to:
  – express it is followed by a noun, a pronoun, an adjective or an adverb:

  C'est mon frère.
  C'est ici.
  C'est trop tard.
  C'est très bien.
  C'est mieux comme ça.

Although the phrase it is is used in English to introduce both singular and plural nouns and pronouns, c'est changes to ce sont in formal French when the following noun or pronoun is plural:

  J'aime beaucoup les Français. *Ce sont* des gens très sympathiques.

  – emphasize a certain part of a sentence:

  Ce que certains n'aiment pas dans les voyages, *c'est* le trajet en avion.
  C'est justement parce qu'il est fatigué que nous ne sortons pas.

  – refer to a word or a whole sentence:

  Il a dit qu'il était furieux contre eux. *C'est* vrai ?

– The form ce is used with the relative pronouns qui, que, dont and à quoi to refer to something indefinite. In these cases, the combined forms normally translate simply as what:

  Ce que je craignais est arrivé.
  Ce que tu devrais faire, c'est leur donner un coup de main.
  Voilà *ce dont* il s'agit.

Je ne me souviens plus de *ce dont* **il m'a parlé.**
Ce n'est pas *ce à quoi* **ils s'attendaient.**

(*See also* **7**.2 for more on ce qui and ce que.)

COMPARE

> **Tout ce qui** is the subject of the following verb and usually
> translates as **all that**:
>
> *Tout ce qui* **nous reste est exposé en vitrine.**
>
> **Tout ce que** is the object of the following verb and usually translates
> as **everything** or **all**:
>
> **J'ai oublié** *tout ce que* **je savais.**

7. Relative pronouns

■ Relative pronouns are used to introduce an adjectival clause. (If you are
unsure what an adjectival clause is, see CLAUSES, **2**.) Their equivalents in
English are who, which, that, and in rather formal English, whom.
Adjectival clauses – like adjectives – always describe something, whether
it is a noun, a pronoun or a whole idea. For example, if you say I enjoyed
the video you lent me, the adjectival clause you lent me describes the
video. The technical name for the thing being described (the video in our
example) is the *antecedent*.

■ There are two important differences between French and English as
regards the use of relative pronouns. These must always be borne in mind.

– It is sometimes possible to leave out the relative pronoun in English. For
example, you can say the book which I am reading or simply the book I
am reading. It is *never* possible to leave out the relative pronoun in French.

– It is perfectly acceptable to put a preposition at the end of an adjectival
clause in English, especially when the relative pronoun is omitted, as
when we say the man I was speaking to or the friend I went to the
cinema with. This is *never* possible in French, where the preposition must
be placed in front of the relative pronoun, as it would be in very formal
English: the man *to whom* I was speaking (l'homme *à qui* je parlais), the
friend *with whom* I went to the cinema (l'ami *avec qui* je suis allé au
cinéma).

7.1 Forms of the relative pronouns

	definite article + quel	à + *lequel*	de + *lequel*
short form	**qui, que (qu'), quoi, dont, où**		
long form	**lequel**	**auquel**	**duquel**
	laquelle	**à laquelle**	**de laquelle**
	lesquels	**auxquels**	**desquels**
	lesquelles	**auxquelles**	**desquelles**

■ *Que* changes to *qu'* before a vowel or a mute h (*see* GUIDE TO SPELLING AND PRONUNCIATION):

Elle ne m'a pas informé de la décision *qu'*elle avait prise.

■ There are both short and long forms of the relative pronouns.

– The short forms of the relative pronouns remain the same for singular and plural, masculine and feminine:

Choisissez l'heure *qui* vous convient.

– The long forms agree in gender and number with the noun they stand for – in other words, with the antecedent:

Je n'étais pas sûr de l'adresse *à laquelle* je devais aller.

In this example, laquelle is feminine singular because the noun it stands for – l'adresse – is also feminine singular.

7.2 Uses of the relative pronouns

■ *Qui*

– Qui is used when the antecedent is the subject of the verb in the adjectival clause. It can stand for either people or things:

Tu connais la personne *qui* vient d'entrer ?
Il y a des gens *qui* disent n'importe quoi.
Je n'aime pas les films *qui* finissent mal.

– Qui is also used after prepositions, but in this case it can only stand for a person or persons. Remember that the preposition can *never* appear at the end of the adjectival clause in French:

La personne *à qui* je me suis adressé est le directeur. (the person I spoke to)
L'homme *avec qui* je parlais est mon oncle. (the man I was talking to)

NOTE:
* **Qui** can only be used if the antecedent is something quite specific, a noun or pronoun which can be clearly identified in the earlier part of the sentence. If this is not the case – in other words, if the adjectival clause refers to a general situation rather than a specific noun – **ce qui** must be used instead:

> Il est arrivé en retard, *ce qui* ne m'a pas plu.
> Elle ne voulait pas le voir, *ce qui* l'a beaucoup déçu.

* **Qui** is not used after the prepositions **parmi** and **entre**. In these cases, the appropriate form of **lequel** is used instead (see below):

> Les candidats *parmi lesquels* il fallait choisir ne semblaient pas très intéressants.
> Les personnes *entre lesquelles* il se trouvait parlaient sans arrêt.

* In proverbs, **qui** sometimes appears without an antecedent. In these cases it means **he who**:

> Rira bien *qui* rira le dernier. (He who laughs last laughs longest.)
> *Qui* vivra verra. (=Time will tell.)

■ *Que*
– Que is used when the antecedent is the object of the verb in the adjectival clause. In such cases the subject of the verb in the adjectival clause is always expressed within that clause itself (j' in the first example below, ils in the second). Que can stand for people or things. It can never be left out in French:

> La robe *que* j'ai achetée ne me plaît plus. (the dress I bought)
> La famille *qu'ils ont* hébergée est restée une semaine. (the family they put up)

NOTE: **Que** can only be used if the antecedent is specific, a noun or pronoun which is clearly identified in the earlier part of the sentence. However, if the adjectival clause refers to a general situation rather than a specific noun, **ce que** must be used instead:

> Il ne tient jamais ses promesses, *ce que* je déteste.
> Ils n'ont pas fini le travail, *ce que* nous ne pouvons pas accepter.

■ *Quoi*

– Quoi is used after prepositions and can only ever stand for the pronoun ce or some other indefinite antecedent which is not actually expressed. It usually translates as what. Remember that the preposition can *never* be placed at the end of the adjectival clause in French:

C'est ce à *quoi* je m'attendais. (It's what I was expecting.)

Je ne sais pas de *quoi* tu parles. (I don't know what you're talking about.)

– Quoi can also appear without an antecedent in phrases such as the following:

Il y a de *quoi* manger. (There's something to eat.)

As-tu de *quoi* écrire ? (Have you got something to write with?)

■ *Dont*

– Dont is a complex but widely used relative pronoun. It stands for any noun or pronoun preceded by the preposition de. Since de has three basic meanings in French – of, from and about – dont can mean of which, about which or from which. Dont can stand for either people or things. Remember that a preposition can *never* appear at the end of an adjectival clause in French:

Il a réalisé plusieurs films, *dont* trois sont des chefs-d'œuvre. (three of which)

J'ai vu le film *dont* tu m'avais parlé. (which you had told me about)

La pièce *dont* il sortait était trop chauffée. (the room he was coming out of)

– Since it can contain the idea of which, another frequent translation of dont is whose. The order of words in a clause beginning with dont is always dont + SUBJECT + VERB + OBJECT/COMPLEMENT, and so the order of words in French is frequently different from what it would be in English:

Le garçon *dont* je connais le père est parti. (whose father I know)

Il vient de sortir un film *dont* on prévoit déjà le succès. (whose success is already being predicted)

La fille *dont* la mère est professeur est très intelligente. (whose mother is a teacher)

> NOTE: **Dont** cannot be used if the noun which is the object of the verb in the adjectival clause is itself preceded by a preposition. In such cases **de qui** must be used instead:
>
> **C'est le garçon avec le père *de qui* j'ai parlé ce matin.**

■ *Où*

– Où most often means where:

L'appartement *où* elle habite est ensoleillé.

– When preceded by d', however, it usually expresses the idea from which. In such circumstances it is often not translated in English:

la ville *d'où* je viens (the town I come from)
la chambre *d'où* il sortait (the room he was coming out of)

– Où can also be used in connection with expressions of time when its antecedent is a noun which refers to a precise length of time (a moment, day, week, evening etc.):

le jour *où* tu es arrivé (the day you arrived)
À l'instant même *où* elle entrait, Jean sortait. (just as she was coming in)

■ *Lequel* (f *laquelle*, mpl *lesquels*, fpl *lesquelles*) and its compounds *auquel* etc. and *duquel* etc.

– Lequel and its compound forms can refer to people or things. It agrees in gender and number with the noun it stands for.

– Lequel is seldom used on its own in everyday French, and is almost always preceded by a preposition:

C'est la personne *à laquelle* je me suis adressée. (the person I spoke to)
Voilà le cinéma *auquel* nous sommes allés hier. (the cinema we went to)

8. Interrogative pronouns and adverbs

8.1 Forms of the interrogative pronouns and adverbs

■ The interrogative pronouns are as follows:

qui	qui est-ce qui	qui est-ce que
que (qu')	qu'est-ce qui	qu'est-ce que
quoi		

lequel	*when*	auquel	*when*	duquel
laquelle	*preceded* →	à laquelle	*preceded* →	de laquelle
lesquels	*by* à	auxquels	*by* de	desquels
lesquelles		auxquelles		desquelles

■ The interrogative adverbs are **pourquoi, quand, combien, comment** and **où**.

8.2 Uses of the interrogative pronouns and adverbs

■ The interrogative *pronouns* are used in direct or indirect questions when we want a person or object or group of persons or objects to be clearly identified. Such questions cannot simply be answered by 'yes' or 'no' (*see* DIFFERENT KINDS OF SENTENCE, **4**.).

■ The subject pronoun **qui** (who) is used to establish the identity of a person. Qui can be replaced by **qui est-ce qui**, though this is less common and less formal:

> *Qui* **vient demain ?**
> *Qui* **a perdu ses clés ?**

Lequel can be used in the same way:

> *Lequel* **d'entre vous pense venir demain ?** (which of you?)

■ When referring to people, the object pronouns are **qui** (who) and **lequel** (which) and lequel's compound forms **auquel** etc. and **duquel** etc.

– When used with prepositions, the pronouns **qui** and **lequel** can be used to enquire about the identity of a specific person or persons. Qui translates as who, and lequel as which. Remember that the preposition must be placed *before* qui or lequel, and cannot come at the end of the question as it can in English:

> **À** *qui* **dois-je m'adresser ?** (Who should I speak to?)
> **À** *qui* **est-ce que je dois m'adresser ?** (Who should I speak to?)
> **De** *qui* **parle-t-elle ?** (Who is she talking about?)
> *Auquel* **d'entre eux avez-vous parlé ?** (Which of them did you speak to?)

– When referring to things, the object pronouns are **que** (what), **quoi** (what) and **lequel** and its compound forms.

– **Que** is used to enquire about the identity of something unknown, and means what. The use of que on its own is rather uncommon in everyday French, where it is normally replaced by **qu'est-ce que**. The subject pronoun is not placed after the verb when qu'est-ce que is used:

> *Que* **veux-tu ?** <u>BUT</u> *Qu'est-ce que* **tu veux ?**

Que cannot be used after a preposition; it has to be replaced by quoi. Remember that the preposition must be placed *before* quoi, and cannot come at the end of the question as it can in English:

À *quoi* penses-tu ? (What are you thinking about?)
De *quoi* parliez-vous en chemin ? (What were you talking about on the way?)

– Lequel, laquelle, lesquels and lesquelles are used to single out an object or person, or group of objects or people, whose identity is already known. They mean which, or which one(s):
Lequel me conseillez-vous ?

■ The interrogative adverbs quand, où, combien, comment and pourquoi refer to time, place, price etc.:

– Quand means when:

Quand arriveront-ils ?
Quand est-ce qu'ils arriveront ?
Je me demande *quand* ils arriveront.

– Où means where:

Où vas-tu ?
Où est-ce que tu vas ?
Dis-moi *où* tu vas.

– Combien means how much or how many:

Il y avait *combien* de monde à ton avis ?
Vous prendrez *combien* de sucres ?

It can also be used to enquire about prices:

Combien coûte cette voiture ?
Tu sais *combien* coûte cette voiture ?

In noun clauses containing the verb être and an adjective, combien can mean how. In such cases, the verb être comes before the adjective in French, whereas the verb to be comes after the adjective in English:

Tu ne sais pas *combien* je te suis redevable. (You don't know how grateful I am to you.)
Je n'avais pas réalisé *combien* elle était fatiguée. (I hadn't realized how tired she was.)

– Pourquoi means why:

> *Pourquoi* **est-ce qu'elle s'est fâchée ?**
> **Je ne comprends pas** *pourquoi* **elle s'est fâchée.**

9. Indefinite pronouns

Indefinite pronouns stand for a person or an object whose identity is unknown:

> *Certains* **disent qu'il va neiger demain.** (some people say)
> *Rien* **n'est sûr.** (Nothing is certain.)

9.1 Forms of the indefinite pronouns

There are many different kinds of indefinite pronoun.

9.2 Uses of the indefinite pronouns

■ *Personne, rien, aucun (f aucune), nul*

These pronouns are always used together with the negative ne, and can be used as either the subject or the object of the verb. Personne (no-one, nobody, not ... anyone, not ... anybody) and rien (nothing, not ... anything) never change their form. Aucun and the feminine aucune mean none. Nul (no-one) is only used in rather formal French:

> *Personne* **n'est venu.**
> **Je** *ne* **connais** *personne.*
> *Rien* **n'est impossible.**
> **Il** *n'a* **rien dit.**
> *Aucun* **d'eux** *n'a* **compris.**
> *Nul* **ne sait ce qu'il est devenu.**

NOTE: When **personne** and **rien** are used with an adjective, **de** is placed between them and the adjective:

> *Personne d'*intéressant n'est venu.
> Il n'y avait *rien de* nouveau.

■ *Tout, tous (fpl toutes), tout le monde*

– Tous (toutes) means all; tout le monde means everyone or everybody:

> **Ils étaient** *tous* **là.**
> *Tout le monde* **le sait.**

> The **-s** at the end of **tous** is always pronounced when **tous** is used
> as a pronoun, but is not pronounced when **tous** is used as an
> adjective (*see* DETERMINERS, **7.2**):
>
> **Je les aime tous** [tus].
> **Les enfants sont tous** [tus] **partis.**
> <u>BUT</u>
> **Tous** [tu] **les enfants sont en vacances.**

– Tout means everything:

> **Je voulais *tout* acheter.**
> ***Tout* l'intéresse.**

■ *Quelqu'un, quelque chose, autre chose, n'importe qui, n'importe lequel (f
laquelle, mpl lesquels, fpl lesquelles), n'importe quoi*

These pronouns mean someone, something, something else, anyone (at
all), any one (at all) and anything (at all) respectively:

> ***Quelqu'un* vous demande au téléphone.**
> **Est-ce que vous auriez *quelque chose* pour écrire ?**
> **Il me faudrait *autre chose*, ce n'est pas très pratique.**
> ***N'importe qui* pourrait le faire.**
> **Il dit *n'importe quoi*.**

> *NOTE:*
> * **Quelque chose** is always written as *two* words.
> * When **quelque chose** is used with an adjective, **de** is placed
> between it and the adjective:
>
> **Tu as acheté *quelque chose d'*intéressant ?**

■ *L'un(e) l'autre (les un(e)s les autres), quelques-un(e)s, plusieurs,
beaucoup, certain(e)s, la plupart, chacun(e)*

These pronouns are used to refer to different members of a group of
people or things:

> **Ils nous ont déjà rendu visite *l'un* et *l'autre*.** (both of them)
> **Vous pouvez acheter soit *l'un* soit *l'autre*.** (either of them)
> **Les *uns* sont absents, les *autres* en retard.** (some … others)
> **J'ai lu *quelques-uns* de ses livres.** (some of his books)

Plusieurs **d'entre eux se sont plaints.** (several of them)

Je pensais qu'il y aurait du monde mais il n'y en a pas *beaucoup*. (a lot)

Certains **pensent qu'un changement est nécessaire.** (some people)

La plupart **des élèves de la classe ont eu leur bac.** (most of)

Chacun **sait que ce n'est pas facile.** (everybody)

NOTE:

* **L'un l'autre** means **each other** or **one another**. It is only used with reflexive verbs (*see* VERBS, **6.**):

   Ils se sont insultés *l'un l'autre*. (They insulted each other.)

If the verb normally requires a preposition before its object, this preposition is placed between **l'un** and **l'autre**:

   Ils se méfiaient l'un *de* **l'autre.** (They distrusted each other.)

* The word **quelques** is an *adjective* and not a pronoun. Consequently, it can never be used on its own to mean **some**. In such cases **quelques-un(e)s** must be used:

   'Tu as vu ses films ?' 'J'en ai vu *quelques-uns*.'

   'Tu connais ses chansons ?' 'J'en connais *quelques-unes*.'

* Although **la plupart** is a singular noun, the verb used with it goes into the third person plural because it refers to several people or things:

   La plupart **des spectateurs** *étaient* **déjà partis.**

---

10. The pronoun *on*

Technically, the pronoun on is the equivalent of the English pronoun one when it is used to mean 'people in general', as in sentences such as one cannot believe everything one hears. The main difference between French and English, however, is that in English one is only used in very formal speech, whereas on in French is widely used in everyday conversation and in writing. It is therefore closer to the use of you in English when this means 'people in general'. For example, it would be much more usual in everyday English to say you can't believe everything you hear. On can sometimes be translated simply as people, or even just as they.

PRONOUNS

■ **On** can only ever be used as the *subject* of the verb. The verb is always in the third person singular:

On *dirait* que la pluie s'est arrêtée. (You'd think it had stopped raining.)

■ The object pronoun **vous** can be used with **on**:

Où que l'on aille, ils *vous* traitent comme un enfant. (Wherever you go, they treat you like a child.)

■ When **on** is used with a reflexive verb, the reflexive pronouns (*see* **2.**) used are **se** (unstressed) and **soi** (stressed):

Si *on* veut s'améliorer, il faut travailler.
On ne pense jamais que ce genre de mésaventure arrive aussi à *soi*.
(You never think this kind of misfortune is going to happen to you.)

■ The possessive adjective used with **on** is **son/sa/ses** (*see* DETERMINERS, **4.**):

On doute parfois de *ses* chances.

■ In everyday speech **on** is very widely used in the sense of *we*, and is in fact often combined with the pronoun **nous**. The verb is still in the third person singular:

On a marché toute la journée. (we've been walking)
On y va ? (Shall we go?)
On en a assez de tes histoires ! (We've had enough of your nonsense!)
Nous, *on* n'en sait rien. (We don't know anything about it.)

■ **On** can also be used to refer vaguely to people in general, other people, most people and the like:

On croit qu'il fait toujours beau ici.
On dit qu'elle est très gentille.
On pense souvent le contraire.

■ It can also mean *someone*:

On a frappé.
On vous demande au téléphone.

■ It can also often be used to express what would be a passive in English (*see* VERBS, **5.**):

On a construit cette maison en 1890. (This house was built in 1890.)

> *NOTE*: In written French the form **l'on** is sometimes used at the beginning of a sentence or after **que**, **et**, **ou** and **où**:
> **Où que *l'on* aille, il y a toujours du monde.** (wherever you go)

ADVERBS

1. Forms of Adverb

2. Uses of Adverbs

3. Types of Adverb

4. How Adverbs Work

5. Groups of Words which can Function as Adverbs

Adverbs are most commonly used to provide more information about a verb. For example, if we say in English **she sang beautifully**, the adverb **beautifully** gives us more information about the verb **sang** (it tells us *how* she sang). When used with verbs, adverbs can provide information about time, place, quantity, how something is done, and so on. However, adverbs can also be used to provide more information about adjectives: for example, **this is an extremely enjoyable film** (the adverb **extremely** gives extra emphasis to the adjective **enjoyable**). They can also be used to provide more information about other adverbs: for example, **she sang extremely beautifully** (where **extremely** adds emphasis to the adverb **beautifully**).

Adverbs in French never change their form, no matter which verb, adjective or other adverb they relate to.

1. Forms of adverb

Adverbs can take very different forms in French. However, those adverbs ending in -ment are formed from adjectives and follow certain rules.

1.1 Adverbs formed from adjectives

■ The vast majority of adverbs ending in -**ment** are formed from the feminine form of the adjective to which the ending -**ment** is added. For example:

doux	→	douce	→	doucement
naïf	→	naïve	→	naïvement
sec	→	sèche	→	sèchement
long	→	longue	→	longuement
lent	→	lente	→	lentement
naturel	→	naturelle	→	naturellement

■ Some adverbs ending in -ment, however, are based on the masculine form of the adjective, to which the ending -ment is added. These adverbs are formed from masculine adjectives which end in a vowel. For example:

poli	→	poliment
joli	→	joliment
vrai	→	vraiment
carré	→	carrément
absolu	→	absolument

■ Adjectives ending in -ant and -ent form adverbs in -amment and -emment. For example:

évident	→	évidemment
prudent	→	prudemment
violent	→	violemment
courant	→	couramment
constant	→	constamment

BUT

lent	→	lentement
présent	→	présentement

NOTE: The following adverbs are slightly irregular:

bref	→	brièvement
gentil	→	gentiment
précis	→	précisément
énorme	→	énormément
intense	→	intensément
profond	→	profondément
commun	→	communément
aveugle	→	aveuglément

1.2 Adverbs formed in other ways

Other types of adverb are not formed according to strict rules and in fact come in many different forms. Some have no corresponding adjective: beaucoup, souvent, très, peu, ici, là, maintenant, déjà, bientôt etc.

> NOTE: Some adjectives can also be used as adverbs. In such cases it is always the masculine singular form of the adjective which is used. The most common of these adverbs are **bas, bon, cher, court, dur, faux, fort, haut, juste, mauvais** and **net**:
>
> Il parle *fort*.
> Elle chante *faux*.
> Ça coûte très *cher*.

1.3 Forming the comparative of adverbs

The comparatives of adverbs are formed in exactly the same way as those of adjectives (*see* ADJECTIVES, **5.**):

> **plus**
> **moins**   +   ADVERB   +   **(que)**
> **aussi**

> Il pleut *moins fort* que tout à l'heure.
> Tu devrais travailler *plus souvent*.
> Elle parle l'italien *aussi couramment* que lui.

> NOTE:
> * The comparative of the adverb **bien** is **mieux (better)**:
>
>   Elle chante *mieux* que lui.
>
> * The comparative of the adverb **peu** is **moins**:
>
>   Tu manges *moins* que moi.
>
> * The comparative of the adverb **beaucoup** is **plus**:
>
>   Je mange *plus* que toi.

1.4 Forming the superlative of adverbs

The superlative of adverbs is the same as the comparative, but is always preceded by the definite article le. Remember that, like all adverbs, the superlative never changes its form:

> C'est elle qui chante *le mieux*.
> Ce sont eux qui travaillent *le plus dur*.

2. Uses of adverbs

Adverbs can be used to provide more information about:
– a verb:

> Elle dort *profondément*.
> Il marche *beaucoup*.

– an adjective:

> Il me paraît *très* grand.
> La journée promet d'être *très* belle.
> C'est *absolument* exact.

– another adverb:

> Il prend *trop* souvent la parole.
> Elle va *très* bien.
> Elle roule *trop* vite.

– a whole sentence:

> *Franchement*, tu exagères.
> *Malheureusement*, il pleut encore.
> *Justement*, j'allais vous appeler.
> *Évidemment*, on pourrait mieux faire.

An important group of adverbs used in this way are pourtant, cependant, toutefois and néanmoins, all of which mean however or none the less:

> *Pourtant*, ce n'est pas vrai.
> J'ai *cependant* décidé de le faire.

3. Types of adverb

■ Adverbs of manner provide information on *how* something is done. Many end in -ment, but this group also includes other adverbs such as bien (well), mal (badly), vite (quickly) etc.:

> Ils ont *poliment* refusé l'invitation.

Il faut en finir *rapidement*.
Parle plus *lentement*.
Le chauffage marche *mal*.

■ Adverbs of quantity, frequency or intensity provide information on the *extent* to which something is done (i.e. a lot, a little, enough etc.). The most common are assez, fort, très, peu, moins, plus, trop, souvent, à peine and beaucoup:

Je l'aime *beaucoup*.
Est-ce qu'il en reste *assez* ?
Son cœur battait *fort*.

COMPARE

Peu and **un peu** do not mean the same thing at all:

Ce genre de film m'intéresse *peu*. (This kind of film holds little interest for me.)
Ce genre de film m'intéresse *un peu*. (This kind of film interests me a little.)

In fact, when used with adjectives, **peu** has the effect of making the adjective negative, or of turning it into its opposite:

J'ai trouvé ce film *peu* intéressant. (= I found this film uninteresting.)
Cela me paraît *peu* probable. (= I find that unlikely.)
L'eau était *peu* profonde. (= The water was shallow.)

■ Comparative adverbs are used when two or more actions of the same kind are compared. The most common are mieux (better), plus (more), moins (less), autant (as much) and aussi (as). Than or as is expressed by que:

Il travaille *plus* que moi.
Je les apprécie *autant* l'un que l'autre.

■ Adverbs of time provide information on *when* something is done. The most common are hier (yesterday), aujourd'hui (today), demain (tomorrow), alors (then), enfin (finally), après (afterwards), soudain (suddenly), maintenant (now), désormais (from now on), jamais (never), parfois (sometimes), souvent (often), toujours (always, still) and encore (still, yet). Adverbs like d'abord, ensuite and puis show sequence:

> **Je reviendrai** *demain*.
> **Elle est** *toujours* **à l'heure**.
> **Les voilà** *enfin* !

■ Adverbs of place provide information on *where* something is done. The most common are ici (here), là (there), là-bas (over there), autour (around), ailleurs (elsewhere), dedans (inside), dehors (outside), derrière (behind), dessus (on top), devant (in front), dessous (underneath) and partout (everywhere):

> **Viens** *ici*.
> **C'est** *là*.
> **Je suis allé le chercher** *ailleurs*.

■ Adverbs of affirmation are used to give a positive answer to a question or request. The most common are oui (yes), bien sûr (of course, certainly), certainement (certainly) and volontiers (willingly):

> **'Vous venez avec moi ?'** *'Oui.'*
> **'Vous voulez encore un café ?'** **'** *Volontiers*, **merci.'**

■ Adverbs of negation are used to make the action of the verb negative in some way. The most common are non, ne ... pas, ne ... plus, ne ... jamais, ne ... rien, ne ... personne and ne ... aucun (*see* MAKING VERBS NEGATIVE):

> **Il** *n'a pas* **envie de le rencontrer**.
> **Il** *n'a aucune* **chance de réussir**.

■ Interrogative adverbs are used in questions (*see* PRONOUNS, **8.**):

> *Pourquoi* **sont-ils déjà partis ?**
> *Quand* **comptes-tu finir ?**

4. How adverbs work

■ Sometimes an adverb is necessary to complete the meaning of a sentence. In the examples below, il habite and mets ton livre would not make sense on their own:

> **Il habite** *loin*.
> **Mets ton livre** *là-dessus*.

■ In other cases adverbs provide additional information without which the sentence would still make sense:

> **Elle se promène *lentement* dans la ville.**
> **Je vais vous répondre *tout de suite*.**

NOTE:

* An adverb used with a verb is placed *after* the verb. However, an adverb used with an adjective or another adverb is placed *in front of* it:

> **Il parle *lentement*.**
> **Ne va pas *trop* vite.**
> **Il est *très* intelligent.**

* The adverb **tout** (**very**) is rather different from other adverbs. When it is followed by a feminine adjective beginning with a vowel or a mute **h** (*see* GUIDE TO SPELLING AND PRONUNCIATION), its form does not change:

> **Elle paraissait *tout* étonnée.**
> **Leur petite fille était *tout* heureuse de les revoir.**

However, when it is followed by a feminine adjective beginning with a consonant, it agrees with it in both gender and number:

> **Elle est *toute* contente aujourd'hui.**
> **Elles semblent *toutes* tristes.**

---

5. Groups of words which can function as adverbs

5.1 Adverbial phrases

These are adverbs which consist of more than one word:

> **Revenez *tout à l'heure*.**
> **Je reviens *tout de suite*.**
> **Il est parti *d'un air décidé*.**
> **Elle la regardait *avec envie*.**

5.2 Adverbial clauses

These are introduced by a conjunction other than **que**, or by a compound conjunction which combines another word with **que**. They are described more fully in CLAUSES, **4.**

5.3 Uses of adverbial phrases and adverbial clauses

Like adverbs, adverbial phrases and adverbial clauses can be used to provide additional information in relation to a verb (*see* BUILDING SENTENCES, **6.**). Compare:

Il marche *péniblement*. (= adverb)
Il marche *avec beaucoup de peine*. (= adverbial phrase)
Elle se lève *tôt*. (= adverb)
Elle se lève *de bon matin*. (= adverbial phrase)
Elle se lève *dès que son réveil sonne*. (= adverbial clause)

PREPOSITIONS

---

1. Forms of Prepositions

2. Prepositions used to indicate Place, Time, Means etc.
  à ▲ après ▲ avant etc.

3. Prepositions used Before the Object of Certain Verbs

4. Prepositions used Before an Infinitive

5. Use of Prepositions in Compound Words
  un verre à vin/un verre de vin

Prepositions never change their form. They can be used:

– to introduce the object of a verb (as in **this depends *on* the weather**)

– to provide additional information within the sentence relating, for example, to time (as in **we met *on* a Saturday**), place (**the book is *on* the table**) and the like.

---

1. Forms of prepositions

There are two kinds of preposition:

– prepositions which consist of a single word. Here are the most common:

> à ▲ après ▲ avant ▲ avec ▲ chez ▲ contre ▲ dans ▲ de ▲ depuis ▲ derrière ▲ dessous ▲ dessus ▲ devant ▲ durant ▲ en ▲ entre ▲ envers ▲ jusque ▲ par ▲ parmi ▲ pendant ▲ pour ▲ sans ▲ sauf ▲ selon ▲ sous ▲ sur ▲ vers

> *NOTE*: For the contraction of **à** and **de** when used with the definite article, *see* DETERMINERS, **1**.

– prepositional phrases consisting of more than one word. For example:

> à cause de ▲ afin de ▲ à l'extérieur de ▲ à l'intérieur de ▲ au milieu de ▲ au bout de ▲ de la part de ▲ en dépit de ▲ en vue de ▲ jusqu'à

2. Prepositions used to indicate place, time, means etc.

There are many prepositions in French, and they are used, as in English, to introduce a reference to time, place, manner, means, cause and so on. Most of them have more than one meaning.

preposition	*translated as (refers to)*	*example*
à	to (place)	**Je rentre *à* Paris.**
		Tu veux aller *à* la piscine avec moi ?
	in (place)	**Ils habitent *à* Dublin.**
	at (place)	**Il était *à* la maison**
	at (time)	**Ils seront là *à* huit heures.**
après	after (place)	**Tournez *après* le deuxième feu rouge.**
	after (time)	**Elle est arrivée *après* tout le monde.**
avant	before (place)	**Tournez *avant* l'église.**
	before (time)	**Soyez-y *avant* huit heures.**
avec	with (means)	**Essaie *avec* un ouvre-boîte.**
	with (accompaniment)	**Il est venu *avec* ses quatre enfants.**
	with (manner)	**Elle marche *avec* difficulté.**
chez	at (the home of)	**Il était *chez* son oncle.**
	at (shop, office)	**J'ai rendez-vous *chez* le dentiste.**
	at (work)	**Il travaille *chez* Renault.**
contre	against (place)	**Il vaut mieux l'appuyer *contre* le mur.**
	against (opposition)	**Ils se sont déclarés *contre* la grève.**
dans	in (place)	**J'ai déjà cherché *dans* la cuisine**
	in (time)	**Je reviens *dans* cinq minutes.**
de	from	**Elle revient *du* cinéma.**
	of	**Il a bu un verre *de* vin.**
		C'est le cousin *d'*Isabelle.
	about	**Ils ont parlé *du* temps.**
depuis	since (time)	**Il habite ici *depuis* 1990.**
	for (time)	**Il habite ici *depuis* cinq ans.**
derrière	behind	**Les clés sont *derrière* la porte.**
devant	in front of	**Arrêtez-vous *devant* le portail.**

durant	during	Il a plu *durant* tout le mois d'octobre.
en	to (place)	Nous allons *en* France.
	in (place)	Il habite *en* Écosse.
	in (time)	Elle a lu le livre *en* une semaine.
entre	between (place)	L'école est *entre* la mairie et l'église.
	between (alternatives)	Ils hésitent *entre* les deux solutions.
envers	to	Il est aimable *envers* tout le monde.
par	through (place)	L'autoroute passe *par* Nantes.
	by (agent)	Le voleur a été arrêté *par* la police.
parmi	among	Votre document doit être *parmi* cette pile de papiers.
pendant	during	Il est mort *pendant* la guerre.
	for (time)	Nous les avons attendus *pendant* deux heures.
pour	for (intended for)	Prends-le, c'est *pour* toi.
	for (place)	Ils partent *pour* l'Italie demain
	for (time)	Est-ce que vous pourrez avoir fini *pour* demain ?
	for (in favour of)	Des millions d'électeurs ont voté *pour* lui
	for (instead of)	Vas-y *pour* moi.
sans	without	Allez-y *sans* moi.
		Il boit son thé *sans* sucre.
sous	beneath, under	Les casseroles sont *sous* l'évier.
sur	on	Les clés sont *sur* mon bureau.
vers	towards (place)	Elle s'est retournée *vers* lui
	around (time)	Ils sont arrivés *vers* dix heures

3. Prepositions used before the object of certain verbs

As in English, certain verbs in French are always linked to their object by a preposition. A list of the most common verbs is given below. Note that the preposition is not necessarily the same as the English preposition in all cases, and that there are some verbs which require a preposition in French which do not require one in English. Equally, some verbs which require a preposition in English do not require one in French.

accuser (qqn) de (qqch)
s'adapter à (qqch)
adresser (qqch) à (qqn)
s'adresser à (qqn)
annoncer (qqch) à (qqn)
s'apercevoir de (qqch)
apprendre (qqch) à (qqn)
s'approcher de (qqn/qqch)
appuyer sur (qqch)
s'attendre à (qqch)
avertir (qqn) de (qqch)
avouer (qqch) à (qqn)
causer (qqch) à (qqn)
changer de (qqch)
charger (qqn) de (qqch)
compter sur (qqn/qqch)
confier (qqch) à (qqn)
confondre (qqn/qqch) avec (qqn/qqch)
conseiller (qqch) à (qqn)
consister en (qqch)
convaincre (qqn) de (qqch)
croire à OR en (qqch)
demander (qqch) à (qqn)
dépendre de (qqn/qqch)
dire (qqch) à (qqn)
donner (qqch) à (qqn)
échanger (qqch) contre (qqch)/avec (qqn)
écrire (qqch) à (qqn)
enseigner (qqch) à (qqn)
envoyer (qqch) à (qqn)
s'excuser de (qqch)
s'habituer à (qqch)

indiquer (qqch) à (qqn)
interdire (qqch) à (qqn)
s'intéresser à (qqch/qqn)
jouer à OR de (qqch)
laisser (qqch) à (qqn)
lancer (qqch) à (qqn)
manquer de (qqch)
se marier avec (qqn)
se méfier de (qqn/qqch)
montrer (qqch) à (qqn)
nuire à (qqn/qqch)
obtenir (qqch) de (qqn)
s'occuper de (qqch/qqn)
offrir (qqch) à (qqn)
pardonner (qqch) à (qqn)
parler de (qqch/qqn) à (qqn)
penser à (qqn/qqch)
préférer (qqch/qqn) à (qqch/qqn)
prêter (qqch) à (qqn)
prévenir (qqn) de (qqch)
profiter de (qqch)
promettre (qqch) à (qqn)
proposer (qqch) à (qqn)
rappeler (qqch) à (qqn)
refuser (qqch) à (qqn)
rendre (qqch) à (qqn)
répondre (qqch) à (qqn)
rêver de (qqch/qqn)
souhaiter qqch à (qqn)
se souvenir de (qqch/qqn)
succéder à (qqn/qqch)
suffire à (qqn/qqch)
tenir à (qqn/qqch) (to be attached to)
tenir de (qqn) (to look like)

4. Prepositions used before an infinitive

Many verbs in French are linked to the following infinitive by a preposition. A list of the most common is given below. Note that the preposition is not necessarily the same as that required by the corresponding verb in English. Rather than being followed by an infinitive, many of the English verbs would be followed by a form ending in -ing, e.g. to refrain from *doing* something. In the list, 'inf' = 'infinitive'.

s'abstenir de (+ inf)
accepter de (+ inf)
accuser (qqn) de (+ inf)
s'agir: il s'agit de (+ inf)
aider (qqn) à (+ inf)
s'arranger pour (+inf)
arriver à (+ inf)(to succeed in)
s'attendre à (+ inf)
avoir à (+ inf) (to have to)
chercher à (+ inf) (to try to)
commencer à OR de (+ inf)
conseiller à (qqn) de (+ inf)
consentir à (+ inf)
consister à (+ inf)
continuer à (+ inf)
convaincre (qqn) de (+inf)
convenir de (+ inf)
décider de (+inf)
défendre à (qqn) de (+ inf)
demander à (qqn) de (+ inf)
empêcher (qqn) de (+ inf)
envisager de (+ inf)
essayer de (+ inf)

s'excuser de (+ inf)
finir de (+ inf)
forcer (qqn) à (+ inf)
s'habituer à (+ inf)
interdire à (qqn) de (+ inf)
se mettre à (+ inf)
obliger (qqn) à (+ inf)
offrir à (qqn) de (+ inf)
ordonner à (qqn) de (+ inf)
pardonner à (qqn) de (+ inf)
parvenir à (+ inf)(to succeed in)
penser à (+ inf)
permettre à (qqn) de (+ inf)
se préparer à (+ inf)
promettre à (qqn) de (+ inf)
proposer à (qqn) de (+ inf)
rappeler à (qqn) de (+ inf)
refuser de (+ inf)
regretter de (+ inf)
réussir à (+ inf)
tarder à (+ inf)
tenter de (+ inf)
venir de (+ inf) (to have just)

> *NOTE:* When any preposition is followed by a verb in French, that verb must be in the infinitive:
>
> **Il est sorti sans me voir.** (He went out without seeing me.)
> **Il a frappé avant d'entrer.** (He knocked before going in.)
>
> The exception to this rule is **en** (*see* VERBS, **8.8**).

5. Use of prepositions in compound words

À and de are often used in the formation of compound words.

COMPARE

> Note the difference between:
>
> **un verre à vin** (= a wine glass) ▲ **un verre de vin** (= a glass of wine)
> **une tasse à thé** (= a tea cup) ▲ **une tasse de thé** (= a cup of tea)
> **une corbeille à fruits** (= a fruit basket) ▲ **une corbeille de fruits** (= a basket of fruit)

CONJUNCTIONS

> **1. Coordinating Conjunctions**
> et ▲ ni ... ni ▲ mais ▲ soit ... soit
>
> **2. Subordinating Conjunctions**
> que ▲ comme ▲ pourvu que ▲ bien que
>
> Conjunctions are words which join different parts of a sentence together. There are two types of conjunction in French, as in English: coordinating conjunctions and subordinating conjunctions.

1. Coordinating conjunctions

Coordinating conjunctions are used to link together:

– two words of the same kind: two nouns, two verbs, two adjectives and so on

– two phrases of the same kind, or two clauses of the same kind. An important feature of clauses joined together by coordinating conjunctions is that each clause makes sense without the other. For example, if you say in English it was cold and it was raining, both it was cold and it was raining would make sense on their own even if they were not joined together. This is not the case, as we shall see, with clauses joined together by subordinating conjunctions.

1.1 Forms of the coordinating conjunctions

The following table indicates the most common coordinating conjunctions, as well as those phrases which operate like coordinating conjunctions:

	conjunctions	*phrases*
adding, negating	**et, ni**	**ni ... ni**
consequences	**donc**	**c'est pourquoi, par conséquent**
cause	**car**	**parce que**
opposition	**mais, or**	
alternatives	**ou**	**ou bien (... ou bien), soit ... soit**

1.2 Uses of the coordinating conjunctions

■ *Et*

– Et (and) joins together two words of the same kind – noun, adjective, verb etc.:

Paul *et* Anne viennent de sortir.
Je voudrais du lait *et* du sucre.

– Et can also link two clauses of the same kind:

La rivière a débordé *et* les champs ont été inondés.

– As in English, et only appears before the last member of a list:

Il faudrait acheter du lait, du beurre, des œufs *et* de la margarine.

NOTE: There are three ways of translating **both** into French:

* When **both** refers to two items of the same kind (e.g. **two books**, **two sisters**), it is translated as **les deux** when it is an adjective, and as **tous les deux** or **toutes les deux** when it is a pronoun:

J'aime *les deux* chansons. → **Je les aime *toutes les deux*.**
Ils sont venus *tous les deux*.

* When **both ... and** is used to join two nouns which are different (e.g. **a book** and **a magazine**, **a dog** and **a cat**), the commonest translation in modern French is **tant ... que**:

Tant les professeurs ***que*** les élèves ont apprécié le film.

Alternatively, et ... et can be used instead:

Cette région offre *et* le soleil *et* la mer.

* When **both ... and** joins two adjectives or adverbs, it is most commonly translated by **à la fois**:

Ce livre est *à la fois* intéressant et utile.
Il travaille *à la fois* vite et bien.

■ *Ni*

– Ni ... ni (neither ... nor) joins together two or more items which are being excluded. The verb in the sentence is always preceded by ne:

Ce tissu *ne* réclame *ni* repassage *ni* séchage. (This cloth requires neither ironing nor drying.)

> *NOTE*: When two or more verbs are joined by **ni**, **ne** is repeated before each verb:
>
> Il *ne* fume ni *ne* boit.
> Il *ne* veut ni *ne* peut le faire.
>
> A more common way of linking two verbs in spoken French would be to repeat **ne** and **pas**:
>
> Il *ne* fume *pas* et *ne* boit *pas* (non plus).

– Ni l'un(e) ni l'autre usually translates as neither of them:

Je *ne* les connais *ni l'un ni l'autre.*

– Ni is also used together with sans, in which case it is translated into English as or:

Il prend son café *sans* lait *ni* sucre. (without milk or sugar)

■ *Ou (… ou), ou bien (… ou bien), soit … soit*

If they appear only once in a sentence, ou and ou bien both mean or. If they are repeated, they then mean either … or, which is also the meaning of soit … soit:

Tu veux venir *ou* non ?
Prends l'un *ou* l'autre, comme tu voudras.
Vous pouvez vous adresser *ou bien* à lui *ou bien* à son assistant.
Tu peux venir *soit* jeudi, *soit* vendredi.

> *NOTE*: Like **or** in English, **ou** is used to explain a difficult word or expression by adding a more simple word or expression after it. **Ou** then becomes the equivalent of phrases such as **c'est-à-dire** (that is to say) or **autrement dit** (in other words). In such cases, the second word or expression is not preceded by a determiner:
>
> le carassin doré *ou* poisson rouge ▲ le silure *ou* poisson-chat

■ *Mais*

– Mais means but:

Ce n'est pas ta faute *mais* la sienne.
Je vous accompagnerais bien *mais* je n'ai pas le temps.
Elle est gentille *mais* distraite.

– It is used to emphasize both oui and si. In this case their meaning becomes of course:

> Tu le connais déjà ? *Mais oui !*
> Tu ne veux pas venir ? *Mais si !*

■ *Or*

Or is used to express a contradiction between two words or clauses, and can be translated as whereas or however:

> Il pensait que ses prévisions se vérifieraient, *or* elles étaient fausses. (whereas)
> Ce matériel nous serait utile; *or*, faute de crédits, nous ne pouvons pas l'acheter. (however)

■ *Donc, par conséquent, c'est pourquoi, aussi*

– Donc, par conséquent and c'est pourquoi all mean therefore or so:

> Il a refusé; il est *donc* inutile d'insister.
> Il est faible et *par conséquent* influençable.
> Lui seul était disponible, *c'est pourquoi* j'ai fait appel à lui.

– Aussi also means therefore if it is followed by a verb whose subject is placed *after* that verb:

> Il a tort. *Aussi* devrait-il s'excuser.

This use of aussi is only found in literary French.

■ *Car*

Car means for or because, and is only used in very formal or in written French:

> Il n'insista pas *car* au fond, il n'y tenait pas vraiment.
> Il ne parlait pas beaucoup *car* tel était son caractère.

2. Subordinating conjunctions

Subordinating conjunctions are always used to join clauses of different types together. One of the clauses would make sense on its own, but the other would not. The clause which would make sense on its own is called the *main clause*, while the clause which cannot stand on its own is called the *subordinate clause*. For example, in the sentence if it rains, I'll go to the cinema, I'll go to the cinema makes sense on its own and is therefore the main clause. The clause if it rains does not make sense on its own, however. It only makes sense if there is another clause to tell you what will happen if it rains, or if it is functioning as the answer to a question such as **Will you go to the cinema?** Since it cannot form a sentence on its own, it is the subordinate clause. The subordinating conjunction which joins these two clauses together is **if**. To take a second example, in a sentence such as **I'll leave when I've finished**, the main clause is **I'll leave**, the subordinate clause is **when I've finished**, and the subordinating conjunction is **when**.

2.1 Forms of the subordinating conjunctions

Note the distinction between que and the other subordinating conjunctions.

■ *Que*

Que (that) introduces what is known as a noun clause. It is called a noun clause because if you replaced it with a noun the sentence would still make sense (though it might mean something different). For example, if you say **I believe that he is telling the truth**, you could replace the noun clause **that he is telling the truth** with the noun **his story** – **I believe his story** – and the sentence would still be perfectly meaningful. Noun clauses can be either the subject or the object of the verb in the main clause.

An important difference between French and English is that the word **that** can often be left out before a noun clause in English. Que can never be left out before a noun clause in French, and this rule must always be borne in mind (*see* CLAUSES):

> **Je ne pense pas *qu*'il ait raison.** (I do not think he is right.)
> **_Qu_'il ait raison m'étonnerait beaucoup.** (I would be surprised if he was right.)
> **La raison de son départ est *qu*'il n'est pas satisfait.** (The reason he is leaving is that he is not satisfied.)

■ Other subordinating conjunctions

These are used to introduce other kinds of subordinate clause which express conditions (si, pourvu que, au cas où), relationships of time (quand, lorsque, aussitôt que, dès que), cause (parce que, puisque), purpose (pour que, afin que) and the like. Some subordinating conjunctions (comme or alors que, for example) have more than one meaning, and quite a few require the verb that follows to be in the subjunctive (*see* VERBS, **8.4**).

2.2 Uses of the subordinating conjunctions

Uses of the subordinating conjunctions are explained in CLAUSES.

VERBS

1. **Different Groups of Verbs**
   chanter ▲ finir ▲ vendre

2. **Special Verbs used to form Certain Tenses:**
   avoir and *être*

3. **Verbs which may be followed by Another Verb**
   faire ▲ laisser ▲ pouvoir ▲ devoir ▲ vouloir ▲ savoir ▲ falloir

4. **Verbs indicating States rather than Actions**
   être ▲ devenir ▲ sembler ▲ paraître ▲ rester ▲ demeurer ▲ passer pour ▲ avoir l'air

5. **Active and Passive Use of Verbs**
   La police l'a arrêté → Il a été arrêté par la police
   Sa femme l'a accompagné → Il a été accompagné de sa femme

6. **Reflexive Verbs**
   se laver ▲ se blesser ▲ s'apercevoir ▲ se souvenir

7. **Impersonal Constructions**
   il neige ▲ il faut que ▲ il y a

8. **Tenses and Moods**
   present ▲ perfect ▲ future etc.
   indicative ▲ subjunctive ▲ imperative etc.

9. **Forming the Different Tenses of the Verb**

10. **Verb Tables**

When we say that verbs *conjugate*, we mean that the ending of the verb changes, depending on whether its subject is **I, you, they** etc., whether the verb refers to the present or the past, and so on. For example, in English we add an **-s** in the present if the subject is **he, she** or **it** – as in **he listens, it rains**; some verbs add **-ed** in the past – **he listened, it rained**; and some change their vowel – **he sings** → **he sang, they fall** → **they fell** – and so on. However, the conjugation of verbs in French involves rather more verb endings than it does in English.

Any form of any French verb can be broken down into two parts:

– the *stem* of the verb, which almost never changes (or if it does, it only changes very slightly)

– the *ending*, which is added to the end of the stem.

The stem indicates the meaning of the verb; the ending varies according to the *subject* and *tense* of the verb, and whether it is in the *indicative* or the *subjunctive*. For example, if we take the English verb **listens, listen-** is the stem and **-s** is the ending. In the French verb **il préparait (he prepared), prépar-** is the stem of the verb, and **-ait** is the ending.

Numbers in square brackets used after verbs throughout this chapter (e.g. chanter [1]) refer to a verb's number in the VERB TABLES, **10.**

1. Different groups of verbs

Verbs in French are divided into three groups, or conjugations. Which group they belong to depends primarily on the ending of the *infinitive*. The infinitive, which corresponds to the verb preceded by **to** in English – for example, **to read, to listen** and the like – is the form of the verb you will always find if you look the word up in a dictionary.

■ Verbs whose infinitive ends in -er belong to the first group:

chant*er* (to sing) ▲ **aim***er* (to love, to like) ▲ **cri***er* (to shout)

■ Verbs whose infinitive ends in -ir and whose present participle ends in -issant belong to the second group (the present participle – *pp* – corresponds in English to the part of the verb which ends in -ing: singing, reading etc.):

fin*ir* (*pp* **finissant**) (to finish) ▲ **sub***ir* (*pp* **subissant**) (to undergo) ▲ **guér***ir* (*pp* **guérissant**) (to heal)

■ Verbs ending in -oir and -re, as well as those verbs ending in -ir whose present participle ends in -ant (not -issant) all belong to the third group:

 voir (to see) ▲ **s'asseoir** (to sit down) ▲ **devoir** (to owe, to have)
 vendre (to sell) ▲ **croire** (to believe) ▲ **naître** (to be born)
 courir (*pp* **courant**) (to run) ▲ **mourir** (*pp* **mourant**) (to die) ▲ **dormir**
 (*pp* **dormant**) (to sleep)

■ In most cases, the stem of a verb is found by removing the ending (-er,
-ir, -oir or -re) from the infinitive, for example:

 chanter: stem **chant-**
 finir: stem **fin-**
 vendre: stem **vend-**

However, verbs of the second group have two stems, as explained below
(*see* 1.2), and a few other irregular verbs have three or more stems
depending on the tense and subject of the verb:

 *all*er: je *v*ais → j'*ir*ai
 *pouv*oir: je *p*eux → nous *pourr*ons → que je *puiss*e

1.1 Verbs belonging to the first group

■ With the notable exception of **aller** and **envoyer**, the conjugation of
most verbs belonging to the first group is regular. They conjugate in
exactly the same way as the verb **chanter** [1] (*see* VERB TABLES, **10.**).

> *NOTE*: All newly created French verbs, in fields such as electronics
> or information technology, go automatically into the first group:
>
> **informatiser** (to computerize) ▲ **formater** (to format)

■ However, the following spelling changes should be borne in mind:
– with verbs whose stem ends in -g, -g changes to -ge if the ending begins
with -a or -o:

 manger: stem **mang-** <u>BUT</u> **je mangeais**
 nager: stem **nag-** <u>BUT</u> **je nageais, nous nageons**

– with verbs whose stem ends in -c, -c changes to -ç if the ending begins
with -a, -o or -u:

 commencer: stem **commenc-**, **je commence** <u>BUT</u> **nous commençons**
 lancer: stem **lanc-** <u>BUT</u> **je lançais, nous lançons**

– with verbs whose stem ends in -y, -y changes to -i before -e (but not
before -é):

envoyer: stem **envoy-** <u>BUT</u> **j'envoie**
nettoyer: stem **nettoy-** <u>BUT</u> **tu nettoies**

– with verbs whose stem ends in -et or -el, an additional t or l is added to the stem before -e (but not before -é):

jeter: stem **jet-** <u>BUT</u> **je jette** (jeter [38])
appeler: stem **appel-** <u>BUT</u> **elles appellent** (appeler [10])

However, some verbs whose stem ends in -et or -el do not add an extra t or l. Instead a grave accent is placed on the e which comes before the t or l. This is the case for verbs like peler [49]. Here are some others:

geler: stem **gel-** <u>BUT</u> **je gèle**
modeler: stem **model-** <u>BUT</u> **elle modèle**
harceler: stem **harcel-** <u>BUT</u> **il harcèle**

It is also the case for verbs like acheter [8].

– this also happens to a number of other verbs whose stem contains the vowel e:

lever: **tu lèves** <u>BUT</u> **tu levais**
mener: **je mène** <u>BUT</u> **nous menons**

> NOTE: If the last vowel of the stem is **-é**, this **-é** changes to **-è** if the ending of the verb is **-e**, **-es** or **-ent**:
>
> espérer: **j'espère** <u>BUT</u> **j'espérais**

1.2 Verbs belonging to the second group

The conjugation of verbs belonging to the second group is regular. Some forms are based on the normal stem, found by removing the -ir of the infinitive, and some on the longer stem which is obtained by removing the -ant of the present participle. They are conjugated like the verb finir [2] (*see* VERB TABLES, **10.**):

finir (finissant): je finis → nous finissons → il finissait

> NOTE: In the case of the verb **haïr** (**to hate**), **ï** changes to **i** in the singular of the present tense:
>
> haïr: je hais → tu hais → il hait

1.3 Verbs belonging to the third group

Verbs of the third conjugation are the most irregular of all, since most of them have two or more stems:

peindre: vous *peindre*z <u>BUT</u> je *peins*, nous *peignons*
résoudre: vous *résoudre*z <u>BUT</u> je *résous*, nous *résolvons*, *résolu*
venir: nous *venons* <u>BUT</u> je *viens*, ils *viendront*

You should therefore check the VERB TABLES, **10.** if you are unsure about how to conjugate any of these verbs.

NOTE: In the case of verbs whose infinitive ends in **-aître**, and also in the case of the verb **plaire**, a circumflex accent is placed on the **i** of the stem when the next letter is a **t**:

para*î*tre: il para*î*t	→	nous para*i*ssons
conna*î*tre: il conna*î*t	→	nous conna*i*ssons
pla*i*re: il pla*î*t	→	nous pla*i*sons

---

2. Special verbs used to form certain tenses: *avoir* and *être*

As well as being ordinary verbs in their own right – **avoir** means to have and **être** means to be – these two verbs are also used to form certain tenses of other verbs. When used in this way, they are known as *auxiliary verbs*, because they *help* to form these other tenses. Since these tenses themselves consist of more than one word, they are known as *compound tenses*, like have read or had eaten in English. In compound tenses, these auxiliary verbs are always followed by the *past participle* of the verb which is being put into the compound tense (*see* **8.7**):

Je l'*ai rencontré* hier.
Lui me l'*aurait permis*.
Il s'*est passé* quelque chose.

2.1 *Avoir*

Avoir is used as an auxiliary verb to form the compound tenses of:

– the verb être and the verb avoir itself:

> J'*ai été* **malade.** (I have been ill.)
> Ils *avaient été* **étonnés.** (They had been astonished.)
> Nous *avons eu* **des cadeaux à Noël.** (We got some presents at Christmas.
> Il *aurait eu* **trop peur.** (He would have been too frightened.)

– all transitive as well as those intransitive verbs not described in **2.**2 below (*see* BUILDING SENTENCES, **3.** if you are unsure of the difference between transitive and intransitive verbs):

> Il *aura* oublié quelque chose.
> Nous *avions* perdu du temps.
>
> Elle *a* bien joué.
> Tu *as* dormi.

2.2 Être

Être is used as an auxiliary verb to form the compound tenses of:
– most verbs indicating motion or a change of state of some kind (*see* BUILDING SENTENCES, **3.**). The most commonly used of these verbs are:

> aller ▲ arriver ▲ devenir ▲ entrer ▲ monter ▲ mourir ▲ naître ▲ partir ▲ rentrer ▲ repartir ▲ rester ▲ retourner ▲ revenir ▲ sortir ▲ venir

> Ce sont eux qui y *sont* allés.
> Nous *sommes* arrivées.
> Elle *est* descendue.
> Elle *est* devenue grande.
> Elle *est* entrée.
> Ils *sont* montés au deuxième étage.
> Il *est* mort il y a longtemps.
> Elle *est* née ici.
> Ils *sont* partis.
> Il *est* passé nous voir.
> Ils *sont* restés quelques instants seulement.
> Ils *sont* retournés les chercher.
> Marie *est* revenue.
> Ils *sont* sortis.
> Paul *est* venu me voir.

> NOTE: There are some verbs of motion and some verbs indicating a change of state which are not conjugated with **être**, but with **avoir**:
>
> Il *a* couru.
> Elle *a* marché.
> Il les *avait* suivis.
> Il *a* grossi.
> Elle *a* maigri.

COMPARE

> Demeurer is conjugated with **être** when it means **to remain**, and with **avoir** when it means **to live**:
>
> Elle *était* demeurée silencieuse. (= She remained silent.)
> Ils *ont* demeuré ici. (= They lived here.)

– all purely reflexive verbs (*see* **6**.), and indeed any verbs which are used with a reflexive pronoun (*see* PRONOUNS, **2**.):

Il s'en *était* repenti.
Elle s'*est* avancée.
Ils se *sont* regardés.
Nous nous *sommes* bien entendus.
Je m'en *suis* aperçu.
L'avion se *serait* écrasé.

2.3 Forming the passive with *être*

Être is always used as the auxiliary to form the passive, just as the verb to be is used to form the passive in English (*see* **5**.):

Elle *est* attendue par toute la délégation. (she is expected)
Elle *a été* consternée par cette nouvelle. (she was dismayed)
La décision *sera* prise ultérieurement. (the decision will be taken)
L'avion *aurait été* détourné par des terroristes. (The plane would appear to have been hijacked.)

2.4 Agreement of the past participle when verbs are conjugated with *être*

The forms of the past participle used in compound tenses (in other words, the perfect, the pluperfect, the past anterior, the future perfect, the conditional perfect, the perfect subjunctive and the pluperfect subjunctive) always agree in gender and number with the *subject* of the verb when these tenses are formed with the auxiliary verb être:

Elle *est* venue nous voir.
Elles *sont* venues nous voir.
Jean et elle *sont* venus nous voir.
Jean et Yves *sont* venus nous voir.

NOTE: The past participle of verbs used reflexively also agrees in gender and number with the subject of the verb:

Ils s'en *sont* repentis.
Elles se *sont* regardées.
Ils se *sont* fâchés.

However, the past participle of a reflexive verb does *not* agree:
* when the reflexive pronoun is an indirect object pronoun, some other noun or pronoun being the object of the verb:

Ils se sont *lavé* les mains. (the object of *lavé* is *les mains*, not *se*)
Elles se sont *réparti* la tâche. (the object of *réparti* is *la tâche*)
Ils se sont *envoyé* des colis. (the object of *envoyé* is *des colis*)

If for any reason the direct object is placed *before* the reflexive verb, the past participle then agrees with the object:

Les fleurs qu'ils se sont *envoyées* n'ont pas encore été livrées.

* in cases where the reflexive verb cannot take a direct object because the verb is always linked to its object by a preposition when it is not reflexive:

Elles se sont *parlé*. (parler *à* qqn)
Ils se sont *téléphoné*. (téléphoner *à* qqn)

2.5 Agreement of the past participle when verbs are conjugated with *avoir*

■ The past participle in compound tenses of verbs conjugated with avoir does not change if the direct object, when there is one, is placed *after* the verb:

> **Elle a *appris* la nouvelle hier.**
> **Elle a *posté* cette lettre ce matin.**
> **Elles m'ont *donné* des gâteaux.**
> **Ils ont *su* que vous veniez.**
> **Elle a *couru* tout le long du chemin.**

■ The past participle *does* agree with the direct object when the latter is placed before the verb. In practice this only occurs in three situations:

– in adjectival clauses (*see* CLAUSES, **2.**)

– in questions

– when the object is replaced by a pronoun.

> **Les gâteaux qu'elles m'ont *donnés* étaient délicieux.**
> **La robe qu'elle m'a *montrée* m'a plu.**
> **La lettre qu'elle a *postée* ce matin ne peut pas être déjà arrivée.**
> **La nouvelle qu'elle a *apprise* hier l'a *bouleversée*.**
> **Quelle robe as-tu *choisie* ?**
> **Les papiers, je les ai *jetés*.**

3. Verbs which may be followed by another verb

Occasionally verbs other than avoir and être can be used as auxiliaries, in which case they are followed by a verb in the infinitive:

> **Elle *fait* rire tout le monde.** (She makes everyone laugh.)
> **Il n'*a* pas *pu* achever sa phrase.** (He could not finish his sentence.)

3.1 The auxiliaries *faire* and *laisser*

■ *Faire*

When used as an auxiliary, faire often has the same meaning as the verb to have carries in English in sentences such as he had his car repaired or they had their house painted. It indicates that the action of the second verb is actually carried out by someone other than the subject of the sentence:

> **Ils se sont fait *construire* une maison.** (They had a house built.)
> **Elle s'est fait *couper* les cheveux.** (She had her hair cut.)

Note that faire used as an auxiliary in this way can be followed by another **faire** which retains its usual meaning, the two verbs together meaning to have something done:

> **À l'école, elle *fait faire* beaucoup de coloriages aux enfants.** (At school she has the children colour in a lot.)
> **Il s'est *fait faire* un bilan de santé.** (He had a checkup carried out.)

Se faire + INFINITIVE is also used commonly in spoken French to form a passive (*see* **5.**):

> **Il *s'est fait mordre* par un chien.** (He was bitten by a dog.)
> **Je *me suis fait gronder* par le prof.** (I was told off by the teacher.)

■ *Laisser*

Laisser can also be used as an auxiliary, meaning to let:

> ***Laisse*-la parler.**
> **Le dessous de la porte *laisse* passer tous les courants d'air.**
> **Ses parents le *laissent* faire tout ce qu'il veut.**

3.2 The auxiliaries *pouvoir* and *devoir*

■ When they are used as auxiliaries, **pouvoir** and **devoir** are always followed by a verb in the infinitive:

> **Tu *peux* venir ce soir.** (You can come this evening.)
> **Je n'ai pas *pu* sortir hier.** (I could not get out yesterday.)
> **Nous *devons* rentrer chez nous.** (We must go home.)
> **Ils *doivent* aller à Paris.** (They must go to Paris.)

■ *Pouvoir*

Pouvoir has various meanings:

– It can express possibility, and is translated into English as **can** or **could**, or one of the tenses of the phrase **to be able**:

> **Tu *peux* porter ça tout seul ?** (Can you carry that on your own?)
> **Je ne *peux* pas lire de loin.** (I cannot read from a distance.)
> **Je *n'ai pas pu* l'en empêcher.** (I could not stop him.)
> **Elle *n'avait pas pu* sortir.** (She had not been able to go out.)

– It can express probability, in which case it is usually translated as **may** or **might**:

> **Ils *peuvent* avoir été retardés par des embouteillages.** (They might have been held up in traffic jams.)

Elle *a pu* se tromper. (She might have been wrong.)

– It can express the fact that permission has been given to do something, in which case it translates as **can** in everyday English, or as **may** or **might** in more formal circumstances:

Tu *peux* rester, tu ne nous déranges pas. (you can/may stay)
Vous *pouvez* sortir. (You can/may go out.)
Si je *peux* faire une remarque, c'est un peu tard pour s'inquiéter. (if I may say so)

– It is used in the conditional to express the idea of **could** in a polite request:

Pourriez-vous me tenir ceci ? (Could you hold this for me?)
Pourriez-vous m'accorder un instant ? (Could you give me a moment of your time?)

> NOTE:
> * When **pouvoir** is used as an auxiliary it can only ever be followed by a normal infinitive. Consequently, to express the idea **could have**, the conditional of **avoir** is placed before the past participle of **pouvoir** (**pu**) and the following infinitive remains unchanged:
>
> **Tu *aurais pu* venir.** (You could have come.)
> **Il *aurait pu* accepter.** (He could have accepted.)
>
> * The impersonal expression **il se peut que** also expresses probability, and consequently usually translates as **may** or **might**. It is always followed by a subjunctive:
>
> **Il se peut qu'il accepte.** (He might accept.)
> **Il se pourrait qu'il y ait une erreur.** (There might be a mistake.)

■ *Devoir*

Devoir also has various meanings:

– It can express obligation, in which case it is translated as **must** or one of the tenses of the phrase to **have to**:

Vous *devez* réserver une place. (You must book a seat.)
Ce billet *doit* être composté. (This ticket must be stamped.)
Il *a dû* le faire lui-même. (He had to do it himself.)
Il *devra* résoudre ce problème. (He will have to solve this problem.)

– When used in the imperfect, **devoir** expresses the fact that something which was supposed to happen did not happen. In such cases it translates into English as **was supposed to**, or simply **was to**:

> **Ils *devaient* être là à quinze heures, mais leur train a eu du retard.**
> (they were (supposed) to be there at three o'clock)

– When used in the conditional, **devoir** expresses a moral obligation, and is usually translated into English as **should** or **ought to**:

> **Tu *devrais* essayer.** (You should/ought to try.)
> **Tu ne *devrais* pas sortir si peu couvert.** (you should not/ought not to go out)

NOTE: As was the case with **pouvoir**, **devoir** can only ever be followed by a normal infinitive. Consequently, to express the idea **should have**, the conditional of **avoir** is placed in front of the past participle of **devoir** (**dû**) and the following infinitive remains unchanged:

> **Ils *auraient dû* arriver hier.** (They should have arrived yesterday.)
> **Tu *aurais dû* venir.** (You should have come.)

– In certain cases, **devoir** can express probability, and is then usually translated into English as **must**:

> **Allons-y, ils *doivent* s'impatienter.** (they must be getting impatient)
> **Tes parents *doivent* être furieux.** (Your parents must be furious.)

NOTE: The auxiliary verb **avoir** is placed in front of the past participle of **devoir** in compound tenses:

> **Il *a dû* oublier.** (He must have forgotten.)
> **Nous *avons dû* nous tromper.** (We must have made a mistake.)

3.3 *Vouloir, savoir* and *falloir*

■ *Vouloir*

– Vouloir means to want. While to want is used only with an infinitive in

English, **vouloir** can be used with an infinitive in French only when the subject of the second verb is the same as the subject of **vouloir**. If the subject of **vouloir** and the subject of the second verb are different, then **que** + SUBJUNCTIVE *must* be used:

> **Les enfants *veulent* venir aussi.** (The children want to come too.)
> **Je *veux* qu'ils viennent.** (I want them to come.)

– When used in the conditional, **vouloir** expresses a polite request, and is usually translated into English as **would like to**:

> **Je *voudrais* avoir votre avis sur cette question.** (I would like to have your opinion on this matter.)
> **Quelqu'un *voudrait* vous parler.** (Someone would like to speak to you.)

■ *Savoir*

Savoir can be followed by an infinitive, or by **que** or **si** + INDICATIVE:

– When followed by an infinitive, it is usually translated into English as **can**:

> **Elle ne *sait* pas skier.** (She cannot ski.)
> **Tu *sais* nager ?** (Can you swim?)

– Otherwise it translates as **to know**:

> **Je *sais* qu'elle a raison.**
> **Il ne *sait* pas qu'ils sont tous là, c'est une surprise.**
> **Je ne *sais* pas si j'aurai le temps.**

■ *Falloir*

- Falloir is an impersonal verb (*see* **7.**): in other words, it is only ever found with **il** as its subject, or else in the infinitive.

– Falloir can be followed by the infinitive or by **que** + SUBJUNCTIVE. It is almost always translated into English as **must** or **have to**. The person who has to do the thing in question is expressed as the subject:

> **Il *faut* partir tout de suite.** (We must leave immediately.)
> **Il *faut* que je vous laisse.** (I must leave you.)
> **Il *faut* qu'elle le lui dise tout de suite.** (She must tell him immediately.)
> **Il va *falloir* partir.** (We will have to leave.)

NOTE: When used in compound tenses, the auxiliaries **faire** and **laisser**, as well as **pouvoir**, **devoir**, **vouloir**, **savoir** and **falloir**, all place the appropriate form of **avoir** in front of their past participles, which are **fait**, **laissé**, **pu**, **dû**, **voulu**, **su** and **fallu** respectively:

Ils *ont fait* repeindre leur maison.
Il ne m'*a* pas *laissé* parler.
Elle n'*aura* pas *pu* venir.
Tu n'*aurais* pas *dû* t'énerver.
Il *a voulu* s'en occuper seul.
Elle *a su* s'y prendre avec eux.
Il *aurait fallu* faire preuve de plus de patience.

3.4 Other verbs and phrases which function like auxiliary verbs

The verbs aller, venir de and commencer à, as well as the phrases être sur le point de and être en train de, are used to provide more information about *when* the action of the verb happened, is happening or will happen. They indicate that the action or state expressed by the verb is just about to begin or finish, has just begun, is in the process of happening, or has just ended.

■ **Aller** + INFINITIVE is used to indicate that an action will begin shortly. It is very close in meaning to to be going to in English, but is used more frequently:

Nous *allons* **partir dans une minute.** (we're going to leave)
Ils *vont* **s'endormir.** (They're going to fall asleep.)

■ The phrase être sur le point de + INFINITIVE means to be about to or to be on the point of:

Il *est sur le point de* **s'endormir.** (He's about to go to sleep.)

■ Commencer à + INFINITIVE means to begin to:

Cette histoire *commence à* **me faire rire.** (This story is beginning to make me laugh.)
Tu *commences à* **m'ennuyer.** (You're beginning to annoy me.)

■ The phrase être en train de + INFINITIVE indicates that an action is actually taking place. It is frequently translated into English by forms such as he is reading, we are listening and so on:

Elle *est en train de* gagner la partie. (She is winning the game.)

■ Venir de + INFINITIVE means to have just. Note that it is followed by the infinitive in French, whereas in English we use a past participle:

Il *vient de* partir. (He has just left.)
Le disque *vient de* se terminer. (The record has just finished.)

NOTE: When they are used as auxiliaries, **aller** and **venir de** cannot be used in a compound tense. **Commencer** à, however, can be; it is conjugated with **avoir**:

Il *a commencé à* apprendre ses leçons.

Être sur le point de is seldom found in compound tenses.

4. Verbs indicating states rather than actions

■ The verbs être (to be), devenir (to become), sembler (to seem), paraître (to seem), rester (to remain) and demeurer (to remain) are used to refer to a state rather than an action. To these verbs we should also add the phrases passer pour (to pass for) and avoir l'air (to look/seem).

■ Verbs of state are different from other verbs in that, like all intransitive verbs, they cannot be put into the passive. The nouns or adjectives which follow them always describe the *subject* of the verb in some way (see BUILDING SENTENCES, **1.** and ADJECTIVES):

Elle semble *contente*.
La situation me paraît *favorable*.

5. Active and passive use of verbs

■ In French, as in English, many (though not all) verbs can be conjugated in either an *active* or a *passive* form.

– When a verb is active, the subject of the verb is the person or thing which carries out the action expressed by the verb, or which is in the state described by the verb:

La télévision a diffusé son reportage. (The subject of the verb – television – is what broadcast his report.)

Tout le monde l'apprécie. (The subject of the verb – **everyone** – is who appreciates him.)

– In the passive, however, the subject of the verb is not the person or thing carrying out the action of the verb. On the contrary, the action expressed by the verb is now carried out *on the subject*. In other words, in the change from active to passive, the *object* of the active verb becomes the *subject* of the passive verb. In these cases the person or thing carrying out the action of the verb – the subject of the active verb – is now introduced by the prepositions **par** or (less frequently) **de**, both of which translate into English as **by**.

Son reportage a été diffusé *par la télévision.* (His report was broadcast by television.)

NOTE:
* **De** is normally used in place of **par** after verbs which express some kind of emotion, and also after the past participle **accompagné**:

Il est apprécié *de tout le monde.* (He is appreciated by everyone.)
Il était accompagné *de sa femme.* (He was accompanied by his wife.)

* **De** is also used if what is indicated is not who or what carried out the action, but the implement which was used:

Il a été tué *d'un coup de revolver.* (He was killed by a gunshot.)

– Sometimes the person or thing by whom the action is carried out is not expressed:

Son reportage a été diffusé.
Il est très apprécié.

■ As in English, the passive is formed in French by the auxiliary verb to be, **être**, together with the past participle of the verb which is being put into the passive (*see* **9.6**). The past participle agrees in number and gender with the subject of the verb.

■ In the passive, the verb **être** may appear in any tense:

Les passeports *sont* **délivrés par la préfecture ou par les ambassades.** (passports are issued)

Cette nouvelle *a été* annoncée hier. (this piece of news was announced)
Le gâteau *sera* cuit pour le goûter. (the cake will be baked)

■ Only *transitive* verbs (i.e. those which can take a direct object) can be put into the passive (*see* BUILDING SENTENCES, **3.**).

■ An *indirect object* cannot become the subject of a passive verb in French, although this is perfectly possible in English. For example, we can say both I gave the book to John (active), and John was given the book by me (passive); the indirect object in the first sentence, John, has become the subject of the passive verb was given in the second. To take another example, we can rephrase The jury awarded first prize to the singer (active) as The singer was awarded first prize by the jury (passive), the indirect object the singer becoming the subject of the passive verb was awarded. Such passive sentences are *never* possible in French. Either the active verb must be used, or the *direct object* of the active verb must be made the subject of the passive verb:

Le jury a attribué le prix au chanteur. (– active)
Le prix a été attribué au chanteur par le jury. (= passive: the direct object of the first sentence, *le prix*, becomes the subject of the passive verb in the second; *le chanteur* remains the indirect object in both sentences.)

■ When using être + PAST PARTICIPLE, it is not always easy to know whether to use the perfect or imperfect tense. Basically, the perfect tense is used to describe *actions*, whereas the imperfect is used to describe *states* or *conditions*:

Quand nous sommes entrés, nous avons vu que la fenêtre *était* cassée. (= When we went in, the window was already broken: what we are describing here is the *condition* of the window, so the verb être is in the *imperfect*.)
Pendant la leçon, la fenêtre *a été* cassée par une pierre. (= In this case the window is actually broken while we are sitting there: what we are talking of here is an *action,* so the verb être is in the perfect.)

Other examples:

Le village *était* abandonné. (= state)
Le village *a été* abandonné par ses habitants. (= action)
La porte *était* ouverte. (= state)
La porte *a été* ouverte par le vent. (= action)

COMPARE

> It is a very common mistake to mix up the imperfect of active verbs and the perfect of passive verbs, since their translations sound somewhat similar in English. It is important to keep the difference between the two clear in your mind:
>
> **Le garçon *chantait* la chanson.** (The boy *was singing* the song.)
> **La chanson *a été chantée* par le garçon.** (The song *was sung* by the boy.)
> **Le patron *construisait* l'usine.** (The boss *was building* the factory.)
> **L'usine *a été construite* par le patron.** (The factory *was built* by the boss.)

■ In spoken French, **se faire** + INFINITIVE is used to form a passive (*see* **3.**1).

6. Reflexive verbs

■ Reflexive verbs are preceded by a reflexive pronoun (*see* PRONOUNS, **2.**). The reflexive pronoun always corresponds to the subject of the verb: in other words, if the subject is I, the pronoun will be **myself**; if the subject is **they**, the pronoun will be **themselves**, and so on. It is important to bear this in mind, since the form of a reflexive verb shown in a dictionary always has the reflexive pronoun **se**. This pronoun *must* be changed if the subject of the verb is something other than a noun, il, elle, ils, elles or on:

se **laver**	→	*je me* **lave**
*s'***habiller**	→	*il s'***habille**
se **baigner**	→	*elle se* **baigne**
se **blesser**	→	*vous vous* **êtes blessés**

> *NOTE*: Remember that the reflexive pronoun is placed after the verb in positive commands, and that in such cases, **te** is replaced by **toi** (*see* PRONOUNS, **2.**2).

■ Some verbs **must** *always* be used with a reflexive pronoun, and never appear on their own:

s'absenter ▲ s'écrier ▲ se souvenir ▲ s'évanouir ▲ s'enfuir

Other verbs change their meaning when they are used reflexively. Sometimes this change of meaning is translated into English as a passive verb:

appeler (to call) → **s'appeler** (to be called)
Je les ai déjà *appelés* deux fois. (I've already called them twice.)
Je *m'appelle* Marianne. (I am called Marianne.)

Sometimes a different verb altogether must be used when translating:

douter (to doubt) → **se douter** (to suspect)
Je *doute* qu'il y parvienne. (I doubt that he'll manage.)
Je *me doute* que ce n'est pas facile. (I suspect that it isn't easy.)

apercevoir (to see) → **s'apercevoir** (to realize)
Je viens de les *apercevoir* au coin de la rue. (I have just seen them on the corner.)
Je viens de *m'apercevoir* que j'ai perdu mes clés. (I have just realized that I have lost my keys.)

■ However, most reflexive verbs indicate that the subject of the verb carries out the action of the verb on himself, herself or itself, so that the appropriate translation is often the appropriate reflexive pronoun in English:

Ils *se sont amusés.* (They enjoyed themselves.)
Elle *se regarde.* (She looks at herself.)

■ There are very many more reflexive verbs in French than in English, though. In English we can often choose between an intransitive verb (he shaves, she dresses) and a reflexive verb (he shaves himself, she dresses herself) or a phrase using the verb get (he gets shaved, she gets dressed). *All* of these must be translated into French by the appropriate reflexive verb. The reflexive pronoun cannot be left out:

Il *se rase.* (He shaves/shaves himself/gets shaved.)
Elle *s'habille.* (She dresses/dresses herself/gets dressed.)

■ As well as having the meaning **myself, yourself** etc., the reflexive pronouns frequently mean **each other** or **one another**. (Each other is used in English when only two people are involved, and one another when there are more than two.):

>**Nous *nous sommes vus* hier.** (We saw each other yesterday.)
>**Ils *se détestent*.** (They hate each other.)
>**Ils *s'observaient* en silence.** (They were looking at one another in silence.)

■ Reflexive verbs can also occasionally have a *passive* meaning:

>**Ce produit *s'abîme* facilement.** (This product is easily spoiled.)
>**Ce livre *se lit* vite.** (This book can be read quickly.)
>**Ça *s'explique* très facilement.** (That can be explained very easily.)
>**Cela ne *se fait* pas.** (That isn't done.)

NOTE: When a reflexive verb is used with a passive meaning, its subject never refers to a person.

7. Impersonal constructions

■ In English, impersonal constructions are usually introduced by **it** or, less frequently, by **there**. In French they are always introduced by **il**. In these cases **il** does not stand for a masculine object, but is in fact neuter; it would usually be very difficult to say precisely what it does stand for.

■ Verbs relating to the weather are always impersonal:

>**Il neige.** (It is snowing.)
>**Il a plu.** (It rained.)
>**Il gèle.** (It is freezing.)

■ The verb **falloir** is also always impersonal. **Falloir** means to be necessary, and is followed either by an infinitive or by a clause whose verb is in the subjunctive (*see* **8**.4). It can be translated into English in different ways:

>**Il faut que tu viennes.** (You have to come.)
>**Il fallait s'y attendre.** (We should have expected it.)
>**Il faut essayer.** (You have to try.)

The indirect object pronoun (*see* PRONOUNS, **1**.) can be used with **falloir** to indicate who has to carry out the action of the verb:

>**Il *lui* faut partir.** (He has to leave.)

*Il **leur** faudra le faire demain.* (They will have to do it tomorrow.)
*Il **me** fallait me lever très tôt.* (I had to get up very early.)

■ However, many other verbs can be used in impersonal constructions:

*Il ne **reste** plus de lait.* (There is no milk left.)
*Il **manque** une chaise.* (There is a chair missing.)

■ Impersonal verbs are always *singular*, even if they refer to more than one person or thing:

*Il **manque** trois tasses.* (There are three cups missing.)

■ Some impersonal phrases, such as il y a, il est, il paraît que, il semble que, il suffit de, il n'y a qu'à and il fait, are very widely used:

– *il y a* *(there is, there are)*

This expression remains unchanged whether it is followed by a singular or a plural noun:

*Il **y a** des œufs dans le frigidaire.*
*Il **y a** quelqu'un qui vous demande.*
*Il **y avait** beaucoup de monde.*
*Il **y aura** trop de chaises.*
*Il **y aurait** 131 morts.* (There would appear to be 131 dead.)
*Il **y a** longtemps que je ne l'ai pas vu.* (It's a long time since I saw him.)

Since the phrase il y a is based on the verb avoir, its infinitive is **y avoir**:

*Il doit **y avoir** une autre solution.* (There must be another solution.)

– *il est* (+ TIME)

*Il **est** cinq heures.* (It is five o'clock.)
*Il **est** tard.* (It is late.)

– *il paraît que* *(it seems that)*

*Il **paraît** qu'il n'était pas content du tout.*

– *il semble que, il me* *(te/lui/nous/vous/leur)* *semble que* *(it seems that, it seems to me etc. that)*

*Il **semble** qu'il aille mieux.*

When used with an indirect object pronoun (*see* PRONOUNS, **2.1**), this phrase can sometimes be translated into English by the verb **to think**:

Il me semble qu'elle a encore grandi. (I think she's grown even more.)

> *NOTE:* **Il semble que** is followed by the subjunctive (*see* **8**.4), but when it is used with an indirect object pronoun it is followed by the indicative:
>
> **Il semble qu'ils** *aient* **raison.** (= subjunctive)
> **Il me semble que vous** *avez* **raison.** (= indicative)

– *il suffit de* (+ INFINITIVE)

Il suffit d'essayer. (All you have to do is try.)

– *il n'y a qu'à* (+ INFINITIVE)

Il n'y a qu'à essayer. (We'll just have to try.)

– *il fait* (+ ADJECTIVE)

This expression is used mostly when describing the weather:

Il fait beau. (The weather is nice.)
Il fait froid. (It's cold.)

■ Here are some more commonly used impersonal expressions:

Il s'agit de se dépêcher. (il s'agit de + INFINITIVE) (We have to get a move on.)
Il s'agit d'une affaire importante. (il s'agit de + NOUN) (It's an important matter.)
Il vaut mieux tout lui dire. (il vaut mieux + INFINITIVE) (It's better to tell him everything.)
Il est possible que je me sois trompée. (il est possible/impossible + que + CLAUSE WITH VERB IN THE SUBJUNCTIVE) (It is possible that I am wrong.)
Il est impossible de trouver une réponse satisfaisante. (il est possible/impossible de + INFINITIVE) (It is impossible to find a satisfactory answer.)
Il est vrai qu'il a exagéré. (il est vrai/faux + que + NOUN CLAUSE) (It is true that he exaggerated.)
Il est arrivé une catastrophe. (il est arrivé + NOUN) (A disaster

occurred.)

Il arrive qu'il fasse très froid. (il arrive + que + CLAUSE WITH VERB IN THE SUBJUNCTIVE) (It can get very cold.)

Il s'est trouvé que j'étais là. (il se trouve + que + NOUN CLAUSE) (I happened to be there.)

Il n'empêche que tu as tort. (il n'empêche + que + NOUN CLAUSE) (Be that as it may, you are wrong.)

Il importe de trouver une solution. (il importe de + INFINITIVE) (It is important to find a solution.)

A particularly useful impersonal construction is the following:

il + (INDIRECT OBJECT PRONOUN) + any tense of the verb être + ADJECTIVE + *de* + INFINITIVE

The indirect object pronoun can be left out. If it is included, it is translated into English using the preposition for. The verb être can be put into the negative if required:

Il me sera impossible d'y aller. (It will be impossible for me to go.)
Il lui sera difficile de répondre. (It will be difficult for him to answer.)
Il n'est pas facile de le faire si vite. (It is not easy to do it so quickly.)

NOTE: Verbs in impersonal expressions can be active or passive, and can appear with or without reflexive pronouns.

■ There are a few impersonal expressions which do not start with il. These are set phrases:

– *si bon me* (te/lui/nous/vous/leur) *semble* (if I, you etc. see fit)

Je céderai *si bon me semble.* (I will give in if I see fit.)

– *n'importe* (even so)

Ça n'a pas marché mais *n'importe*, c'était une bonne idée.

– *mieux vaudrait* (it would be better)

Mieux vaudrait le rappeler plus tard.

– *n'empêche* (even so, all the same)

N'empêche, il n'aurait pas dû le faire.

8. Tenses and moods

Tenses are used to place actions or states in time: for example, **I am reading** refers to the present, **I shall read** refers to the future and so on. *Moods* are used to indicate the relationship between the speaker and the event he or she is talking about: whether he sees it as real or doubtful, whether he is simply stating it as a fact or is happy or sad about it, whether the verb is being used to order someone to do something and so on. The moods in French are called the indicative (the normal form of the verb), the subjunctive, the conditional and the imperative. Each of these moods has more than one tense. Other parts of the verb covered in this section are the infinitive, the participles and the gerund.

8.1 Table of moods and tenses

moods	*simple tenses*	*compound tenses*
indicative	**present, imperfect, future, past historic**	**perfect, pluperfect, future perfect, past anterior**
conditional	**present**	**perfect**
subjunctive	**present, imperfect**	**perfect, pluperfect**
imperative	**present**	**perfect**
infinitive	**present**	**perfect**
participle	**present**	**perfect**
gerund		

8.2 Uses of the indicative

■ The indicative is the form in which verbs appear most frequently, and it is the only mood which is capable of expressing *past, present* and *future* time.

We use the indicative when we want to place an event clearly at some point in time, and when we want to present it simply as a fact:

> **Il *a fait* très beau aujourd'hui.**
> **Lorsque la mer s'*est retirée,* il *était* dix-huit heures.**

8.2.1 The simple tenses of the indicative

■ **The present indicative**

– The present tense is used to present an action which is currently taking place:

> **Je la *vois* qui *arrive*.** (I see her arriving.)
> **Elle *dort* profondément.** (She is sleeping deeply.)
> **Elle n'*arrête* pas de parler.** (She never stops talking.)

Remember that there is only one form of the present tense in French: **je parle**, for example, translates not only I **speak** but also I **am speaking** and I **do speak**. If you wish to stress the idea that something is *actually happening*, you can use the phrase **être en train de** + INFINITIVE:

> **Il *est en train de manger*.** (He is (busy) eating.)

– As in English, the present tense can also express an action which is going on all the time, or which occurs habitually:

> **La terre *tourne*.** (The earth turns.)
> **Je me *couche* à onze heures tous les jours.** (I go to bed every day at eleven o'clock.)

– It can be used to refer to an event which will take place in the near future. In such cases it translates into English either as the future tense, or as the present tense of the kind I'm going:

> **Je te *vois* demain.** (I'll see you tomorrow.)
> **Elle *termine* dans un instant.** (She'll finish in a moment.)
> **J'*arrive* !** (I'm coming!)
> **Le bateau *part* demain.** (The boat is leaving tomorrow.)

– When telling a story, the present tense is sometimes used to refer to events which happened in the past:

> **En 1709, un terrible hiver s'*abat* sur l'Europe, et *cause* une des plus graves famines du siècle.**

– It is also frequently found in descriptions:

> **Leur maison *est* grande et spacieuse, mais elle *est* aussi plutôt froide.**

- Note in particular that it is the *present* tense which is used in French to express an action which started in the past but is still continuing in the present. Whereas English uses the perfect tense and the preposition for, French uses the present tense and the preposition **depuis**:

> **Je *travaille* ici depuis dix ans.** (I've been working here for ten years.)
> **Elle *étudie* le français depuis six mois.** (She's been studying French for six months.)

Depuis combien de temps *attendez-***vous ?** (How long have you been waiting?)

As well as **depuis**, both **il y a** and **voilà** are sometimes used to indicate the amount of time involved, but the two latter expressions are both usually placed *before* the verb:

Voilà deux heures que nous t'*attendons* **!**
Il y a dix ans qu'il *habite* **ici.**

However, the verb goes into the perfect tense if it is negative:

Je ne l'*ai* **pas** *vu* **depuis vingt ans.** (I haven't seen him for twenty years.)

In spoken French the expression **ça fait** or **cela fait** … can also be used:

Ça fait deux heures que nous t'*attendons* **!**

■ **The future indicative**

– The future tense is used to refer to actions or states which will happen or come about in the future, whether or not they are seen as likely:

Tu *changeras* **vite d'avis.** (You will soon change your mind.)
Je pense que ça *ira* **comme ça.** (I think it'll be OK like that.)
Est-ce que tu *viendras* **?** (Will you come?)

– In contrast to English, the future tense is also used after conjunctions such as **quand**, **aussitôt que** and **tant que** to refer to future events. In similar circumstances it is the *present* tense which is used in English:

Je le ferai aussitôt que je *pourrai.* (I'll do it as soon as I *can*.)
Je lui parlerai quand j'*aurai* **le temps.** (I'll speak to him when I *have* the time.)

– Just as the present tense can be used to refer to past events, the future can also be used in the same way in historic or journalistic texts. In such cases it would usually be translated into English by the conditional:

Quelques années plus tard, en 1929, la crise économique s'*installera.* (the economic crisis *would* set in)

– As in English, the future can also be used to give an *order*. The order can be either to do something or not to do something, and can be direct or in indirect speech (*see* DIFFERENT KINDS OF SENTENCE, **2.** and REPORTED SPEECH):

Tu n'*oublieras* **pas de laisser les clés bien en évidence.**
Vous y *penserez.*

> NOTE: A near future can be indicated by using the auxiliary verb
> **aller** + INFINITIVE, or by using the phrase **être sur le point de** +
> INFINITIVE:
>
> **Elle *va partir* (dans très peu de temps).** (she's going to leave)
> **Elle *est sur le point de partir*.** (She's about to leave.)

■ The imperfect indicative

– The imperfect is a *past tense*. It is different from the past historic or the
perfect tense in that it views an action or state in the past as still being in
progress when something else happened. In such circumstances it is often
translated into English by forms such as I was doing, they were reading,
and so on:

Il se *promenait* lorsque je l'ai croisé. (He was out walking when I
met him.)
J'ai lu ces livres à l'époque où j'*étais* malade. (I read these books
when I was ill.)

– It can be the equivalent of a *present in the past*. It therefore has some of
the characteristics of the present and can, as a result, express:

– general truths about the past:

En ce temps-là, il *faisait* très froid.

– a near future in the past:

Le bateau *partait* le lendemain. (The boat was leaving the next day.)

– repetition or habit. In this case it is often translated into English using
forms of the kind I used to go, I used to think:

J'*aimais* bien y aller le dimanche. (I used to like going there on
Sundays.)
Paul *était* content d'aller au cinéma. (Paul used to be happy to go to
the cinema.)

– The imperfect is often used to describe the general circumstances in
which other actions took place, or general descriptions of persons:

Seule une petite lampe *éclairait* la pièce.
Il *faisait* presque nuit lorsque Pierre est arrivé.
Il *était* grand et mince.

– It is also used in a conditional clause when the verb in the main clause is in the conditional (*see* CLAUSES, **4**.6):

>   **Si tu *étais* moins distrait, tu y penserais.**

– In the same way as the present tense is used to describe an action which started in the past and is continuing in the present (*see above*), the imperfect is used in sentences such as the following:

>   **Je l'*attendais* depuis plus de dix minutes.** (I *had been waiting* for him for more than ten minutes.)
>   **Nous la *connaissions* depuis très longtemps.** (We *had known* her for a very long time.)

■ **The past historic**

The past historic is never used in spoken French. In written French it is used to refer to an action which is seen as *over and done with*. It is used for narrating past events:

>   **Ce jour-là, il se *leva* très tôt, s'*habilla*, puis *partit*.**
>   **Je me souviens qu'un jour il se *trompa* de route et *mit* beaucoup de temps pour nous rejoindre.**

In story-telling it is used to present the events of the story, while the imperfect is used to present the circumstances within which the events took place:

>   **Le jour se levait quand il *partit*.**

8.2.2 The compound tenses of the indicative

■ **The perfect**

– The perfect is the most commonly used past tense in spoken French, where it has replaced the past historic. It indicates that the action or state referred to by the verb is seen as *over and done with*. In such cases, it is normally translated as the simple past in English:

>   **J'*ai pris* ce train pour venir.** (I got this train to come here.)
>   **Elle m'*a offert* un pull.** (She gave me a pullover.)

– It can also indicate that the consequences of the event can still be felt in the present. In such cases it is usually translated by the perfect tense in English:

>   **Le train *est arrivé*.** (The train has arrived.)

L'année dernière, les enfants *ont* beaucoup *grandi*. (The children have grown a lot this last year.)

> NOTE: The recent past can also be referred to by using the phrase **venir de + INFINITIVE**, which translates into English as **to have just**:
>
> **Il *vient de partir*.** (He has just left.)
> **Tu *viens de dire* le contraire !** (You have just said the opposite!)

■ **The pluperfect**
– The pluperfect tense is in frequent use in French. It is used to situate one event at a point in the past which *precedes* another event. It is translated as the pluperfect in English:

Je l'*avais vu* le jour avant. (I had seen him the day before.)
Il s'*était mis* en tête qu'il avait tort. (He had got it into his head that he was wrong.)

– It presents an action or a state as over and done with in the past:

À vingt-deux heures, il n'*avait* encore rien *gagné* et une heure plus tard, il perdait toujours.

– As in English, it is used in the main clause when the verb in a conditional clause is in the conditional perfect (*see* CLAUSES, **4**.6):

Si j'*avais su*, j'aurais commandé autre chose. (if I had known)

■ **The past anterior**
– This tense is seldom used and is found only in written French. It has the same meaning as the pluperfect, and appears mainly after conjunctions of time:

Quand il *eut fini* de parler, le silence régna de nouveau.

– If it appears in a main clause, it places a *completed* event in a *distant past*:

Enfin il *eut fini*.

■ **The future perfect**
– This tense is used in both spoken and written French. Like the same tense in English, it indicates that a particular event will already have happened when another takes place in the future:

Il l'*aura* déjà *trouvé*. (He will already have found it, i.e. before something else happens.)

À ce moment-là, le match *aura commencé*. (The match will have started by then.)

– It is also used after conjunctions of time such as **quand**, **dès que** and the like where English would use a perfect tense:

Quand tu *auras vu* ce film, tu me le raconteras. (When you *have seen* the film you can tell me all about it.)

8.3 Uses of the conditional

– We use the conditional mood to refer to events which *might or might not* happen, and which are therefore situated in the *future*:

Il se *pourrait* bien qu'il vienne. (He *could* well come.)

– It is also used to refer to events which did not happen in the past:

J'*aurais* bien *aimé* le voir, mais il n'est pas venu.

– The conditional mood is used in the main clauses which accompany conditional clauses containing an *imperfect* or a *pluperfect* tense (*see* CLAUSES, **4.**6):

S'il ne pleuvait pas, nous *pourrions* sortir.

– It can express what is called *future in the past*. It is called 'future in the past' because the original statement contained a future tense, but the entire event is now situated in the past:

J'étais certain qu'il ne *pourrait* pas venir. (= At the time mentioned, I would have said 'je suis certain qu'il ne pourra pas venir' – future tense.)

- Both the conditional and the conditional perfect are often used in French to indicate that the person speaking or writing does not feel able to guarantee that what he/she is describing is actually the case. The use of the conditional places responsibility for the accuracy of the information on someone else. In such cases the conditional is usually translated by a simple past tense in English:

Selon la police, il y *aurait* cinq blessés. (According to the police there are five injured people.)

D'après lui, il *serait* rentré vers cinq heures. (According to him, he came home about five o'clock.)

8.3.1 The tenses of the conditional

■ The conditional present

– The conditional present is used above all to indicate that the event being referred to is only a possibility which may or may not happen:

Il *serait* bien agréable que l'été arrive.

– It is frequently used to express what would happen if a certain condition was fulfilled:

J'*achèterais* cette voiture si elle était un peu moins chère.

– In a noun clause introduced by **que** or **si**, the conditional present can also be used to express 'future in the past' (*see* AGREEMENT OF TENSES, **1.**):

Il m'avait dit qu'il le *ferait*. (= What he originally said was 'je le ferai' – future.)

Je ne savais pas qu'il *viendrait*. (= This implies an original statement 'il ne viendra pas' made at some point in the past.)

Je lui ai demandé s'il *serait* là. (= The original question was 'seras-tu là ?')

– As in English, the conditional present is often used to make a polite request or to express a wish in a slightly indirect way:

J'*aimerais* beaucoup que tu lises ce livre. (I would very much like you to read this book.)

Pourriez-vous me donner l'heure, s'il vous plaît ? (Could you tell me the time, please?)

Je *voudrais* bien venir mais cela m'est impossible. (I would very much like to come but it's impossible.)

■ The conditional perfect

– In general, the conditional perfect is used to refer to something which *could have happened* in the past but which *did not happen*:

Il *aurait pu* parler, mais il n'a finalement rien dit.

– It is frequently used in main clauses linked to conditional clauses to refer to events which did not in fact take place:

Si nous avions été prévenus à temps, nous *aurions* peut-être *pu* faire quelque chose. (= We did not do anything because we were not warned in time.)

Si tu avais voulu, nous *aurions pu* y aller ensemble. (= We did not go together since you did not want to.)

– It presents an event (or non-event, to be more precise) as *over and done with*:

> **Je pensais que vous l'*auriez cru*.**

– It is used after conjunctions of time such as **quand**, **dès que** and so on, where in English a pluperfect tense would be used:

> **Je pensais que tu commencerais dès que tu *aurais terminé* ton autre travail.** (as soon as you *had finished* your other work)

– As in English, it can be used to make a polite request or to express something in an indirect manner:

> **J'*aurais aimé* que vous m'en parliez.** (I would have liked you to speak to me about it.)

8.4 Uses of the subjunctive

■ Though the subjunctive was once widely used in English, it has now almost entirely disappeared from everyday speech. It still survives in a few phrases such as if I *were* rich or I insist that he *finish* this work now, but such expressions can sound rather formal and many people prefer to say if I *was* rich or I insist that he *finishes* this work now, using the normal indicative forms instead. The subjunctive also survives in certain set expressions such as so *be* it, or *come* what may. In French, however, the subjunctive is still very much alive and is an important part of everyday speech. It is important to understand what it means and how to use it correctly.

■ Whereas the indicative presents an event as a fact, the use of the subjunctive often suggests that the person speaking or writing cannot guarantee that the event being mentioned is actually the case, or that it will definitely happen. The subjunctive therefore frequently expresses *doubt* or *uncertainty*:

> **Je ne crois pas qu'il *soit* prêt.** (I do not think he is ready.)
> **Il se peut qu'ils *soient* en retard.** (It is possible they will be late.)
> **Il est impossible qu'elle *ait eu* cette réaction.** (She could not have reacted that way.)
> **Il est peu probable qu'il *accepte*.** (It is unlikely he will accept.)

■ There are numerous occasions when the grammar of the sentence makes the use of a subjunctive obligatory. It is most often found in noun clauses introduced by a verb which expresses *fear, doubt* or *regret*, as well as after verbs which are used to give orders, express *wishes, emotions* or *desires*, or verbs which indicate that a particular event is only a *possibility*, one which might happen or might not.

> **On craint qu'il n'y *ait* pas de survivants.**
> **J'ai bien peur que cela ne *soit* pas facile.**
> **Il a toujours redouté que tout le monde *apprenne* la vérité.**
> **Je doute qu'il *revienne* à temps.**
> **Je souhaite qu'elle *réussisse*.**
> **J'exige qu'il *fasse* des excuses.**
> **Je voudrais qu'elle *vienne*.**
> **Il se peut qu'il *ait* tort.**
> **Il arrive qu'on ne s'*aperçoive* pas de ses erreurs.**
> **C'est dommage qu'il ne *soit* pas venu.**

■ For the use of ne with the subjunctive in positive sentences, *see* MAKING VERBS NEGATIVE, **1**.

8.4.1 The simple tenses of the subjunctive

■ **The present subjunctive**

– When it is used in a main clause, the subjunctive always indicates that the speaker feels involved in the event in some way (*see above*), whereas the indicative merely presents the event as a fact. The subjunctive can express a feeling of some kind, a wish or enthusiasm, and is often used in exclamations:

> **Il n'est pas encore arrivé, que je *sache*.** (as far as I know)
> **Qu'on se le *dise* !** (Let it be known!)

- It can also express indignation or anger:

> **Qu'il *se débrouille* !** (Let him sort it out himself!)
> **Qu'il *fasse* comme il veut !** (Let him do what he wants!)

– It can also express a third person command:

> **Qu'il *parte*, je l'exige !** (I demand that he leaves!)

– The subjunctive is, however, most often used in noun clauses (see CLAUSES, **3.**). These noun clauses follow verbs expressing:

– fear, a wish or regret:

> **Je crains qu'il ne s'*aperçoive* pas de l'heure.**

> **Je souhaite qu'il *réussisse*.**
> **Il veut que nous *sortions*.**
> **Il faut que nous *poursuivions*.**
> **Je regrette qu'il n'*attende* pas.**
> **J'ai peur qu'il n'y en *ait* pas assez.**

NOTE: The subjunctive is only used if the subject of the second verb is different from that of the first. If the two subjects are the same, the second verb is simply put into the infinitive:

> **Il craint de se *faire* mal.**
> **Je veux *sortir*.**
> **Je regrette de vous le *dire*.**

– doubt and disbelief:

> **Je ne crois pas qu'il *soit* venu.** (I don't believe he has come.)
> **Je doute qu'il *vienne*.** (I doubt he'll come.)

– emotions:

> **Ça m'étonne que tu *sois* de cet avis.** (I'm astonished that that's your opinion.)
> **Je suis heureux que vous *ayez* réussi.** (I'm glad you've succeeded.)

– something thought about, but not real, i.e. after verbs of *imagining*:

> **Imaginons que tout cela *soit* absolument vrai, qu'il ne *mente* pas un seul instant.**

– an obstacle or contradiction of some kind introduced by pour peu que (however little), bien que and quoique (although), si … que (however):

> **Pour peu qu'il le *veuille* vraiment, il y arrivera.** (however little he really wants to)
> **Bien qu'il ne *soit* pas très aimable, il est compétent.** (although he's not very likeable)
> **Si gentille qu'elle *puisse* être, elle ne me plaît pas.** (however kind she might be)
> **Si peu que ce *soit*, cela nous est nécessaire.** (however little it is)

– It is also found after pour que, afin que, de sorte que, de manière que and de façon que to indicate purpose. All these expressions are translated as so that:

> Il se dépêche *pour que* je *puisse* sortir à mon tour.

NOTE: **Pour que** and **afin que** are used only if the subject of the second verb is different from that of the first. If the two subjects are the same, **pour que** becomes **pour**, **afin que** becomes **afin de** and both are followed simply by the infinitive:

> Il a travaillé *pour gagner* de l'argent.
> Ils ont offert le meilleur prix *afin de gagner* le contrat.

– It is used after avant que (before) and jusqu'à ce que (until) in expressions of time:

> Il faut cueillir ces fruits *avant* qu'ils ne *soient* trop mûrs.
> Je resterai là *jusqu'à ce* qu'il *revienne*.

– The present subjunctive is also used in French in the following cases:

– after conjunctions expressing conditions: à condition que, à moins que and pourvu que and conjunctions expressing fear – de peur que and de crainte que (*see* CLAUSES, **4.6**)

– in concessive clauses introduced by qui que, quoi que and the like (*see* CLAUSES, **4.5**)

– after expressions of possibility or impossibility like il est possible/impossible que and il se peut que (*see* **3.2**)

– after expressions of necessity like il est nécessaire que and il faut que (*see* **3.3**)

– in adjectival clauses following a superlative (*see* ADJECTIVES, **5.2**).

Note that the present subjunctive usually replaces the imperfect subjunctive in French. It is therefore used even when the verb in the main clause is in the imperfect or conditional perfect:

> Il voulait que je le *fasse*. (He wanted me to do it.)
> Il aurait préféré que vous le lui *disiez*. (He would have preferred you to tell him.)

The imperfect subjunctive can still be found in literary texts.

■ **The imperfect subjunctive**

The imperfect subjunctive is almost never used now, not even in literary

French. It could only ever be found in extremely formal language:

> **Il n'a rien trouvé qui le *satisfît*.**
> **Nous cherchions quelqu'un qui *pût* le faire.**

8.4.2 The compound tenses of the subjunctive

■ **The perfect subjunctive**

The perfect subjunctive is used in the same kind of situation as the present subjunctive, but it is used to refer to events which took place in the past:

> **Je regrette qu'il n'en *ait* jamais rien *su*.** (I'm sorry he never knew about it.)
> **J'ai bien peur qu'il n'*ait été* malade.** (I'm afraid he's been ill.)

■ **The pluperfect subjunctive**

In a main clause it expresses an event which might have happened, but which did not:

> **Vous *eussiez* sans doute *pu* vous entendre.**

However, it is never used nowadays (though it can still be found in old texts), and has been replaced by the conditional perfect in main clauses:

> **Vous *auriez* sans doute *pu* vous entendre.**

8.5 Uses of the imperative

■ The imperative is used to give an order:

> *Allez-y, partez* !
> *Montre*-moi ça !

■ When it is followed by another clause, it can, as in English, express a condition:

> *Fais* un geste et tu verras ! (= si tu fais un geste, tu verras)

■ When verbs are used in the imperative the subject is not expressed. Only the ending of the verb shows whether it is singular or plural.

8.5.1 The present and perfect imperative

■ The present imperative is used to give an order without any indication as to whether it will be completed or not (*see* DIFFERENT KINDS OF SENTENCE, **2.**)

> **N'*oublie* pas tes clés.**
> **Pense à téléphoner au médecin.**

■ The difference between the present and the perfect imperative is that the perfect imperative indicates that the action to be undertaken has to be finished. In this sense it does not really refer to the past:

Travaille bien et surtout aie fini à l'heure. (and make sure you finish on time)

8.6 Uses of the infinitive

■ The infinitive is the form of the verb always found in dictionaries. It functions both as a verb and as a noun. It is therefore frequently used instead of those forms of the verb which end in -ing in English:

Se plaindre **serait inutile.** (Complaining would be pointless.)
Sauter **en parachute demande du courage.** (Parachuting requires courage.)

■ However, it is also frequently translated as **to** + Verb in English:

Il serait inutile de *se plaindre.* (It would be pointless to complain.)
Il faut du courage pour *sauter* **en parachute.** (You need courage to parachute.)

■ Whereas prepositions in English are all followed by the form of the verb ending in -ing, in French they are all – with one exception – followed by the infinitive:

Il est resté sans *bouger.* (He stood there without moving.)
Elle est sortie sans *dire* **un mot.** (She went out without saying a word.)
Nous irons au cinéma après *avoir dîné.* (We'll go to the cinema after eating.)

> NOTE: **En** is the only preposition in French which is followed by the present participle:
>
> **Je l'ai vu** *en sortant.* (I saw him on leaving.)
> **Il l'a regardé** *en souriant.* (He looked at her, smiling.)

■ The infinitive is always used after certain verbs and adjectives which take a preposition:

Ils ont décidé *de partir.*
Je suis prête *à y aller.*

(*See* Prepositions, **4.** for more information on these verbs.)

■ The infinitive may also be used in giving impersonal instructions, for instance on road signs and in recipes:

> **Ralentir.** (Slow down.)
> **Ajouter la farine, le beurre et le sucre et mixer.** (Add the flour, butter and sugar, and mix.)

■ As well as the normal infinitive there is also a perfect infinitive:

> **Il aurait été impossible de le faire sans lui en *avoir parlé*.** (It would have been impossible to do it without having spoken to him about it.)

■ Contrary to English usage, it is the *perfect* infinitive which is used after the preposition **après**, and also after certain verbs if they refer to events which took place in the past:

> **Il est sorti après *avoir vu* le film.** (He went out after seeing the film.)
> **Il m'a remercié de l'*avoir aidé*.** (He thanked me for helping him.)
> **Nous regrettons de vous *avoir dérangé*.** (We are sorry for disturbing you.)

8.7 Uses of the present, past and perfect participles

■ Present and past participles can operate like verbs. For example, a present participle can take an object, and a past participle can be like a passive without the verb être:

> ***Connaissant* leur situation, il aurait pu les aider.**
> **C'est un détail *ignoré* de tous.**

■ Both can also have the function of adjectives:

> **Les résultats *obtenus* sont *satisfaisants*.**

8.7.1 The present participle

■ The present participle ends in -ant.

■ It often functions primarily as a verb, in which case it can take its own object. When it functions as a verb it is *invariable*. For example, if it could be replaced by an adjectival clause beginning with **qui** without the meaning of the sentence changing, it does not change its form:

> **Les gens *ayant* un parapluie ont pu sortir.** (*ayant = qui avaient*, the object being *un parapluie*)

It is also invariable if it could be replaced by a clause of time:

> ***Lisant* le journal, elle s'est souvenu de tout.** (*lisant = quand elle lisait*, the object being *le journal*)
> ***Rentrant* assez tard, nous avons rencontré notre père.** (*rentrant = quand nous rentrions*)

It is invariable if it could be replaced by a clause of reason:

N'*ayant* pas assez d'argent, elles n'y sont pas allées. (*n'ayant pas = puisqu'elles n'avaient pas*, the object being *assez d'argent*)

> NOTE: A present participle can *never* be used with **être** to form tenses in French. **I am speaking** is either **je parle** or **je suis en train de parler; they were eating** is either **ils mangeaient** or **ils étaient en train de manger**.

■ Sometimes a present participle is used just like an adjective and describes a noun. In these cases it cannot take an object, and it agrees with the noun just as any other adjective would:

Il fait une chaleur *étouffante*.

Ils sont rentrés à la nuit *tombante*.

Indeed, some present participles have entirely lost their verbal function, and now exist only as adjectives:

Elle était *ravissante*. (She was beautiful.)

> NOTE:
> * There is sometimes a difference in spelling between a present participle which still has a verbal function and a similar form which now exists only as an adjective. For example, adjectival forms sometimes end in **-cant** or **-gant** whereas the present participle ends in **-quant** or **-guant**:
>
> | *present participle* | | *adjective* |
> |---|---|---|
> | communiquant | → | communicant |
> | convainquant | → | convaincant |
> | intriguant | → | intrigant |
> | provoquant | → | provocant |
> | fatiguant | → | fatigant |
>
> * Sometimes adjectives ending in **-ent** correspond to present participles ending in **-ant**:
>
> | *present participle* | | *adjective* |
> |---|---|---|
> | adhérant | → | adhérent |
> | différant | → | différent |
> | excellant | → | excellent |
> | négligeant | → | négligent |

8.7.2 The past participle

■ Regular past participles end in -é, -i or -u:

■ The past participle is used to form compound tenses (*see* **9.**):

> **Elle a *ri*.**
> **Ils se sont *amusés*.**
> **Elles ont *couru*.**

■ It can also be used as an adjective, in which case it agrees with the noun it describes:

> **Ses cheveux sont bien *coiffés*.**

■ A number of past participles are used in French to express ideas which are expressed by present participles in English:

> **Il était *assis* au coin.** (He was sitting in the corner.)
> **Une lampe était *suspendue* au milieu de la pièce.** (A lamp was hanging in the middle of the room.)

Other similar past participles are accoudé (leaning on one's elbows), agenouillé (kneeling), appuyé (leaning), couché (lying) and étendu (lying).

> NOTE: The past participle used with the auxiliary verb **être** agrees with the *subject*:
>
> > **Mes amis *sont partis*.**
> > **Nous *sommes restés*.**
>
> However, when it is used with the auxiliary verb **avoir**, it only agrees with a direct object placed *before* the verb:
>
> > **Les *fleurs* qu'elles ont *reçues* sont très jolies.**
>
> If the direct object is placed *after* the verb, the past participle does not agree with it:
>
> > **Elles ont reç*u* de très jolies fleurs.**
>
> (For more detailed rules on the agreement of past participles, *see* 2.4 and 2.5.)

8.7.3 The perfect participle

There is also a perfect participle in French, formed from the present participle of avoir (ayant) or être (étant), and the past participle of the verb. When formed with étant, the past participle must agree with the subject. The equivalent in English is having done, having seen and so on:

Ayant fini **leur travail, ils sont partis.** (having finished)
Étant arrivée **tard, elle avait raté le train.** (having arrived)

8.8 Uses of the gerund

■ The gerund consists of the preposition en followed by the present participle.

■ It is used to refer to one action which is taking place at the same time as another. It is often translated into English as while ...ing or on ...ing:

Il parle *en dormant.* (while sleeping)
En les voyant, **il leur a fait signe.** (on seeing them)
En passant **près d'eux, il leur a fait signe.** (on passing by)

■ The gerund is also the only way of translating by ...ing into French (par can *never* be used to express this idea):

Il a gagné l'argent *en travaillant.* (He earned the money by working.)
Il l'a trouvé *en cherchant.* (He found it by looking.)

> NOTE:
> * The gerund is often the only way of translating verbs such as **to run in, to run out** into French:
>
> **Il est entré** *en courant.* (He ran in.)
> **Elle est sortie** *en courant.* (She ran out.)
>
> * The gerund can be used with **tout** to stress the fact that the two actions are taking place at the same time. **Tout** never changes its form, no matter who or what is the subject of the verb:
>
> **Elle essayait de boutonner sa veste** *tout en courant.*

9. Forming the different tenses of the verb

Verb tenses can either be:
– *simple* (consisting of one word)
– *compound* (consisting of more than one word). The compound tenses are

formed using the auxiliary verbs être and avoir + the PAST PARTICIPLE of the verb:

J'ai bien *dormi*. (= perfect)
Tu ne m'*aurais* rien *dit*. (= conditional perfect)

9.1 Forming the simple tenses of the indicative

■ The present tense

The present indicative is formed from the stem of the verb, to which the different endings corresponding to I, you etc. are added. Many verbs have irregular stems, and you should check the VERB TABLES, **10.** if you are in any doubt.

je chant-e ▲ nous finiss-ons ▲ ils reçoiv-ent ▲ je vend-s

These are the endings for the present indicative:

| | Group 1 | | Group 2 | | Group 3 | |
	singular	plural	singular	plural	singular	plural
1st person	-e	-ons	-is	-issons	-s	-ons
2nd person	-es	-ez	-is	-issez	-s	-ez
3rd person	-e	-ent	-it	-issent	-	-ent

> *NOTE*: The third person singular of the verbs **vaincre** and **convaincre** has the ending **-c**:
>
> **il vainc ▲ il convainc**

■ The future tense

The future indicative is formed by adding the endings given below to the *infinitive* of the verb. Note that verbs whose infinitive ends in -re drop the -e from the end of the infinitive before adding the endings for the future tense. Irregular stems are shown in the VERB TABLES, **10.**:

je danser*ai* ▲ tu finir*as* ▲ tu peindr*as* ▲ vous recevr*ez*

These are the endings for the future indicative:

	singular	plural
1st person	-ai	-ons
2nd person	-as	-ez
3rd person	-a	-ont

■ The imperfect tense

The imperfect is formed by adding the endings given below to the stem of the verb.

In the case of those verbs of the second group whose present participle ends in -issant (for example, finir → finissant), the imperfect is formed using the stem of the present participle and not the stem of the infinitive:

tu aim*ais* ▲ tu finiss*ais* ▲ tu peign*ais* ▲ vous recev*iez*

These are the endings for the imperfect indicative:

	singular	*plural*
1st person	**-ais**	**-ions**
2nd person	**-ais**	**-iez**
3rd person	**-ait**	**-aient**

■ The past historic tense

The past historic is no longer used in spoken French, though it may still be found in literature and sometimes in the press. Its forms are often unpredictable in the singular and do not always follow regular rules. However, all verbs have a circumflex (^) on the first and second person plural (*see* ACCENTS, THE DIAERESIS AND THE CEDILLA, **1.**3).

If you are unsure about any of the forms, you should check them in the VERB TABLES, **10.**:

je chant*ai* ▲ tu fin*is* ▲ il batt*it* ▲ nous d*îmes* ▲ tu v*ins*

These are the endings for the past historic:

	Group 1		*Groups 2 & 3*	
	singular	*plural*	*singular*	*plural*
1st person	**-ai**	**-âmes**	**-is**	**-îmes**
2nd person	**-as**	**-âtes**	**-is**	**-îtes**
3rd person	**-a**	**-èrent**	**-it**	**-irent**

> *NOTE*: In the case of verbs from the second group (i.e. those which conjugate like **finir**), some of the forms of the past historic are identical to those of the present tense. The context will make clear which tense is in fact intended:
>
> **finir: je finis** → **tu finis** → **il finit**

9.2 Forming the compound tenses of the indicative

The forms of the compound tenses are always regular in the sense that they are all formed using one of the simple tenses of the two auxiliary verbs **être** and **avoir** followed by the past participle. The only irregularities which ever arise occur in the past participle, since a number of verbs have irregular past participles. Rules for agreement of the past participle are given in **2.4** and **2.5**.

■ **The perfect tense**

The perfect is made up of the *present tense of an auxiliary verb* + the PAST PARTICIPLE of the verb which is being put into the perfect tense:

> Elle *a remarqué* leur absence.
> Ils *sont restés* tard.
> Nous nous *sommes abstenus* de faire une remarque.

■ **The pluperfect tense**

The pluperfect is made up of the *imperfect tense of an auxiliary verb* + the PAST PARTICIPLE of the verb being put into the pluperfect tense:

> il *avait douté* ▲ vous *aviez interdit* ▲ ils *avaient dit*

■ **The past anterior tense**

The past anterior is made up of the *past historic of the auxiliary verb* + the PAST PARTICIPLE of the verb being put into the past anterior tense:

> Ils ne purent partir que quand il *eut fini*.

■ **The future perfect tense**

The future perfect is made up of the *future tense of the auxiliary verb* + the PAST PARTICIPLE of the verb being put into the future perfect tense:

> Je vous rejoindrai quand j'*aurai terminé*.
> Vous nous préviendrez quand vous *aurez délibéré*.

9.3 Forming the conditional

■ **The conditional present**

The conditional present is formed by adding the endings given below to the infinitive. Note that verbs which end in -re in the infinitive drop the -e before adding these endings:

> Il *jouerait* mieux s'il était plus calme.
> Vous vous y *habitueriez* si vous vouliez.
> Je *reprendrais* bien un peu de viande.

These are the endings for the conditional present:

	singular	plural
1st person	-ais	-ions
2nd person	-ais	-iez
3rd person	-ait	-aient

NOTE:
* Any verb which has an irregular stem in the future tense will have the same irregular stem in the conditional:

infinitive	future	conditional
aller	j'irai	j'irais
faire	je ferai	je ferais

Consult the VERB TABLES, **10.** for further information.

* It is important not to confuse the future and the conditional, since their endings can be rather similar:

Je *serais* ravie de le rencontrer. (*serais* = conditional)
Je *serai* là demain. (*serai* = future)

■ **The conditional perfect**

The conditional perfect is made up of the *conditional of the auxiliary verb* + the PAST PARTICIPLE of the verb being put into the conditional perfect tense:

Il *aurait aimé* vous voir.
Nous *aurions voulu* nous joindre à vous.

9.4 Forming the subjunctive

■ **The present subjunctive**

The present subjunctive is made up of the stem of the verb followed by the endings given in the table below.

– The endings for the subjunctive resemble those of the indicative of group 1 verbs, except that an -i- is added in the first and second persons plural:

Qu'est-ce que vous voulez que nous *amenions* ?
Elle voudrait que vous lui *téléphoniez.*

– In the case of verbs of the second group, the stem used is the longer stem of the present participle ending in -iss- (for example finissant, subjunctive stem finiss-):

J'attends qu'il *finisse.*

– The stem for the subjunctive of some other verbs is irregular, as is the case for **aller** and the auxiliary verbs **avoir** and **être**. You should refer to the VERB TABLES, **10.** if you are at all unsure:

Il faut que j'y *aille*.

	singular	plural
1st person	-e	-ions
2nd person	-es	-iez
3rd person	-e	-ent

■ **The perfect subjunctive**

The perfect subjunctive is made up of the *present subjunctive of the auxiliary verb* followed by the PAST PARTICIPLE of the verb being put into the perfect subjunctive tense:

Il aurait mieux valu qu'il *soit venu* seul.
Il est regrettable qu'ils *aient échoué*.

■ **The imperfect subjunctive**

The imperfect subjunctive is no longer used either in written or in spoken French, where it has been replaced by the present subjunctive. None the less, it is still found in older French texts.

The imperfect subjunctive is based on the stem of the infinitive, to which the endings given below are added. In the case of verbs of the second group, the stem used is the one without **-iss** (i.e. **fin-** not **finiss-**):

que tu chantasses ▲ que tu finisses ▲ qu'il offrît ▲ qu'il aimât

These are the endings for the imperfect subjunctive:

	Group 1		Groups 2 & 3	
	singular	plural	singular	plural
1st person	-asse	-assions	-isse	-issions
2nd person	-asses	-assiez	-isses	-issiez
3rd person	-ât	-assent	-ît	-issent

9.5 Forming the imperative

The imperative only exists in the 2nd person singular and plural and in the 1st person plural.

■ **The present imperative**

The endings of the imperative are the same as those of the 2nd person singular and plural (**tu** and **vous**) and the 1st person plural (**nous**) indicative:

pars (2nd person singular)	**regarde** (2nd person singular)
partons (1st person plural)	**regardons** (1st person plural)
partez (2nd person plural)	**regardez** (2nd person plural)

NOTE: Group 1 verbs, as well as group 2 verbs whose 3rd person singular ends in **-e** (**cueillir**, **souffrir**, **offrir**), drop the **-s** at the end of the 2nd person singular and form their imperative simply in **-e**:

nager: nage ▲ **cueillir** (il cueille): **cueille** ▲ **souffrir** (il souffre): **souffre** ▲ **offrir** (il offre): **offre**

However, these verbs keep the **-s** of the second person singular when it is followed by **en** or **y**, in order to make the imperative easier to pronounce:

Manges-en.
Penses-y.

The only exceptions to these general rules are the verbs **être**, **avoir** and **savoir**, whose imperative is identical to the present subjunctive:

	être	*avoir*	*savoir*
2nd person singular	**sois**	**aie**	**sache**
1st person plural	**soyons**	**ayons**	**sachons**
2nd person plural	**soyez**	**ayez**	**sachez**

■ The perfect imperative

The perfect imperative is made up of the *imperative of the auxiliary* + the PAST PARTICIPLE of the verb being put into the perfect imperative tense. It is very seldom used. It translates into English as **make sure you have** or **see to it that you have**:

Ayez relu **vos notes pour demain.** (See to it that you have re-read your notes by tomorrow.)

9.6 Forming the present and past participles

■ The present participle

The present participle of verbs of all three groups is formed by dropping the **-ons** ending from the 1st person plural of the present indicative (the **nous** form) and adding **-ant**:

chantons → **chantant**

commençons	→	commençant
nageons	→	nageant
finissons	→	finissant
vendons	→	vendant
courons	→	courant
devons	→	devant
asseyons	→	asseyant

NOTE: The present participles of these three verbs are irregular:

avoir	→	ayant
être	→	étant
savoir	→	sachant

■ **The past participle**

– Regular verbs form their past participles as follows:

– Verbs ending in -er add -é to their stem:

chanter	→	chanté

– Verbs ending in -ir add -i to their stem:

finir	→	fini

– Verbs ending in -re add -u to their stem:

vendre	→	vendu

– For the past participles of irregular verbs, see the VERB TABLES, **10**.

10. Verb tables

The tables on the following pages show how the most important verbs conjugate.

First of all you will find models for the three main verb groups:

Chanter for verbs whose infinitive ends in -**er**, **finir** for verbs whose infinitive ends in -**ir**, and **vendre** for verbs whose infinitive ends in -**re**.

Next come avoir, être, aller and faire.

For these verbs, you will find that all the tenses are given in full, in the following order: the infinitive, the participles, the simple tenses and then the compound tenses of the indicative. Next you will find the conditional and the subjunctive forms. Finally, the forms of the imperative are given.

After these model verbs **acheter** to **vouloir** are given in alphabetical order. For these verbs we list the main tenses only for ease of reference. Note that the conditional forms can easily be worked out from the future forms (*see* **9**.3).

[1] CHANTER

INFINITIVE
present
chanter
perfect
avoir chanté

PARTICIPLE
present
chantant
perfect
chanté, e
ayant chanté

INDICATIVE
present
je chante
tu chantes
il, elle chante
nous chantons
vous chantez
ils, elles chantent

imperfect
je chantais
tu chantais
il, elle chantait
nous chantions
vous chantiez
ils, elles chantaient

future
je chanterai
tu chanteras
il, elle chantera
nous chanterons
vous chanterez
ils, elles chanteront

past historic
je chantai
tu chantas
il, elle chanta
nous chantâmes
vous chantâtes
ils, elles chantèrent

perfect
j'ai chanté
tu as chanté
il, elle a chanté
nous avons chanté
vous avez chanté
ils, elles ont chanté

pluperfect
j'avais chanté
tu avais chanté
il, elle avait chanté
nous avions chanté
vous aviez chanté
ils, elles avaient chanté

future perfect
j'aurai chanté
tu auras chanté
il, elle aura chanté
nous aurons chanté
vous aurez chanté
ils, elles auront chanté

past anterior
j'eus chanté
tu eus chanté
il, elle eut chanté
nous eûmes chanté
vous eûtes chanté
ils, elles eurent chanté

CONDITIONAL
present
je chanterais
tu chanterais
il, elle chanterait
nous chanterions
vous chanteriez
ils, elles chanteraient

perfect
j'aurais chanté
tu aurais chanté
il, elle aurait chanté
nous aurions chanté
vous auriez chanté
ils, elles auraient chanté

SUBJUNCTIVE
present
que je chante
que tu chantes
qu'il, elle chante
que nous chantions
que vous chantiez
qu'ils, elles chantent

imperfect
que je chantasse
que tu chantasses
qu'il, elle chantât
que nous chantassions
que vous chantassiez
qu'ils, elles chantassent

perfect
que j'aie chanté
que tu aies chanté
qu'il, elle ait chanté
que nous ayons chanté
que vous ayez chanté
qu'ils, elles aient chanté

pluperfect
que j'eusse chanté
que tu eusses chanté
qu'il, elle eût chanté
que nous eussions chanté
que vous eussiez chanté
qu'ils, elles eussent
  chanté

IMPERATIVE
present
chante
chantons
chantez

perfect
aie chanté
ayons chanté
ayez chanté

[2] FINIR

INFINITIVE
present
finir
perfect
avoir fini

PARTICIPLE
present
finissant
perfect
fini, e
ayant fini

INDICATIVE
present
je finis
tu finis
il, elle finit
nous finissons
vous finissez
ils, elles finissent
imperfect
je finissais
tu finissais
il, elle finissait
nous finissions
vous finissiez
ils, elles finissaient
future
je finirai
tu finiras
il, elle finira
nous finirons
vous finirez
ils, elles finiront
past historic
je finis
tu finis
il, elle finit
nous finîmes
vous finîtes
ils, elles finirent

perfect
j'ai fini
tu as fini
il, elle a fini
nous avons fini
vous avez fini
ils, elles ont fini
pluperfect
j'avais fini
tu avais fini
il, elle avait fini
nous avions fini
vous aviez fini
ils, elles avaient fini
future perfect
j'aurai fini
tu auras fini
il, elle aura fini
nous aurons fini
vous aurez fini
ils, elles auront fini
past anterior
j'eus fini
tu eus fini
il, elle eut fini
nous eûmes fini
vous eûtes fini
ils, elles eurent fini

CONDITIONAL
present
je finirais
tu finirais
il, elle finirait
nous finirions
vous finiriez
ils, elles finiraient
perfect
j'aurais fini
tu aurais fini
il, elle aurait fini
nous aurions fini
vous auriez fini
ils, elles auraient fini

SUBJUNCTIVE
present
que je finisse
que tu finisses
qu'il, elle finisse
que nous finissions
que vous finissiez
qu'ils, elles finissent
imperfect
que je finisse
que tu finisses
qu'il, elle finît
que nous finissions
que vous finissiez
qu'ils, elles finissent
perfect
que j'aie fini
que tu aies fini
qu'il, elle ait fini
que nous ayons fini
que vous ayez fini
qu'ils, elles aient fini
pluperfect
que j'eusse fini
que tu eusses fini
qu'il, elle eût fini
que nous eussions fini
que vous eussiez fini
qu'ils, elles eussent fini

IMPERATIVE
present
finis
finissons
finissez
perfect
aie fini
ayons fini
ayez fini

[3] VENDRE

INFINITIVE
present

vendre

perfect

avoir vendu

PARTICIPLE
present

vendant

perfect

vendu, e
ayant vendu

INDICATIVE
present

je vends
tu vends
il, elle vend
nous vendons
vous vendez
ils, elles vendent

imperfect

je vendais
tu vendais
il, elle vendait
nous vendions
vous vendiez
ils, elles vendaient

future

je vendrai
tu vendras
il, elle vendra
nous vendrons
vous vendrez
ils, elles vendront

past historic

je vendis
tu vendis
il, elle vendit
nous vendîmes
vous vendîtes
ils, elles vendirent

perfect

j'ai vendu
tu as vendu
il, elle a vendu
nous avons vendu
vous avez vendu
ils, elles ont vendu

pluperfect

j'avais vendu
tu avais vendu
il, elle avait vendu
nous avions vendu
vous aviez vendu
ils, elles avaient vendu

future perfect

j'aurai vendu
tu auras vendu
il, elle aura vendu
nous aurons vendu
vous aurez vendu
ils, elles auront vendu

past anterior

j'eus vendu
tu eus vendu
il, elle eut vendu
nous eûmes vendu
vous eûtes vendu
ils, elles eurent vendu

CONDITIONAL
present

je vendrais
tu vendrais
il, elle vendrait
nous vendrions
vous vendriez
ils, elles vendraient

perfect

j'aurais vendu
tu aurais vendu
il, elle aurait vendu
nous aurions vendu
vous auriez vendu
ils, elles auraient vendu

SUBJUNCTIVE
present

que je vende
que tu vendes
qu'il, elle vende
que nous vendions
que vous vendiez
qu'ils, elles vendent

imperfect

que je vendisse
que tu vendisses
qu'il, elle vendît
que nous vendissions
que vous vendissiez
qu'ils, elles vendissent

perfect

que j'aie vendu
que tu aies vendu
qu'il, elle ait vendu
que nous ayons vendu
que vous ayez vendu
qu'ils, elles aient vendu

pluperfect

que j'eusse vendu
que tu eusses vendu
qu'il, elle eût vendu
que nous eussions vendu
que vous eussiez vendu
qu'ils, elles eussent vendu

IMPERATIVE
present

vends
vendons
vendez

perfect

aie vendu
ayons vendu
ayez vendu

[4] AVOIR

INFINITIVE

present

avoir

perfect

avoir eu

PARTICIPLE

present

ayant

perfect

eu, e

ayant eu

INDICATIVE

present

j'ai

tu as

il, elle a

nous avons

vous avez

ils, elles ont

imperfect

j'avais

tu avais

il, elle avait

nous avions

vous aviez

ils, elles avaient

future

j'aurai

tu auras

il, elle aura

nous aurons

vous aurez

ils, elles auront

past historic

j'eus

tu eus

il, elle eut

nous eûmes

vous eûtes

ils, elles eurent

perfect

j'ai eu

tu as eu

il, elle a eu

nous avons eu

vous avez eu

ils, elles ont eu

pluperfect

j'avais eu

tu avais eu

il, elle avait eu

nous avions eu

vous aviez eu

ils, elles avaient eu

future perfect

j'aurai eu

tu auras eu

il, elle aura eu

nous aurons eu

vous aurez eu

ils, elles auront eu

past anterior

j'eus eu

tu eus eu

il, elle eut eu

nous eûmes eu

vous eûtes eu

ils, elles eurent eu

CONDITIONAL

present

j'aurais

tu aurais

il, elle aurait

nous aurions

vous auriez

ils, elles auraient

perfect

j'aurais eu

tu aurais eu

il, elle aurait eu

nous aurions eu

vous auriez eu

ils, elles auraient eu

SUBJUNCTIVE

present

que j'aie

que tu aies

qu'il, elle ait

que nous ayons

que vous ayez

qu'ils, elles aient

imperfect

que j'eusse

que tu eusses

qu'il, elle eût

que nous eussions

que vous eussiez

qu'ils, elles eussent

perfect

que j'aie eu

que tu aies eu

qu'il, elle ait eu

que nous ayons eu

que vous ayez eu

qu'ils, elles aient eu

pluperfect

que j'eusse eu

que tu eusses eu

qu'il, elle eût eu

que nous eussions eu

que vous eussiez eu

qu'ils, elles eussent eu

IMPERATIVE

present

aie

ayons

ayez

perfect

aie eu

ayons eu

ayez eu

[5] ÊTRE

INFINITIVE

present

être

perfect

avoir été

PARTICIPLE

present

étant

perfect

été

ayant été

INDICATIVE

present

je suis
tu es
il, elle est
nous sommes
vous êtes
ils, elles sont

imperfect

j'étais
tu étais
il, elle était
nous étions
vous étiez
ils, elles étaient

future

je serai
tu seras
il, elle sera
nous serons
vous serez
ils, elles seront

past historic

je fus
tu fus
il, elle fut
nous fûmes
vous fûtes
ils, elles furent

perfect

j'ai été
tu as été
il, elle a été
nous avons été
vous avez été
ils, elles ont été

pluperfect

j'avais été
tu avais été
il, elle avait été
nous avions été
vous aviez été
ils, elles avaient été

future perfect

j'aurai été
tu auras été
il, elle aura été
nous aurons été
vous aurez été
ils, elles auront été

past anterior

j'eus été
tu eus été
il, elle eut été
nous eûmes été
vous eûtes été
ils, elles eurent été

CONDITIONAL

present

je serais
tu serais
il, elle serait
nous serions
vous seriez
ils, elles seraient

perfect

j'aurais été
tu aurais été
il, elle aurait été
nous aurions été
vous auriez été
ils, elles auraient été

SUBJUNCTIVE

present

que je sois
que tu sois
qu'il, elle soit
que nous soyons
que vous soyez
qu'ils, elles soient

imperfect

que je fusse
que tu fusses
qu'il, elle fût
que nous fussions
que vous fussiez
qu'ils, elles fussent

perfect

que j'aie été
que tu aies été
qu'il, elle ait été
que nous ayons été
que vous ayez été
qu'ils, elles aient été

pluperfect

que j'eusse été
que tu eusses été
qu'il, elle eût été
que nous eussions été
que vous eussiez été
qu'ils, elles eussent été

IMPERATIVE

present

sois
soyons
soyez

perfect

aie été
ayons été
ayez été

[6] ALLER

INFINITIVE

present

aller

perfect

être allé

PARTICIPLE

present

allant

perfect

allé, e

étant allé

INDICATIVE

present

je vais

tu vas

il, elle va

nous allons

vous allez

ils, elles vont

imperfect

j'allais

tu allais

il, elle allait

nous allions

vous alliez

ils, elles allaient

future

j'irai

tu iras

il, elle ira

nous irons

vous irez

ils, elles iront

past historic

j'allai

tu allas

il, elle alla

nous allâmes

vous allâtes

ils, elles allèrent

perfect

je suis allé

tu es allé

il, elle est allé, e

nous sommes allés

vous êtes allés

ils, elles sont allés, es

pluperfect

j'étais allé

tu étais allé

il, elle était allé, e

nous étions allés

vous étiez allés

ils, elles étaient allés, es

future perfect

je serai allé

tu seras allé

il, elle sera allé, e

nous serons allés

vous serez allés

ils, elles seront allés, es

past anterior

je fus allé

tu fus allé

il, elle fut allé, e

nous fûmes allés

vous fûtes allés

ils, elles furent allés, es

CONDITIONAL

present

j'irais

tu irais

il, elle irait

nous irions

vous iriez

ils, elles iraient

perfect

je serais allé

tu serais allé

il, elle serait allé, e

nous serions allés

vous seriez allés

ils, elles seraient allés, es

SUBJUNCTIVE

present

que j'aille

que tu ailles

qu'il, elle aille

que nous allions

que vous alliez

qu'ils, elles aillent

imperfect

que j'allasse

que tu allasses

qu'il, elle allât

que nous allassions

que vous allassiez

qu'ils, elles allassent

perfect

que je sois allé

que tu sois allé

qu'il, elle soit allé, e

que nous soyons allés

que vous soyez allés

qu'ils, elles soient allés, es

pluperfect

que je fusse allé

que tu fusses allé

qu'il, elle fût allé, e

que nous fussions allés

que vous fussiez allés

qu'ils, elles fussent allés, es

IMPERATIVE

present

va

allons

allez

perfect

sois allé

soyons allés

soyez allés

Note: *Aller is conjugated with *être* in compound tenses. *The imperative of *aller* is *vas* when it is followed by *y*: *vas-y*. *S'en aller* in the imperative gives: *va-t'en, allons-nous-en, allez-vous-en*.

[7] FAIRE

INFINITIVE

present
faire

perfect
avoir fait

PARTICIPLE

present
faisant

perfect
fait, e
ayant fait

INDICATIVE

present
je fais
tu fais
il, elle fait
nous faisons
vous **faites**
ils, elles font

imperfect
je faisais
tu faisais
il, elle faisait
nous faisions
vous faisiez
ils, elles faisaient

future
je ferai
tu feras
il, elle fera
nous ferons
vous ferez
ils, elles feront

past historic
je fis
tu fis
il, elle fit
nous fîmes
vous fîtes
ils, elles firent

perfect
j'ai fait
tu as fait
il, elle a fait
nous avons fait
vous avez fait
ils, elles ont fait

pluperfect
j'avais fait
tu avais fait
il, elle avait fait
nous avions fait
vous aviez fait
ils, elles avaient fait

future perfect
j'aurai fait
tu auras fait
il, elle aura fait
nous aurons fait
vous aurez fait
ils, elles auront fait

past anterior
j'eus fait
tu eus fait
il, elle eut fait
nous eûmes fait
vous eûtes fait
ils, elles eurent fait

CONDITIONAL

present
je ferais
tu ferais
il, elle ferait
nous ferions
vous feriez
ils, elles feraient

perfect
j'aurais fait
tu aurais fait
il, elle aurait fait
nous aurions fait
vous auriez fait
ils, elles auraient fait

SUBJUNCTIVE

present
que je fasse
que tu fasses
qu'il, elle fasse
que nous fassions
que vous fassiez
qu'ils, elles fassent

imperfect
que je fisse
que tu fisses
qu'il, elle fît
que nous fissions
que vous fissiez
qu'ils, elles fissent

perfect
que j'aie fait
que tu aies fait
qu'il, elle ait fait
que nous ayons fait
que vous ayez fait
qu'ils, elles aient fait

pluperfect
que j'eusse fait
que tu eusses fait
qu'il, elle eût fait
que nous eussions fait
que vous eussiez fait
qu'ils, elles eussent fait

IMPERATIVE

present
fais
faisons
faites

perfect
aie fait
ayons fait
ayez fait

Note: *The following 2nd persons plural should be remembered: *vous faites*; imperative: *faites*. *Vous faisez, faisez* are wrong!
*The compound verbs *défaire, parfaire, refaire* and *satisfaire* are conjugated in the same way as *faire*.

[8] ACHETER

present participle
achetant
past participle
acheté, e
present indicative
j'achète
tu achètes
il, elle achète
nous achetons
vous achetez
ils, elles achètent
imperfect indicative
j'achetais
tu achetais
il, elle achetait
nous achetions
vous achetiez
ils, elles achetaient

future indicative
j'achèterai
tu achèteras
il, elle achètera
nous achèterons
vous achèterez
ils, elles achèteront
perfect indicative
j'ai acheté
tu as acheté
il, elle a acheté
nous avons acheté
vous avez acheté
ils, elles ont acheté

past historic indicative
j'achetai
tu achetas
il, elle acheta
nous achetâmes
vous achetâtes
ils, elles achetèrent
present subjunctive
que j'achète
que tu achètes
qu'il, elle achète
que nous achetions
que vous achetiez
qu'ils, elles achètent
imperative
achète
achetons
achetez

[9] ACQUÉRIR

present participle
acquérant
past participle
acquis, e
present indicative
j'acquiers
tu acquiers
il, elle acquiert
nous acquérons
vous acquérez
ils, elles acquièrent
imperfect indicative
j'acquérais
tu acquérais
il, elle acquérait
nous acquérions
vous acquériez
ils, elles acquéraient

future indicative
j'acquerrai
tu acquerras
il, elle acquerra
nous acquerrons
vous acquerrez
ils, elles acquerront
perfect indicative
j'ai acquis
tu as acquis
il, elle a acquis
nous avons acquis
vous avez acquis
ils, elles ont acquis

past historic indicative
j'acquis
tu acquis
il, elle acquit
nous acquîmes
vous acquîtes
ils, elles acquirent
present subjunctive
que j'acquière
que tu acquières
qu'il, elle acquière
que nous acquérions
que vous acquériez
qu'ils, elles acquièrent
imperative
acquiers
acquérons
acquérez

[10] APPELER

present participle
appelant
past participle
appelé, e
present indicative
j'appelle
tu appelles
il, elle appelle
nous appelons
vous appelez
ils, elles appellent
imperfect indicative
j'appelais
tu appelais
il, elle appelait
nous appelions
vous appeliez
ils, elles appelaient

future indicative
j'appellerai
tu appelleras
il, elle appellera
nous appellerons
vous appellerez
ils, elles appelleront
perfect indicative
j'ai appelé
tu as appelé
il, elle a appelé
nous avons appelé
vous avez appelé
ils, elles ont appelé
past historic indicative
j'appelai
tu appelas
il, elle appela
nous appelâmes
vous appelâtes
ils, elles appelèrent

present subjunctive
que j'appelle
que tu appelles
qu'il, elle appelle
que nous appelions
que vous appeliez
qu'ils, elles appellent
imperative
appelle
appelons
appelez

Note: Most verbs ending in -eler behave like *appeler* and double the final -l before mute -e: *j'appelle, tu appelleras ...*

[11] APPRENDRE

present participle
apprenant
past participle
appris, e
present indicative
j'apprends
tu apprends
il, elle apprend
nous apprenons
vous apprenez
ils, elles apprennent
imperfect indicative
j'apprenais
tu apprenais
il, elle apprenait
nous apprenions
vous appreniez
ils, elles apprenaient

future indicative
j'apprendrai
tu apprendras
il, elle apprendra
nous apprendrons
vous apprendrez
ils, elles apprendront
perfect indicative
j'ai appris
tu as appris
il, elle a appris
nous avons appris
vous avez appris
ils, elles ont appris

past historic indicative
j'appris
tu appris
il, elle apprit
nous apprîmes
vous apprîtes
ils, elles apprirent
present subjunctive
que j'apprenne
que tu apprennes
qu'il, elle apprenne
que nous apprenions
que vous appreniez
qu'ils, elles apprennent
imperative
apprends
apprenons
apprenez

[12] ARRIVER

present participle
arrivant
past participle
arrivé, e
present indicative
j'arrive
tu arrives
il, elle arrive
nous arrivons
vous arrivez
ils, elles arrivent
imperfect indicative
j'arrivais
tu arrivais
il, elle arrivait
nous arrivions
vous arriviez
ils, elles arrivaient

future indicative
j'arriverai
tu arriveras
il, elle arrivera
nous arriverons
vous arriverez
ils, elles arriveront
perfect indicative
je suis arrivé
tu es arrivé
il, elle est arrivé, e
nous sommes arrivés
vous êtes arrivés
ils, elles sont arrivés, es

past historic indicative
j'arrivai
tu arrivas
il, elle arriva
nous arrivâmes
vous arrivâtes
ils, elles arrivèrent
present subjunctive
que j'arrive
que tu arrives
qu'il, elle arrive
que nous arrivions
que vous arriviez
qu'ils, elles arrivent
imperative
arrive
arrivons
arrivez

[13] S'ASSEOIR

present participle
s'asseyant/assoyant
past participle
assis, e
present indicative
je m'assieds/assois
tu t'assieds/assois
il, elle s'assied/assoit
nous nous asseyons/
  assoyons
vous vous asseyez/
  assoyez
ils, elles s'asseyent/
  assoient
imperfect indicative
je m'asseyais
tu t'asseyais
il, elle s'asseyait
nous nous asseyions
vous vous asseyiez
ils, elles s'asseyaient

future indicative
je m'assiérai/assoirai
tu t'assiéras/assoiras
il, elle s'assiéra/assoira
nous nous assiérons/
  assoirons
vous vous assiérez/
  assoirez
ils, elles s'assiéront/
  assoiront
perfect indicative
je me suis assis
tu t'es assis
il, elle s'est assis, e
nous nous sommes assis
vous vous êtes assis
ils, elles se sont assis, es
past historic indicative
je m'assis
tu t'assis
il, elle s'assit
nous nous assîmes
vous vous assîtes
ils, elles s'assirent

present subjunctive
que je m'asseye/assoie
que tu t'asseyes/assoies
qu'il, elle s'asseye/assoie
que nous nous asseyions/
  assoyions
que vous vous asseyiez/
  assoyiez
qu'ils, elles s'asseyent/
  assoient
imperative
assieds-toi
asseyons-nous
asseyez-vous

Note: *S'asseoir* can also take
the form of the non-reflexive
verb *asseoir*: j'assieds, tu asseyais ... but in compound
tenses it is then conjugated
with the auxiliary *avoir*: j'**ai**
assis, nous **avions** *assis ...*
Je m'assois and *nous nous as-
seyons* are more common than
their alternatives, but the forms
in **ie** and **ey** are preferable to
the forms in **oi**.

[14] ATTENDRE

present participle
attendant
past participle
attendu, e
present indicative
j'attends
tu attends
il, elle attend
nous attendons
vous attendez
ils, elles attendent
imperfect indicative
j'attendais
tu attendais
il, elle attendait
nous attendions
vous attendiez
ils, elles attendaient

future indicative
j'attendrai
tu attendras
il, elle attendra
nous attendrons
vous attendrez
ils, elles attendront
perfect indicative
j'ai attendu
tu as attendu
il, elle a attendu
nous avons attendu
vous avez attendu
ils, elles ont attendu

past historic indicative
j'attendis
tu attendis
il, elle attendit
nous attendîmes
vous attendîtes
ils, elles attendirent
present subjunctive
que j'attende
que tu attendes
qu'il, elle attende
que nous attendions
que vous attendiez
qu'ils, elles attendent
imperative
attends
attendons
attendez

[15] BATTRE

present participle
battant
past participle
battu, e
present indicative
je bats
tu bats
il, elle bat
nous battons
vous battez
ils, elles battent
imperfect indicative
je battais
tu battais
il, elle battait
nous battions
vous battiez
ils, elles battaient

future indicative
je battrai
tu battras
il, elle battra
nous battrons
vous battrez
ils, elles battront
perfect indicative
j'ai battu
tu as battu
il, elle a battu
nous avons battu
vous avez battu
ils, elles ont battu
past historic indicative
je battis
tu battis
il, elle battit
nous battîmes
vous battîtes
ils, elles battirent

present subjunctive
que je batte
que tu battes
qu'il, elle batte
que nous battions
que vous battiez
qu'ils, elles battent
imperative
bats
battons
battez

Note: Compounds of *battre*, such as *abattre*, *combattre*, *débattre*, *s'ébattre* and *rabattre*, are conjugated in the same way.

[16] BOIRE

present participle
buvant

past participle
bu, e

present indicative
je bois
tu bois
il, elle boit
nous buvons
vous buvez
ils, elles boivent

imperfect indicative
je buvais
tu buvais
il, elle buvait
nous buvions
vous buviez
ils, elles buvaient

future indicative
je boirai
tu boiras
il, elle boira
nous boirons
vous boirez
ils, elles boiront

perfect indicative
j'ai bu
tu as bu
il, elle a bu
nous avons bu
vous avez bu
ils, elles ont bu

past historic indicative
je bus
tu bus
il, elle but
nous bûmes
vous bûtes
ils, elles burent

present subjunctive
que je boive
que tu boives
qu'il, elle boive
que nous buvions
que vous buviez
qu'ils, elles boivent

imperative
bois
buvons
buvez

[17] BOUILLIR

present participle
bouillant

past participle
bouilli, e

present indicative
je bous
tu bous
il, elle bout
nous bouillons
vous bouillez
ils, elles bouillent

imperfect indicative
je bouillais
tu bouillais
il, elle bouillait
nous bouillions
vous bouilliez
ils, elles bouillaient

future indicative
je bouillirai
tu bouilliras
il, elle bouillira
nous bouillirons
vous bouillirez
ils, elles bouilliront

perfect indicative
j'ai bouilli
tu as bouilli
il, elle a bouilli
nous avons bouilli
vous avez bouilli
ils, elles ont bouilli

past historic indicative
je bouillis
tu bouillis
il, elle bouillit
nous bouillîmes
vous bouillîtes
ils, elles bouillirent

present subjunctive
que je bouille
que tu bouilles
qu'il, elle bouille
que nous bouillions
que vous bouilliez
qu'ils, elles bouillent

imperative
bous
bouillons
bouillez

[18] COMMENCER

present participle
commençant

past participle
commencé, e

present indicative
je commence
tu commences
il, elle commence
nous commençons
vous commencez
ils, elles commencent

imperfect indicative
je commençais
tu commençais
il, elle commençait
nous commencions
vous commenciez
ils, elles commençaient

future indicative
je commencerai
tu commenceras
il, elle commencera
nous commencerons
vous commencerez
ils, elles commenceront

perfect indicative
j'ai commencé
tu as commencé
il, elle a commencé
nous avons commencé
vous avez commencé
ils, elles ont commencé

past historic indicative
je commençai
tu commenças
il, elle commença
nous commençâmes
vous commençâtes
ils, elles commencèrent

present subjunctive
que je commence
que tu commences
qu'il, elle commence
que nous commencions
que vous commenciez
qu'ils, elles commencent

imperative
commence
commençons
commencez

Note: *Annoncer, avancer, déplacer, effacer, lancer* and *placer* are conjugated in the same way as *commencer*.
*Verbs in **-cer** change **c** to **ç** in front of the vowels **a** and **o**.

[19] CONCLURE

present participle
concluant

past participle
conclu, e

present indicative
je conclus
tu conclus
il, elle conclut
nous concluons
vous concluez
ils, elles concluent

imperfect indicative
je concluais
tu concluais
il, elle concluait
nous concluions
vous concluiez
ils, elles concluaient

future indicative
je conclurai
tu concluras
il, elle conclura
nous conclurons
vous conclurez
ils, elles concluront

perfect indicative
j'ai conclu
tu as conclu
il, elle a conclu
nous avons conclu
vous avez conclu
ils, elles ont conclu

past historic indicative
je conclus
tu conclus
il, elle conclut
nous conclûmes
vous conclûtes
ils, elles conclurent

present subjunctive
que je conclue
que tu conclues
qu'il, elle conclue
que nous concluions
que vous concluiez
qu'ils, elles concluent

imperative
conclus
concluons
concluez

Note: *Exclure, inclure* and *occlure* are conjugated like *conclure*. Remember, however, the past participles *inclus(e)* and *occlus(e)*.
*Note the difference between *exclu(e)* and *inclus(e)*.

[20] CONDUIRE

present participle
conduisant

past participle
conduit, e

present indicative
je conduis
tu conduis
il, elle conduit
nous conduisons
vous conduisez
ils, elles conduisent

imperfect indicative
je conduisais
tu conduisais
il, elle conduisait
nous conduisions
vous conduisiez
ils, elles conduisaient

future indicative
je conduirai
tu conduiras
il, elle conduira
nous conduirons
vous conduirez
ils, elles conduiront

perfect indicative
j'ai conduit
tu as conduit
il, elle a conduit
nous avons conduit
vous avez conduit
ils, elles ont conduit

past historic indicative
je conduisis
tu conduisis
il, elle conduisit
nous conduisîmes
vous conduisîtes
ils, elles conduisirent

present subjunctive
que je conduise
que tu conduises
qu'il, elle conduise
que nous conduisions
que vous conduisiez
qu'ils, elles conduisent

imperative
conduis
conduisons
conduisez

Note: *Construire, cuire* and similar verbs such as *déduire, introduire, produire, réduire, séduire* and *traduire* are all conjugated in the same way.

[21] CONNAÎTRE

present participle
connaissant

past participle
connu, e

present indicative
je connais
tu connais
il, elle connaît
nous connaissons
vous connaissez
ils, elles connaissent

imperfect indicative
je connaissais
tu connaissais
il, elle connaissait
nous connaissions
vous connaissiez
ils, elles connaissaient

future indicative
je connaîtrai
tu connaîtras
il, elle connaîtra
nous connaîtrons
vous connaîtrez
ils, elles connaîtront

perfect indicative
j'ai connu
tu as connu
il, elle a connu
nous avons connu
vous avez connu
ils, elles ont connu

past historic indicative
je connus
tu connus
il, elle connut
nous connûmes
vous connûtes
ils, elles connurent

present subjunctive
que je connaisse
que tu connaisses
qu'il, elle connaisse
que nous connaissions
que vous connaissiez
qu'ils, elles connaissent

imperative
connais
connaissons
connaissez

Note: **Connaître, naître* [43], *paraître* [45] and their compounds such as *reconnaître, apparaître* and *disparaître* are all conjugated in the same way.

*Note the circumflex **î** when **i** comes before **t** in verbs in **-aître**.

[22] COURIR

present participle
courant
past participle
couru, e
present indicative
je cours
tu cours
il, elle court
nous courons
vous courez
ils, elles courent
imperfect indicative
je courais
tu courais
il, elle courait
nous courions
vous couriez
ils, elles couraient

future indicative
je courrai
tu courras
il, elle courra
nous courrons
vous courrez
ils, elles courront
perfect indicative
j'ai couru
tu as couru
il, elle a couru
nous avons couru
vous avez couru
ils, elles ont couru
past historic indicative
je courus
tu courus
il, elle courut
nous courûmes
vous courûtes
ils, elles coururent

present subjunctive
que je coure
que tu coures
qu'il, elle coure
que nous courions
que vous couriez
qu'ils, elles courent
imperative
cours
courons
courez

Note: *Courir* and its compounds *accourir, parcourir* and *secourir* are conjugated in the same way.
*Note the double **r** in the future (it reappears in the conditional present): *je courrai (tu courrais)*.

[23] COUVRIR

present participle
couvrant
past participle
couvert, e
present indicative
je couvre
tu couvres
il, elle couvre
nous couvrons
vous couvrez
ils, elles couvrent
imperfect indicative
je couvrais
tu couvrais
il, elle couvrait
nous couvrions
vous couvriez
ils, elles couvraient

future indicative
je couvrirai
tu couvriras
il, elle couvrira
nous couvrirons
vous couvrirez
ils, elles couvriront
perfect indicative
j'ai couvert
tu as couvert
il, elle a couvert
nous avons couvert
vous avez couvert
ils, elles ont couvert
past historic indicative
je couvris
tu couvris
il, elle couvrit
nous couvrîmes
vous couvrîtes
ils, elles couvrirent

present subjunctive
que je couvre
que tu couvres
qu'il, elle couvre
que nous couvrions
que vous couvriez
qu'ils, elles couvrent
imperative
couvre
couvrons
couvrez

Note: *Découvrir, ouvrir* [44], *offrir* and *souffrir* are all conjugated in the same way.

[24] CRAINDRE

present participle
craignant
past participle
craint, e
present indicative
je crains
tu crains
il, elle craint
nous craignons
vous craignez
ils, elles craignent
imperfect indicative
je craignais
tu craignais
il, elle craignait
nous craignions
vous craigniez
ils, elles craignaient

future indicative
je craindrai
tu craindras
il, elle craindra
nous craindrons
vous craindrez
ils, elles craindront
perfect indicative
j'ai craint
tu as craint
il, elle a craint
nous avons craint
vous avez craint
ils, elles ont craint
past historic indicative
je craignis
tu craignis
il, elle craignit
nous craignîmes
vous craignîtes
ils, elles craignirent

present subjunctive
que je craigne
que tu craignes
qu'il, elle craigne
que nous craignions
que vous craigniez
qu'ils, elles craignent
imperative
crains
craignons
craignez

Note: *Contraindre* and *plaindre* are conjugated in the same way.

[25] CRÉER

present participle
créant
past participle
créé, e
present indicative
je crée
tu crées
il, elle crée
nous créons
vous créez
ils, elles créent
imperfect indicative
je créais
tu créais
il, elle créait
nous créions
vous créiez
ils, elles créaient

future indicative
je créerai
tu créeras
il, elle créera
nous créerons
vous créerez
ils, elles créeront
perfect indicative
j'ai créé
tu as créé
il, elle a créé
nous avons créé
vous avez créé
ils, elles ont créé

past historic indicative
je créai
tu créas
il, elle créa
nous créâmes
vous créâtes
ils, elles créèrent
present subjunctive
que je crée
que tu crées
qu'il, elle crée
que nous créions
que vous créiez
qu'ils, elles créent
imperative
crée
créons
créez

[26] CRIER

present participle
criant

past participle
crié, e

present indicative
je crie
tu cries
il, elle crie
nous crions
vous criez
ils, elles crient

imperfect indicative
je criais
tu criais
il, elle criait
nous criions
vous criiez
ils, elles criaient

future indicative
je crierai
tu crieras
il, elle criera
nous crierons
vous crierez
ils, elles crieront

perfect indicative
j'ai crié
tu as crié
il, elle a crié
nous avons crié
vous avez crié
ils, elles ont crié

past historic indicative
je criai
tu crias
il, elle cria
nous criâmes
vous criâtes
ils, elles crièrent

present subjunctive
que je crie
que tu cries
qu'il, elle crie
que nous criions
que vous criiez
qu'ils, elles crient

imperative
crie
crions
criez

Note: Note the presence of two i's in the 1st and 2nd person plural of the imperfect indicative and the present subjunctive: *criions, criiez*.

[27] CROIRE

present participle
croyant

past participle
cru, e

present indicative
je crois
tu crois
il, elle croit
nous croyons
vous croyez
ils, elles croient

imperfect indicative
je croyais
tu croyais
il, elle croyait
nous croyions
vous croyiez
ils, elles croyaient

future indicative
je croirai
tu croiras
il, elle croira
nous croirons
vous croirez
ils, elles croiront

perfect indicative
j'ai cru
tu as cru
il, elle a cru
nous avons cru
vous avez cru
ils, elles ont cru

past historic indicative
je crus
tu crus
il, elle crut
nous crûmes
vous crûtes
ils, elles crurent

present subjunctive
que je croie
que tu croies
qu'il, elle croie
que nous croyions
que vous croyiez
qu'ils, elles croient

imperative
crois
croyons
croyez

Note: Do not confuse *je crois* from *croire* with *je croîs* from *croître*.

[28] CUEILLIR

present participle
cueillant

past participle
cueilli, e

present indicative
je cueille
tu cueilles
il, elle cueille
nous cueillons
vous cueillez
ils, elles cueillent

imperfect indicative
je cueillais
tu cueillais
il, elle cueillait
nous cueillions
vous cueilliez
ils, elles cueillaient

future indicative
je cueillerai
tu cueilleras
il, elle cueillera
nous cueillerons
vous cueillerez
ils, elles cueilleront

perfect indicative
j'ai cueilli
tu as cueilli
il, elle a cueilli
nous avons cueilli
vous avez cueilli
ils, elles ont cueilli

past historic indicative
je cueillis
tu cueillis
il, elle cueillit
nous cueillîmes
vous cueillîtes
ils, elles cueillirent

present subjunctive
que je cueille
que tu cueilles
qu'il, elle cueille
que nous cueillions
que vous cueilliez
qu'ils, elles cueillent

imperative
cueille
cueillons
cueillez

Note: *Accueillir and recueillir are conjugated in the same way.
*In the future indicative cueillir becomes cueillerai and not cueillirai.

[29] DESCENDRE

present participle
descendant

past participle
descendu, e

present indicative
je descends
tu descends
il, elle descend
nous descendons
vous descendez
ils, elles descendent

imperfect indicative
je descendais
tu descendais
il, elle descendait
nous descendions
vous descendiez
ils, elles descendaient

future indicative
je descendrai
tu descendras
il, elle descendra
nous descendrons
vous descendrez
ils, elles descendront

perfect indicative
je suis descendu
tu es descendu
il, elle est descendu, e
nous sommes descendus
vous êtes descendus
ils, elles sont descendus, es

past historic indicative
je descendis
tu descendis
il, elle descendit
nous descendîmes
vous descendîtes
ils, elles descendirent

present subjunctive
que je descende
que tu descendes
qu'il, elle descende
que nous descendions
que vous descendiez
qu'ils, elles descendent

imperative
descends
descendons
descendez

Note: *Many verbs ending in **-dre** are conjugated as here.
*In compound tenses *descendre* is conjugated with *être* when it is intransitive meaning 'to come/go/get down': *le cavalier est descendu de son cheval*, and with *avoir* when it is transitive meaning 'to bring/take down' and can take a direct object: *nous avons descendu les valises*.

[30] DEVENIR

present participle
devenant

past participle
devenu, e

present indicative
je deviens
tu deviens
il, elle devient
nous devenons
vous devenez
ils, elles deviennent

imperfect indicative
je devenais
tu devenais
il, elle devenait
nous devenions
vous deveniez
ils, elles devenaient

future indicative
je deviendrai
tu deviendras
il, elle deviendra
nous deviendrons
vous deviendrez
ils, elles deviendront

perfect indicative
je suis devenu
tu es devenu
il, elle est devenu, e
nous sommes devenus
vous êtes devenus
ils, elles sont devenus, es

past historic indicative
je devins
tu devins
il, elle devint
nous devînmes
vous devîntes
ils, elles devinrent

present subjunctive
que je devienne
que tu deviennes
qu'il, elle devienne
que nous devenions
que vous deveniez
qu'ils, elles deviennent

imperative
deviens
devenons
devenez

[31] DEVOIR

present participle
devant

past participle
dû, due

present indicative
je dois
tu dois
il, elle doit
nous devons
vous devez
ils, elles doivent

imperfect indicative
je devais
tu devais
il, elle devait
nous devions
vous deviez
ils, elles devaient

future indicative
je devrai
tu devras
il, elle devra
nous devrons
vous devrez
ils, elles devront

perfect indicative
j'ai dû
tu as dû
il, elle a dû
nous avons dû
vous avez dû
ils, elles ont dû

past historic indicative
je dus
tu dus
il, elle dut
nous dûmes
vous dûtes
ils, elles durent

present subjunctive
que je doive
que tu doives
qu'il, elle doive
que nous devions
que vous deviez
qu'ils, elles doivent

Note: The imperative *dois, devons, devez* exists but is seldom used.

[32] DIRE

present participle
disant

past participle
dit, e

present indicative
je dis
tu dis
il, elle dit
nous disons
vous **dites**
ils, elles disent

imperfect indicative
je disais
tu disais
il, elle disait
nous disions
vous disiez
ils, elles disaient

future indicative
je dirai
tu diras
il, elle dira
nous dirons
vous direz
ils, elles diront

perfect indicative
j'ai dit
tu as dit
il, elle a dit
nous avons dit
vous avez dit
ils, elles ont dit

past historic indicative
je dis
tu dis
il, elle dit
nous dîmes
vous dîtes
ils, elles dirent

present subjunctive
que je dise
que tu dises
qu'il, elle dise
que nous disions
que vous disiez
qu'ils, elles disent

imperative
dis
disons
dites

Note: Among the many compounds of *dire*, only *redire* follows the model *dites*, *redites*. *Contredire, dédire, interdire, médire* and *prédire* have the following forms in the present indicative and imperative: *(vous) contredisez, dédisez, interdisez, médisez, prédisez.* As regards *maudire*, it is conjugated like *finir: nous maudissons, vous maudissez, ils maudissent, je maudissais, maudissant* ... except in the past participle: *maudit, e.*

[33] DORMIR

present participle
dormant

past participle
dormi

present indicative
je dors
tu dors
il, elle dort
nous dormons
vous dormez
ils, elles dorment

imperfect indicative
je dormais
tu dormais
il, elle dormait
nous dormions
vous dormiez
ils, elles dormaient

future indicative
je dormirai
tu dormiras
il, elle dormira
nous dormirons
vous dormirez
ils, elles dormiront

perfect indicative
j'ai dormi
tu as dormi
il, elle a dormi
nous avons dormi
vous avez dormi
ils, elles ont dormi

past historic indicative
je dormis
tu dormis
il, elle dormit
nous dormîmes
vous dormîtes
ils, elles dormirent

present subjunctive
que je dorme
que tu dormes
qu'il, elle dorme
que nous dormions
que vous dormiez
qu'ils, elles dorment

imperative
dors
dormons
dormez

Note: *Endormir* also follows this model, its past participle being *endormi, endormie.*
*The feminine form of the past participle of *dormir: dormie,* is scarcely ever used.

[34] ÉCRIRE

present participle
écrivant
past participle
écrit, e
present indicative
j'écris
tu écris
il, elle écrit
nous écrivons
vous écrivez
ils, elles écrivent
imperfect indicative
j'écrivais
tu écrivais
il, elle écrivait
nous écrivions
vous écriviez
ils, elles écrivaient

future indicative
j'écrirai
tu écriras
il, elle écrira
nous écrirons
vous écrirez
ils, elles écriront
perfect indicative
j'ai écrit
tu as écrit
il, elle a écrit
nous avons écrit
vous avez écrit
ils, elles ont écrit

past historic indicative
j'écrivis
tu écrivis
il, elle écrivit
nous écrivîmes
vous écrivîtes
ils, elles écrivirent
present subjunctive
que j'écrive
que tu écrives
qu'il, elle écrive
que nous écrivions
que vous écriviez
qu'ils, elles écrivent
imperative
écris
écrivons
écrivez

[35] ENTRER

present participle
entrant
past participle
entré, e
present indicative
j'entre
tu entres
il, elle entre
nous entrons
vous entrez
ils, elles entrent
imperfect indicative
j'entrais
tu entrais
il, elle entrait
nous entrions
vous entriez
ils, elles entraient

future indicative
j'entrerai
tu entreras
il, elle entrera
nous entrerons
vous entrerez
ils, elles entreront
perfect indicative
je suis entré
tu es entré
il, elle est entré, e
nous sommes entrés
vous êtes entrés
ils, elles sont entrés, es

past historic indicative
j'entrai
tu entras
il, elle entra
nous entrâmes
vous entrâtes
ils, elles entrèrent
present subjunctive
que j'entre
que tu entres
qu'il, elle entre
que nous entrions
que vous entriez
qu'ils, elles entrent
imperative
entre
entrons
entrez

Note: In compound tenses, *entrer* is conjugated with the auxiliary *être*.

[36] ENVOYER

present participle
envoyant
past participle
envoyé, e
present indicative
j'envoie
tu envoies
il, elle envoie
nous envoyons
vous envoyez
ils, elles envoient
imperfect indicative
j'envoyais
tu envoyais
il, elle envoyait
nous envoyions
vous envoyiez
ils, elles envoyaient

future indicative
j'enverrai
tu enverras
il, elle enverra
nous enverrons
vous enverrez
ils, elles enverront
perfect indicative
j'ai envoyé
tu as envoyé
il, elle a envoyé
nous avons envoyé
vous avez envoyé
ils, elles ont envoyé

past historic indicative
j'envoyai
tu envoyas
il, elle envoya
nous envoyâmes
vous envoyâtes
ils, elles envoyèrent
present subjunctive
que j'envoie
que tu envoies
qu'il, elle envoie
que nous envoyions
que vous envoyiez
qu'ils, elles envoient
imperative
envoie
envoyons
envoyez

[37] FALLOIR

INFINITIVE
present
falloir
PARTICIPLE
perfect
fallu
INDICATIVE
present
il faut
imperfect
il fallait
future
il faudra

past historic
il fallut
perfect
il a fallu
pluperfect
il avait fallu
future perfect
il aura fallu
past anterior
il eut fallu
CONDITIONAL
present
il faudrait
perfect
il aurait fallu

SUBJUNCTIVE
present
qu'il faille
imperfect
qu'il fallût
perfect
qu'il ait fallu
pluperfect
qu'il eût fallu

Note: *Falloir* is an impersonal verb. It has no imperative.

[38] JETER

present participle
jetant

past participle
jeté, e

present indicative
je jette
tu jettes
il, elle jette
nous jetons
vous jetez
ils, elles jettent

imperfect indicative
je jetais
tu jetais
il, elle jetait
nous jetions
vous jetiez
ils, elles jetaient

future indicative
je jetterai
tu jetteras
il, elle jettera
nous jetterons
vous jetterez
ils, elles jetteront

perfect indicative
j'ai jeté
tu as jeté
il, elle a jeté
nous avons jeté
vous avez jeté
ils, elles ont jeté

past historic indicative
je jetai
tu jetas
il, elle jeta
nous jetâmes
vous jetâtes
ils, elles jetèrent

present subjunctive
que je jette
que tu jettes
qu'il, elle jette
que nous jetions
que vous jetiez
qu'ils, elles jettent

imperative
jette
jetons
jetez

Note: Most verbs in **-eter** behave like *jeter* and double the final **-t** before a mute **-e**: *je jette, tu jetteras ...*

[39] LIRE

present participle
lisant

past participle
lu, e

present indicative
je lis
tu lis
il, elle lit
nous lisons
vous lisez
ils, elles lisent

imperfect indicative
je lisais
tu lisais
il, elle lisait
nous lisions
vous lisiez
ils, elles lisaient

future indicative
je lirai
tu liras
il, elle lira
nous lirons
vous lirez
ils, elles liront

perfect indicative
j'ai lu
tu as lu
il, elle a lu
nous avons lu
vous avez lu
ils, elles ont lu

past historic indicative
je lus
tu lus
il, elle lut
nous lûmes
vous lûtes
ils, elles lurent

present subjunctive
que je lise
que tu lises
qu'il, elle lise
que nous lisions
que vous lisiez
qu'ils, elles lisent

imperative
lis
lisons
lisez

Note: *Élire* and *relire* follow the same model.

[40] MANGER

present participle
mangeant
past participle
mangé, e
present indicative
je mange
tu manges
il, elle mange
nous mangeons
vous mangez
ils, elles mangent
imperfect indicative
je mangeais
tu mangeais
il, elle mangeait
nous mangions
vous mangiez
ils, elles mangeaient

future indicative
je mangerai
tu mangeras
il, elle mangera
nous mangerons
vous mangerez
ils, elles mangeront
perfect indicative
j'ai mangé
tu as mangé
il, elle a mangé
nous avons mangé
vous avez mangé
ils, elles ont mangé
past historic indicative
je mangeai
tu mangeas
il, elle mangea
nous mangeâmes
vous mangeâtes
ils, elles mangèrent

present subjunctive
que je mange
que tu manges
qu'il, elle mange
que nous mangions
que vous mangiez
qu'ils, elles mangent
imperative
mange
mangeons
mangez

Note: Verbs in **-ger**, such as *juger* and *manger*, retain an **e** after the **g** in front of the vowels **a** and **o**.

[41] METTRE

present participle
mettant
past participle
mis, e
present indicative
je mets
tu mets
il, elle met
nous mettons
vous mettez
ils, elles mettent
imperfect indicative
je mettais
tu mettais
il, elle mettait
nous mettions
vous mettiez
ils, elles mettaient

future indicative
je mettrai
tu mettras
il, elle mettra
nous mettrons
vous mettrez
ils, elles mettront
perfect indicative
j'ai mis
tu as mis
il, elle a mis
nous avons mis
vous avez mis
ils, elles ont mis
past historic indicative
je mis
tu mis
il, elle mit
nous mîmes
vous mîtes
ils, elles mirent

present subjunctive
que je mette
que tu mettes
qu'il, elle mette
que nous mettions
que vous mettiez
qu'ils, elles mettent
imperative
mets
mettons
mettez

Note: The compounds of *mettre* such as *admettre, commettre, émettre, promettre* and *remettre*, are conjugated in the same way.

[42] MOURIR

present participle
mourant

past participle
mort, e

present indicative
je meurs
tu meurs
il, elle meurt
nous mourons
vous mourez
ils, elles meurent

imperfect indicative
je mourais
tu mourais
il, elle mourait
nous mourions
vous mouriez
ils, elles mouraient

future indicative
je mourrai
tu mourras
il, elle mourra
nous mourrons
vous mourrez
ils, elles mourront

perfect indicative
je suis mort
tu es mort
il, elle est mort, e
nous sommes morts
vous êtes morts
ils, elles sont morts, es

past historic indicative
je mourus
tu mourus
il, elle mourut
nous mourûmes
vous mourûtes
ils, elles moururent

present subjunctive
que je meure
que tu meures
qu'il, elle meure
que nous mourions
que vous mouriez
qu'ils, elles meurent

imperative
meurs
mourons
mourez

Note: *The **r** is doubled in the future tense (and also in the conditional present): *je mourrai, (je mourrais)*.
*The auxiliary *être* is used in compound tenses.

[43] NAÎTRE

present participle
naissant

past participle
né, e

present indicative
je nais
tu nais
il, elle naît
nous naissons
vous naissez
ils, elles naissent

imperfect indicative
je naissais
tu naissais
il, elle naissait
nous naissions
vous naissiez
ils, elles naissaient

future indicative
je naîtrai
tu naîtras
il, elle naîtra
nous naîtrons
vous naîtrez
ils, elles naîtront

perfect indicative
je suis né
tu es né
il, elle est né, e
nous sommes nés
vous êtes nés
ils, elles sont nés, es

past historic indicative
je naquis
tu naquis
il, elle naquit
nous naquîmes
vous naquîtes
ils, elles naquirent

present subjunctive
que je naisse
que tu naisses
qu'il, elle naisse
que nous naissions
que vous naissiez
qu'ils, elles naissent

Note: *Connaître* [21], *naître, paraître* [45] and their compounds *reconnaître, apparaître* and *disparaître*, are conjugated in the same way.
*There is a circumflex on **î** when **i** comes before **t** in verbs in **-aître**.

[44] OUVRIR

present participle
ouvrant
past participle
ouvert, e
present indicative
j'ouvre
tu ouvres
il, elle ouvre
nous ouvrons
vous ouvrez
ils, elles ouvrent
imperfect indicative
j'ouvrais
tu ouvrais
il, elle ouvrait
nous ouvrions
vous ouvriez
ils, elles ouvraient

future indicative
j'ouvrirai
tu ouvriras
il, elle ouvrira
nous ouvrirons
vous ouvrirez
ils, elles ouvriront
perfect indicative
j'ai ouvert
tu as ouvert
il, elle a ouvert
nous avons ouvert
vous avez ouvert
ils, elles ont ouvert
past historic indicative
j'ouvris
tu ouvris
il, elle ouvrit
nous ouvrîmes
vous ouvrîtes
ils, elles ouvrirent

present subjunctive
que j'ouvre
que tu ouvres
qu'il, elle ouvre
que nous ouvrions
que vous ouvriez
qu'ils, elles ouvrent
imperative
ouvre
ouvrons
ouvrez

Note: *Couvrir* [23], *découvrir, offrir* and *souffrir* are conjugated in the same way.

[45] PARAÎTRE

present participle
paraissant
past participle
paru, e
present indicative
je parais
tu parais
il, elle paraît
nous paraissons
vous paraissez
ils, elles paraissent
imperfect indicative
je paraissais
tu paraissais
il, elle paraissait
nous paraissions
vous paraissiez
ils, elles paraissaient

future indicative
je paraîtrai
tu paraîtras
il, elle paraîtra
nous paraîtrons
vous paraîtrez
ils, elles paraîtront
perfect indicative
j'ai paru
tu as paru
il, elle a paru
nous avons paru
vous avez paru
ils, elles ont paru
past historic indicative
je parus
tu parus
il, elle parut
nous parûmes
vous parûtes
ils, elles parurent

present subjunctive
que je paraisse
que tu paraisses
qu'il, elle paraisse
que nous paraissions
que vous paraissiez
qu'ils, elles paraissent
imperative
parais
paraissons
paraissez

Note: *Connaître* [21], *naître* [43], *paraître* and their compounds such as *reconnaître, apparaître* and *disparaître* are conjugated in the same way.
*There is a circumflex on î when i comes before -t in verbs in -aître.

[46] PARTIR

present participle
partant
past participle
parti, e
present indicative
je pars
tu pars
il, elle part
nous partons
vous partez
ils, elles partent
imperfect indicative
je partais
tu partais
il, elle partait
nous partions
vous partiez
ils, elles partaient

future indicative
je partirai
tu partiras
il, elle partira
nous partirons
vous partirez
ils, elles partiront
perfect indicative
je suis parti
tu es parti
il, elle est parti, e
nous sommes partis
vous êtes partis
ils, elles sont partis, es
past historic indicative
je partis
tu partis
il, elle partit
nous partîmes
vous partîtes
ils, elles partirent

present subjunctive
que je parte
que tu partes
qu'il, elle parte
que nous partions
que vous partiez
qu'ils, elles partent
imperative
pars
partons
partez

Note: *Mentir, sentir* and *sortir* are conjugated in the same way.
*The auxiliary *être* is used in compound tenses.

[47] PAYER

present participle
payant
past participle
payé, e
present indicative
je paie/paye
tu paies/payes
il, elle paie/paye
nous payons
vous payez
ils, elles paient/payent
imperfect indicative
je payais
tu payais
il, elle payait
nous payions
vous payiez
ils, elles payaient

future indicative
je paierai/payerai
tu paieras/payeras
il, elle paiera/payera
nous paierons/payerons
vous paierez/payerez
ils, elles paieront/payeront
perfect indicative
j'ai payé
tu as payé
il, elle a payé
nous avons payé
vous avez payé
ils, elles ont payé
past historic indicative
je payai
tu payas
il, elle paya
nous payâmes
vous payâtes
ils, elles payèrent

present subjunctive
que je paie/paye
que tu paies/payes
qu'il, elle paie/paye
que nous payions
que vous payiez
qu'ils, elles paient/payent
imperative
paie/paye
payons
payez

Note: *Verbs in **-ayer** such as *payer* can either keep the **y** in all their forms or replace the **y** by **i** before mute **e** (in the endings: **e**, **es**, **ent**, **erai**). The pronunciation changes depending on which form is chosen: **je paye** [pɛj] or **je paie** [pɛ].
*There is an **i** after the **y** in the 1st and 2nd persons plural of the imperfect indicative and the present subjunctive.

[48] PEINDRE

present participle
peignant
past participle
peint, e
present indicative
je peins
tu peins
il, elle peint
nous peignons
vous peignez
ils, elles peignent
imperfect indicative
je peignais
tu peignais
il, elle peignait
nous peignions
vous peigniez
ils, elles peignaient

future indicative
je peindrai
tu peindras
il, elle peindra
nous peindrons
vous peindrez
ils, elles peindront
perfect indicative
j'ai peint
tu as peint
il, elle a peint
nous avons peint
vous avez peint
ils, elles ont peint
past historic indicative
je peignis
tu peignis
il, elle peignit
nous peignîmes
vous peignîtes
ils, elles peignirent

present subjunctive
que je peigne
que tu peignes
qu'il, elle peigne
que nous peignions
que vous peigniez
qu'ils, elles peignent
imperative
peins
peignons
peignez

Note: *Atteindre, feindre, enfreindre, teindre* are conjugated in the same way.

[49] PELER

present participle
pelant
past participle
pelé, e
present indicative
je pèle
tu pèles
il, elle pèle
nous pelons
vous pelez
ils, elles pèlent
imperfect indicative
je pelais
tu pelais
il, elle pelait
nous pelions
vous peliez
ils, elles pelaient

future indicative
je pèlerai
tu pèleras
il, elle pèlera
nous pèlerons
vous pèlerez
ils, elles pèleront
perfect indicative
j'ai pelé
tu as pelé
il, elle a pelé
nous avons pelé
vous avez pelé
ils, elles ont pelé
past historic indicative
je pelai
tu pelas
il, elle pela
nous pelâmes
vous pelâtes
ils, elles pelèrent

present subjunctive
que je pèle
que tu pèles
qu'il, elle pèle
que nous pelions
que vous peliez
qu'ils, elles pèlent
imperative
pèle
pelons
pelez

Note: *Unlike most verbs in **-eler** such as *appeler* [10], which double the final **-l**, *peler* takes a grave accent on the **-e** before the **-l**.
Celer, ciseler, démanteler, écarteler, geler, marteler, modeler, harceler are conjugated in the same way.

[50] PERDRE

present participle
perdant
past participle
perdu, e
present indicative
je perds
tu perds
il, elle perd
nous perdons
vous perdez
ils, elles perdent
imperfect indicative
je perdais
tu perdais
il, elle perdait
nous perdions
vous perdiez
ils, elles perdaient

future indicative
je perdrai
tu perdras
il, elle perdra
nous perdrons
vous perdrez
ils, elles perdront
perfect indicative
j'ai perdu
tu as perdu
il, elle a perdu
nous avons perdu
vous avez perdu
ils, elles ont perdu

past historic indicative
je perdis
tu perdis
il, elle perdit
nous perdîmes
vous perdîtes
ils, elles perdirent
present subjunctive
que je perde
que tu perdes
qu'il, elle perde
que nous perdions
que vous perdiez
qu'ils, elles perdent
imperative
perds
perdons
perdez

[51] PLAIRE

present participle
plaisant
past participle
plu
present indicative
je plais
tu plais
il, elle plaît
nous plaisons
vous plaisez
ils, elles plaisent
imperfect indicative
je plaisais
tu plaisais
il, elle plaisait
nous plaisions
vous plaisiez
ils, elles plaisaient

future indicative
je plairai
tu plairas
il, elle plaira
nous plairons
vous plairez
ils, elles plairont
perfect indicative
j'ai plu
tu as plu
il, elle a plu
nous avons plu
vous avez plu
ils, elles ont plu

past historic indicative
je plus
tu plus
il, elle plut
nous plûmes
vous plûtes
ils, elles plurent
present subjunctive
que je plaise
que tu plaises
qu'il, elle plaise
que nous plaisions
que vous plaisiez
qu'ils, elles plaisent
imperative
plais
plaisons
plaisez

[52] PLEUVOIR

INFINITIVE
present
pleuvoir

PARTICIPLE
perfect
plu

INDICATIVE
present
il pleut
imperfect
il pleuvait
future
il pleuvra

past historic
il plut
perfect
il a plu
pluperfect
il avait plu
future perfect
il aura plu
past anterior
il eut plu

CONDITIONAL
present
il pleuvrait
perfect
il aurait plu

SUBJUNCTIVE
present
qu'il pleuve
imperfect
qu'il plût
perfect
qu'il ait plu
pluperfect
qu'il eût plu

Note: *Pleuvoir* is an impersonal verb. It has no imperative.
Pleuvoir can be used in the plural in a figurative sense:
les injures pleuvaient sur le pauvre homme.

[53] POUVOIR

present participle
pouvant
past participle
pu
present indicative
je peux
tu peux
il, elle peut
nous pouvons
vous pouvez
ils, elles peuvent
imperfect indicative
je pouvais
tu pouvais
il, elle pouvait
nous pouvions
vous pouviez
ils, elles pouvaient

future indicative
je pourrai
tu pourras
il, elle pourra
nous pourrons
vous pourrez
ils, elles pourront
perfect indicative
j'ai pu
tu as pu
il, elle a pu
nous avons pu
vous avez pu
ils, elles ont pu

past historic indicative
je pus
tu pus
il, elle put
nous pûmes
vous pûtes
ils, elles purent

present subjunctive
que je puisse
que tu puisses
qu'il, elle puisse
que nous puissions
que vous puissiez
qu'ils, elles puissent

Note: *Pouvoir* has no imperative.
"Can I?" is not **peux-je ?** but **puis-je ?**

[54] PRENDRE

present participle
prenant
past participle
pris, e
present indicative
je prends
tu prends
il, elle prend
nous prenons
vous prenez
ils, elles prennent
imperfect indicative
je prenais
tu prenais
il, elle prenait
nous prenions
vous preniez
ils, elles prenaient

future indicative
je prendrai
tu prendras
il, elle prendra
nous prendrons
vous prendrez
ils, elles prendront
perfect indicative
j'ai pris
tu as pris
il, elle a pris
nous avons pris
vous avez pris
ils, elles ont pris
past historic indicative
je pris
tu pris
il, elle prit
nous prîmes
vous prîtes
ils, elles prirent

present subjunctive
que je prenne
que tu prennes
qu'il, elle prenne
que nous prenions
que vous preniez
qu'ils, elles prennent
imperative
prends
prenons
prenez

Note: The compounds of *prendre: apprendre, comprendre, entreprendre, surprendre,* are conjugated in the same way.

[55] RECEVOIR

present participle
recevant
past participle
reçu, e
present indicative
je reçois
tu reçois
il, elle reçoit
nous recevons
vous recevez
ils, elles reçoivent
imperfect indicative
je recevais
tu recevais
il, elle recevait
nous recevions
vous receviez
ils, elles recevaient

future indicative
je recevrai
tu recevras
il, elle recevra
nous recevrons
vous recevrez
ils, elles recevront
perfect indicative
j'ai reçu
tu as reçu
il, elle a reçu
nous avons reçu
vous avez reçu
ils, elles ont reçu
past historic indicative
je reçus
tu reçus
il, elle reçut
nous reçûmes
vous reçûtes
ils, elles reçurent

present subjunctive
que je reçoive
que tu reçoives
qu'il, elle reçoive
que nous recevions
que vous receviez
qu'ils, elles reçoivent
imperative
reçois
recevons
recevez

Note: *C changes to ç when it comes before **o** or **u**. *Apercevoir, concevoir, décevoir, percevoir* are conjugated in the same way as *recevoir*.

[56] RENDRE

present participle
rendant
past participle
rendu, e
present indicative
je rends
tu rends
il, elle rend
nous rendons
vous rendez
ils, elles rendent
imperfect indicative
je rendais
tu rendais
il, elle rendait
nous rendions
vous rendiez
ils, elles rendaient

future indicative
je rendrai
tu rendras
il, elle rendra
nous rendrons
vous rendrez
ils, elles rendront
perfect indicative
j'ai rendu
tu as rendu
il, elle a rendu
nous avons rendu
vous avez rendu
ils, elles ont rendu

past historic indicative
je rendis
tu rendis
il, elle rendit
nous rendîmes
vous rendîtes
ils, elles rendirent
present subjunctive
que je rende
que tu rendes
qu'il, elle rende
que nous rendions
que vous rendiez
qu'ils, elles rendent
imperative
rends
rendons
rendez

[57] RÉPONDRE

present participle
répondant
past participle
répondu, e
present indicative
je réponds
tu réponds
il, elle répond
nous répondons
vous répondez
ils, elles répondent
imperfect indicative
je répondais
tu répondais
il, elle répondait
nous répondions
vous répondiez
ils, elles répondaient

future indicative
je répondrai
tu répondras
il, elle répondra
nous répondrons
vous répondrez
ils, elles répondront
perfect indicative
j'ai répondu
tu as répondu
il, elle a répondu
nous avons répondu
vous avez répondu
ils, elles ont répondu

past historic indicative
je répondis
tu répondis
il, elle répondit
nous répondîmes
vous répondîtes
ils, elles répondirent
present subjunctive
que je réponde
que tu répondes
qu'il, elle réponde
que nous répondions
que vous répondiez
qu'ils, elles répondent
imperative
réponds
répondons
répondez

[58] RÉSOUDRE

present participle
résolvant

past participle
résolu, e

present indicative
je résous
tu résous
il, elle résout
nous résolvons
vous résolvez
ils, elles résolvent

imperfect indicative
je résolvais
tu résolvais
il, elle résolvait
nous résolvions
vous résolviez
ils, elles résolvaient

future indicative
je résoudrai
tu résoudras
il, elle résoudra
nous résoudrons
vous résoudrez
ils, elles résoudront

perfect indicative
j'ai résolu
tu as résolu
il, elle a résolu
nous avons résolu
vous avez résolu
ils, elles ont résolu

past historic indicative
je résolus
tu résolus
il, elle résolut
nous résolûmes
vous résolûtes
ils, elles résolurent

present subjunctive
que je résolve
que tu résolves
qu'il, elle résolve
que nous résolvions
que vous résolviez
qu'ils, elles résolvent

imperative
résous
résolvons
résolvez

[59] RIRE

present participle
riant

past participle
ri

present indicative
je ris
tu ris
il, elle rit
nous rions
vous riez
ils, elles rient

imperfect indicative
je riais
tu riais
il, elle riait
nous riions
vous riiez
ils, elles riaient

future indicative
je rirai
tu riras
il, elle rira
nous rirons
vous rirez
ils, elles riront

perfect indicative
j'ai ri
tu as ri
il, elle a ri
nous avons ri
vous avez ri
ils, elles ont ri

past historic indicative
je ris
tu ris
il, elle rit
nous rîmes
vous rîtes
ils, elles rirent

present subjunctive
que je rie
que tu ries
qu'il, elle rie
que nous riions
que vous riiez
qu'ils, elles rient

imperative
ris
rions
riez

Note: *Rire* takes two **i**'s in the 1st and 2nd persons plural of the imperfect indicative and the present subjunctive: **(que) nous riions, (que) vous riiez**.

[60] ROMPRE

present participle

rompant

past participle

rompu, e

present indicative

je romps
tu romps
il, elle rompt
nous rompons
vous rompez
ils, elles rompent

imperfect indicative

je rompais
tu rompais
il, elle rompait
nous rompions
vous rompiez
ils, elles rompaient

future indicative

je romprai
tu rompras
il, elle rompra
nous romprons
vous romprez
ils, elles rompront

perfect indicative

j'ai rompu
tu as rompu
il, elle a rompu
nous avons rompu
vous avez rompu
ils, elles ont rompu

past historic indicative

je rompis
tu rompis
il, elle rompit
nous rompîmes
vous rompîtes
ils, elles rompirent

present subjunctive

que je rompe
que tu rompes
qu'il, elle rompe
que nous rompions
que vous rompiez
qu'ils, elles rompent

imperative

romps
rompons
rompez

Note: *Rompre, interrompre* and *corrompre* are conjugated in the same way as verbs in **-dre**. Note, however, the presence of **t** after the **p** of the 3rd person singular of the present indicative: il **rompt**.

[61] SAVOIR

present participle

sachant

past participle

su, e

present indicative

je sais
tu sais
il, elle sait
nous savons
vous savez
ils, elles savent

imperfect indicative

je savais
tu savais
il, elle savait
nous savions
vous saviez
ils, elles savaient

future indicative

je saurai
tu sauras
il, elle saura
nous saurons
vous saurez
ils, elles sauront

perfect indicative

j'ai su
tu as su
il, elle a su
nous avons su
vous avez su
ils, elles ont su

past historic indicative

je sus
tu sus
il, elle sut
nous sûmes
vous sûtes
ils, elles surent

present subjunctive

que je sache
que tu saches
qu'il, elle sache
que nous sachions
que vous sachiez
qu'ils, elles sachent

imperative

sache
sachons
sachez

[62] SUFFIRE

present participle
suffisant

past participle
suffi

present indicative
je suffis
tu suffis
il, elle suffit
nous suffisons
vous suffisez
ils, elles suffisent

imperfect indicative
je suffisais
tu suffisais
il, elle suffisait
nous suffisions
vous suffisiez
ils, elles suffisaient

future indicative
je suffirai
tu suffiras
il, elle suffira
nous suffirons
vous suffirez
ils, elles suffiront

perfect indicative
j'ai suffi
tu as suffi
il, elle a suffi
nous avons suffi
vous avez suffi
ils, elles ont suffi

past historic indicative
je suffis
tu suffis
il, elle suffit
nous suffîmes
vous suffîtes
ils, elles suffirent

present subjunctive
que je suffise
que tu suffises
qu'il, elle suffise
que nous suffisions
que vous suffisiez
qu'ils, elles suffisent

imperative
suffis
suffisons
suffisez

Note: *Suffire* is conjugated like *confire* and *frire*. However, the past participle is **suffi** (without **t**).
*An important use of this verb is in the expression **ça suffit** (that's enough).

[63] SUIVRE

present participle
suivant

past participle
suivi, e

present indicative
je suis
tu suis
il, elle suit
nous suivons
vous suivez
ils, elles suivent

imperfect indicative
je suivais
tu suivais
il, elle suivait
nous suivions
vous suiviez
ils, elles suivaient

future indicative
je suivrai
tu suivras
il, elle suivra
nous suivrons
vous suivrez
ils, elles suivront

perfect indicative
j'ai suivi
tu as suivi
il, elle a suivi
nous avons suivi
vous avez suivi
ils, elles ont suivi

past historic indicative
je suivis
tu suivis
il, elle suivit
nous suivîmes
vous suivîtes
ils, elles suivirent

present subjunctive
que je suive
que tu suives
qu'il, elle suive
que nous suivions
que vous suiviez
qu'ils, elles suivent

imperative
suis
suivons
suivez

[64] TENIR

present participle
tenant

past participle
tenu, e

present indicative
je tiens
tu tiens
il, elle tient
nous tenons
vous tenez
ils, elles tiennent

imperfect indicative
je tenais
tu tenais
il, elle tenait
nous tenions
vous teniez
ils, elles tenaient

future indicative
je tiendrai
tu tiendras
il, elle tiendra
nous tiendrons
vous tiendrez
ils, elles tiendront

perfect indicative
j'ai tenu
tu as tenu
il, elle a tenu
nous avons tenu
vous avez tenu
ils, elles ont tenu

past historic indicative
je tins
tu tins
il, elle tint
nous tînmes
vous tîntes
ils, elles tinrent

present subjunctive
que je tienne
que tu tiennes
qu'il, elle tienne
que nous tenions
que vous teniez
qu'ils, elles tiennent

imperative
tiens
tenons
tenez

Note: *Tenir* and its compounds: *s'abstenir, appartenir, contenir, détenir, entretenir, maintenir, obtenir, retenir* and *soutenir,* are conjugated in the same way.

[65] VAINCRE

present participle
vainquant

past participle
vaincu, e

present indicative
je vaincs
tu vaincs
il, elle vainc
nous vainquons
vous vainquez
ils, elles vainquent

imperfect indicative
je vainquais
tu vainquais
il, elle vainquait
nous vainquions
vous vainquiez
ils, elles vainquaient

future indicative
je vaincrai
tu vaincras
il, elle vaincra
nous vaincrons
vous vaincrez
ils, elles vaincront

perfect indicative
j'ai vaincu
tu as vaincu
il, elle a vaincu
nous avons vaincu
vous avez vaincu
ils, elles ont vaincu

past historic indicative
je vainquis
tu vainquis
il, elle vainquit
nous vainquîmes
vous vainquîtes
ils, elles vainquirent

present subjunctive
que je vainque
que tu vainques
qu'il, elle vainque
que nous vainquions
que vous vainquiez
qu'ils, elles vainquent

imperative
vaincs
vainquons
vainquez

Note: *The only irregularity of the verb *vaincre* is that it does not take a **t** at the end of the 3rd person singular of the present indicative.
*Remember that **c** becomes **qu** in front of all vowels except **u**.
Convaincre is conjugated in the same way as *vaincre*.

[66] VALOIR

present participle
valant
past participle
valu, e
present indicative
je vaux
tu vaux
il, elle vaut
nous valons
vous valez
ils, elles valent
imperfect indicative
je valais
tu valais
il, elle valait
nous valions
vous valiez
ils, elles valaient

future indicative
je vaudrai
tu vaudras
il, elle vaudra
nous vaudrons
vous vaudrez
ils, elles vaudront
perfect indicative
j'ai valu
tu as valu
il, elle a valu
nous avons valu
vous avez valu
ils, elles ont valu

past historic indicative
je valus
tu valus
il, elle valut
nous valûmes
vous valûtes
ils, elles valurent
present subjunctive
que je vaille
que tu vailles
qu'il, elle vaille
que nous valions
que vous valiez
qu'ils, elles vaillent
imperative
vaux
valons
valez

[67] VENIR

present participle
venant
past participle
venu, e
present indicative
je viens
tu viens
il, elle vient
nous venons
vous venez
ils, elles viennent
imperfect indicative
je venais
tu venais
il, elle venait
nous venions
vous veniez
ils, elles venaient

future indicative
je viendrai
tu viendras
il, elle viendra
nous viendrons
vous viendrez
ils, elles viendront
perfect indicative
je suis venu
tu es venu
il, elle est venu, e
nous sommes venus
vous êtes venus
ils, elles sont venus, es
past historic indicative
je vins
tu vins
il, elle vint
nous vînmes
vous vîntes
ils, elles vinrent

present subjunctive
que je vienne
que tu viennes
qu'il, elle vienne
que nous venions
que vous veniez
qu'ils, elles viennent
imperative
viens
venons
venez

Note: *Venir* and its compounds: *advenir, convenir, devenir, intervenir, parvenir, prévenir, provenir, revenir* and *se souvenir*, are all conjugated in the same way.
*The auxiliary *être* is used in the compound tenses.

[68] VIVRE

present participle
vivant
past participle
vécu, e
present indicative
je vis
tu vis
il, elle vit
nous vivons
vous vivez
ils, elles vivent
imperfect indicative
je vivais
tu vivais
il, elle vivait
nous vivions
vous viviez
ils, elles vivaient

future indicative
je vivrai
tu vivras
il, elle vivra
nous vivrons
vous vivrez
ils, elles vivront
perfect indicative
j'ai vécu
tu as vécu
il, elle a vécu
nous avons vécu
vous avez vécu
ils, elles ont vécu
past historic indicative
je vécus
tu vécus
il, elle vécut
nous vécûmes
vous vécûtes
ils, elles vécurent

present subjunctive
que je vive
que tu vives
qu'il, elle vive
que nous vivions
que vous viviez
qu'ils, elles vivent
imperative
vis
vivons
vivez

[69] VOIR

present participle
voyant
past participle
vu, e
present indicative
je vois
tu vois
il, elle voit
nous voyons
vous voyez
ils, elles voient
imperfect indicative
je voyais
tu voyais
il, elle voyait
nous voyions
vous voyiez
ils, elles voyaient

future indicative
je verrai
tu verras
il, elle verra
nous verrons
vous verrez
ils, elles verront
perfect indicative
j'ai vu
tu as vu
il, elle a vu
nous avons vu
vous avez vu
ils, elles ont vu

past historic indicative
je vis
tu vis
il, elle vit
nous vîmes
vous vîtes
ils, elles virent
present subjunctive
que je voie
que tu voies
qu'il, elle voie
que nous voyions
que vous voyiez
qu'ils, elles voient
imperative
vois
voyons
voyez

[70] VOULOIR

present participle
voulant

past participle
voulu, e

present indicative
je veux
tu veux
il, elle veut
nous voulons
vous voulez
ils, elles veulent

imperfect indicative
je voulais
tu voulais
il, elle voulait
nous voulions
vous vouliez
ils, elles voulaient

future indicative
je voudrai
tu voudras
il, elle voudra
nous voudrons
vous voudrez
ils, elles voudront

perfect indicative
j'ai voulu
tu as voulu
il, elle a voulu
nous avons voulu
vous avez voulu
ils, elles ont voulu

past historic indicative
je voulus
tu voulus
il, elle voulut
nous voulûmes
vous voulûtes
ils, elles voulurent

present subjunctive
que je veuille
que tu veuilles
qu'il, elle veuille
que nous voulions
que vous vouliez
qu'ils, elles veuillent

imperative
veuille/veux
voulons/veuillons
veuillez

Note: The irregular imperative of *vouloir* is used in the polite phrase: **veuillez agréer mes respectueuses salutations**.

BUILDING SENTENCES

1. The Subject
2. The Object
3. The Verb
4. The Complement
5. Noun Phrases
6. Adverbs and Adverbial Phrases

1. The subject

Any sentence must have a verb, and any verb must have a subject. The subject is the person or thing, or persons or things, who either carries out the action of the verb in the case of verbs of action, or who is in the state described by the verb in the case of verbs of state. For example, in the sentence **John listens to music**, **John** is the subject since he is the person listening (an action). In the sentence **Mary seems enthusiastic**, **Mary** is the subject since she is the person who seems enthusiastic (a state). Occasionally the subject of the verb is not expressed, for example when giving commands, as in **Venez !** or **Tais-toi !**

■ With the exception of questions which do not contain the phrase **est-ce que**, the subject in French is almost always placed *before* the verb.

> SUBJECT + VERB:
> *L'élève* a fermé la porte en sortant.
> *Les magasins* n'ouvrent pas le dimanche.
> *Je* n'ai pas vu ce film.
> Quand est-ce que *tu* arrives ?

■ If est-ce que *is* used in questions containing compound tenses, the order SUBJECT + VERB is maintained (*see* DIFFERENT KINDS OF SENTENCE, **4.**):

> Est-ce qu'*ils* sont rentrés à la maison ?
> À quelle heure est-ce qu'*ils* sont rentrés à la maison ?

■ However, in questions which do not contain est-ce que, the subject is placed *after* the verb:

VERB + SUBJECT:

Qu'en pensez-*vous* ?
Quand serez-*vous* là ?
Combien coûte *cette jupe* ?

■ If the verb in such questions is in a compound tense (i.e. a tense formed with the auxiliaries avoir or être + PAST PARTICIPLE), the subject is placed between the auxiliary verb and the past participle:

AUXILIARY VERB + SUBJECT + PAST PARTICIPLE:

Qu'en ont-*ils* pensé ?
Avaient-*ils* eu le temps de vous mettre au courant ?

■ The subject is placed after the verb in sentences beginning with aussi (meaning therefore), à peine (scarcely, hardly) and peut-être (perhaps):

AUSSI/À PEINE/PEUT-ÊTRE + VERB + SUBJECT:

Il s'est trompé. Aussi doit-*il* en souffrir les conséquences. (therefore he has to suffer the consequences)
À peine était-*il* sorti qu'elle est arrivée. (Scarcely had he left when she arrived.)
Peut-être ont-*ils* raison. (Perhaps they are right.)

> NOTE:
> * **Aussi** meaning **also** does not affect the normal word order:
>   *Il est venu aussi.*
>   J'ai *aussi* fait la vaisselle.
> * If peut-être is followed by **que** the normal word order is retained:
>   **Peut-être qu'*ils* ont raison.**

■ The verb is placed before the subject if it comes immediately after direct speech:

'Entrez', a-t-*il* dit.
'Asseyez-vous !', ordonna *le professeur*.

2. The object

2.1 The direct object

■ The object of a verb is the person or thing on whom the subject of the verb carries out the action expressed by the verb. For example, in a sentence such as **they watch television**, television is the object since that is what **they** (the subject) are watching. A *direct object* is one which can be placed after the verb without the need for a preposition of any kind. Television in the sentence given above is a direct object. The picture in **he looked at the picture** is not a direct object, since it has to be linked to the verb by the preposition **at**.

▪ Direct objects answer questions such as **what** or **who**:

Il a lu *ce roman*. (What did he read? This novel.)

Il a rencontré *un ami*. (Who did he meet? A friend.)

▪ Direct objects can consist of someone's name, a noun, a group of words which function as a noun, a pronoun, a clause or a verb in the infinitive. In all cases except pronouns, they are placed *after* the verb:

Appelle *Anne* tout de suite. (= name)

J'ai retrouvé *mes clés*. (= noun)

J'ai vu *le père de ton amie*. (= group of words functioning as a noun)

Je pense *que tu as raison*. (= clause)

Il veut *partir* tout de suite. (= verb in the infinitive)

However, direct objects are placed *before* the verb if they take the form of pronouns:

Ils regardent la télé. → **Ils *la* regardent.**

▪ When the verb is in a compound tense, the direct object pronoun is placed before the auxiliary verb. The past participle agrees with the preceding direct object in number and gender:

Ils *l*'ont achetée.

Je *les* ai retrouvées.

▪ Direct objects can also be placed before the verb in questions (*see* DIFFERENT KINDS OF SENTENCE, **4.**):

Quel film as-tu vu hier ?

▪ It is important to bear in mind that some verbs which can take a direct object in English require a preposition in French, and some verbs which require a preposition in English can take a direct object in French:

Les fleurs lui rappelaient le printemps. (The flowers reminded him *of* spring.)

Il approche *de* la cinquantaine. (He is approaching fifty.)

Il a résisté *à* la tentation de le faire. (He resisted the temptation to do it.)

Even if a preposition is used in both languages, it is not always a direct equivalent:

Il pense *à* son départ. (He is thinking *about* his departure.)
Il va réfléchir *à* votre proposition. (He will think *about* your proposal.)

For a list of French verbs which require a preposition before their object, *see* PREPOSITIONS, **3**.

2.2 The indirect object

■ The difference between a direct and an indirect object is a very important one, and has to be borne in mind at all times when working with French verbs. An indirect object always contains the idea of *to* (or, less frequently, *for*), and will *always* be preceded by the preposition *à* when expressed as a noun in French. In English the preposition *to* can frequently be left out, so that it is not always easy for us to tell which is a direct object and which is an indirect one. For example, we can say **he gave a bone to the dog**; it is easy to spot the indirect object (the dog). If we take the sentence **he gave the dog a bone** (which means the same thing and is more common), *to* has disappeared and the indirect object is more difficult to find. If a verb appears to have two objects (the dog/a bone), one of them will *always* be an indirect object. To find out which it is, ask yourself which one contains the idea of *to*. (Did he give the bone to the dog, or did he give the dog to the bone?)

■ Indirect objects answer questions such as **to what** or **to whom**:

Il a envoyé une lettre *à sa sœur*. (Who did he send the letter to? His sister.)
Mon père a prêté mille francs *à mon frère*. (Who did he lend the money to? My brother.)

■ The indirect object can be a name, a noun, a group of words functioning as a noun, or a pronoun:

Je donne le livre *à Sophie*. (= name)
Il a accordé une augmentation *au personnel*. (= noun)
J'ai parlé *à la fille d'Anne* hier. (= group of words functioning as a noun)
Donne-la-*lui*. (= pronoun)

■ Indirect objects can appear as the only object of the verb:

Il a parlé *au patron*.

However, they are more frequently combined with direct objects. When they are both expressed as nouns, the order is SUBJECT + VERB + DIRECT

OBJECT + à + INDIRECT OBJECT:

> **Elle a offert des fleurs** *à sa mère.*
> **Il a rapporté des jouets** *aux enfants.*

> NOTE: If the indirect object consists of a group of words which is longer than the direct object, then the indirect object can be placed between the verb and the direct object:
>
> **Il a rapporté** *aux enfants* **de très beaux jouets.**

■ The indirect object is placed before the verb if it takes the form of a pronoun:

> **Je** *lui* **ai fait un cadeau.**

■ The indirect object is also placed before the verb in a question. Remember that the preposition à can never be placed at the end of a question in French:

> *À qui* **as-tu donné le livre ?** (Who did you give the book to?)

■ Verbs which can take an indirect as well as a direct object often express an action which is close to the idea of *giving* or *showing*. Here are some of the most commonly used ones:

> **envoyer** (to send) ▲ **faire voir** (to show) ▲ **indiquer** (to show) ▲
> **montrer** (to show) ▲ **offrir** (to offer) ▲ **prêter** (to lend) ▲ **rendre** (to give back)

■ Some verbs take an indirect object in French, whereas they take a direct object in English, and vice versa:

> **Elle téléphone** *à sa mère.* (She telephones her mother.)
> **Il faut obéir** *à tes parents.* (You must obey your parents.)
> **Je** *lui* **ai demandé son avis.** (I asked him his opinion.)
> BUT:
> **Nous écoutons la radio.** (We are listening *to* the radio.)

Some French verbs take an indirect object and are preceded by à but need a quite different preposition in English:

> **Il a caché l'argent** *aux autres.* (He hid the money *from* the others.)
> **Elle a acheté la voiture** *à sa voisine.* (She bought the car *from* her neighbour.)

See PREPOSITIONS, **3.** for a list of these verbs.

■ Finally, although almost all objects introduced by à *are* indirect objects, there are a few which are not. When a true indirect object is replaced by a pronoun, it is the corresponding indirect object pronoun which is placed before the verb. If a noun preceded by à is not an indirect object, it will be replaced by the pronoun y before the verb if it refers to a thing, and by the preposition à + the appropriate stressed object pronoun after the verb if it refers to a person (*see* PRONOUNS, **1.**):

> **Il a donné le livre à Pierre.** → **Il *lui* a donné le livre.** (= indirect object)
> **Elle pense à Pierre.** → **Elle pense *à lui*.** (= not an indirect object)
> **Nous avons résisté à la tentation de le faire.** → **Nous *y* avons résisté.** (= not an indirect object)

COMPARE

It is important to distinguish between an indirect object introduced by à, and a phrase beginning with à which merely indicates *where* something is happening:

> **Il enseigne le russe *à des étudiants*.** (= indirect object)
> **Il enseigne le russe *à l'université*.** (= indication of place)

3. The verb

All sentences must contain a verb. The verb expresses an action carried out by the subject, or describes the state of the subject.

3.1 Transitive verbs

Verbs which can take a direct object are called transitive verbs. For example, the verb to fix in English is transitive, since it is possible to fix *something* (a television, record player, and so on). However, the verb to arrive is not transitive, since it is not possible to arrive *something*:

> **Ils *ont acheté une maison*.**
> **Ils *l'apprécient* beaucoup.**

In most cases, the direct object of a transitive verb must be expressed in order for the sentence to make sense:

> **Il a lu *un roman*.** (*Il a lu* does not make sense on its own.)
> **Il a écrit *une lettre*.** (*Il a écrit* does not make sense on its own.)

> NOTE: Only transitive verbs may be put into the passive in French
> (see VERBS, 5.):
>
> **La presse a *diffusé* les résultats.** → **Les résultats *ont été diffusés*
> par la presse.**

3.2 Intransitive verbs

Verbs which do not need to be followed by a direct object are called
intransitive. In the case of intransitive verbs of action, it makes no sense to
ask the question *what* in connection with the action expressed by the verb:

Le bébé *est tombé* et il *pleure*.

You cannot ask *what* the baby is falling – it simply falls. Nor can you ask
what it is crying – it is simply crying. (The expression to cry tears needs a
different verb in French, which is in fact transitive: **verser des larmes.**)

> NOTE: Many verbs of motion and all verbs of state are intransitive:
>
> **aller ▲ courir ▲ devenir ▲ être ▲ marcher ▲ mourir ▲ naître ▲
> partir ▲ pleurer ▲ rester ▲ tomber ▲ trembler ▲ venir ▲ vivre**
>
> However, some verbs which are usually intransitive can sometimes
> be used with a direct object. In some cases, this occurs in set phrases
> in which the object is very closely linked to the meaning of the verb:
>
> **vivre *sa vie*** (to live one's life)
>
> In others the verb in fact acquires a new meaning:
>
> ***vivre* une période de crise** (to be going through a period of crisis)
> ***vivre* un grand amour** (to experience a great love)

■ Many verbs, in French and in English, can be used both transitively and
intransitively:

Il *a fermé* la fenêtre. (= transitive, object *la fenêtre*)
Le magasin *ferme* à six heures. (= intransitive, no object)
Elles *ont mangé* les gâteaux. (= transitive, object *les gâteaux*)
Tu *as* déjà *mangé* ? (= intransitive, no object)

■ Some verbs used intransitively in English require a different construction
in French, in many cases a reflexive verb:

Ce disque *se vend* bien. (This record is selling well.)
Il *se lève* vers huit heures. (He gets up around eight.)

4. The complement

4.1 Describing the subject

A verb of state is always followed by an adjective, a past participle or a noun which describes the *subject* of the verb, whether it refers to a permanent or momentary characteristic. The technical name for an adjective, a past participle or a noun used in this way is the *complement*. The complement must always be expressed in order for the sentence to make sense.

■ The complement agrees in number and gender with the subject of the verb:

L'hôtel a l'air *agréable*.
Ça devient *compliqué*.
Elle est *épanouie*.
Ils sont *architectes*.

■ If the complement is a noun, it can only agree in gender with the subject if the noun has both a masculine and a feminine form. This is not always the case (*see* NOUNS, **2.**):

Il est *instituteur*. → **Elle est** *institutrice*.
Elle est *dentiste*.
Cet oiseau, c'est une *hirondelle*.

4.2 Describing the direct object

A verb of opinion (trouver, juger, estimer, considérer, croire) will be followed by an adjective which describes the *object* of the verb in some way, whether it refers to a permanent or a momentary characteristic. This adjective is also called a complement, and must be expressed in order for the sentence to make sense.

■ The complement agrees in gender and number with the object of the verb.

Je trouve cette ville *merveilleuse*.
Je les crois *capables* **de tout.**

■ If the object of the verb is a pronoun, the order is:

SUBJECT + PRONOUN + VERB + COMPLEMENT:
Je *le* **trouve** *gentil*.

■ If the object of the verb is a noun, the order is:

SUBJECT + VERB + NOUN + COMPLEMENT:
Je trouve *ces gens aimables*.
Il juge *cette idée stupide*.

5. Noun phrases

A noun phrase is a group of words which are closely linked in the sentence, and which have the same function as a noun. A noun phrase can consist of:

– two or more nouns linked by prepositions. The order is:

NOUN + PREPOSITION + NOUN (+ PREPOSITION + NOUN):

Je voudrais bien un *verre d'eau*.

Est-ce que vous auriez un *plan de la ville* ?

La *vente de livres scolaires d'occasion* ne commencera qu'en août.

– a noun group in apposition (which provides more information about the first noun), with or without a determiner:

M. Paul Durant, *directeur des ventes*, assistera à la réunion.

M. Paul Durant, *le directeur des ventes*, assistera à la réunion.

> *NOTE:* Some nouns can be used as invariable adjectives to describe other nouns:
>
> **un gâteau maison** (a home-made cake) ▲ **une visite éclair** (a flying visit)
>
> The most commonly used nouns of this type can also appear in the plural and can be linked to the noun they are describing by a dash:
>
> **les industries(-)clé(s)** (the key industries, i.e. the most important)

– a noun and an adjective, the adjective appearing either before or after the noun (*see* ADJECTIVES, **4.**):

une *grande* maison

une vie *mouvementée*

– a noun followed by an adjectival clause (*see* CLAUSES, **2.**):

Une personne *qui n'a pas dit son nom* vous demande au téléphone.

– a noun clause introduced by que (*see* CLAUSES, **3.**):

J'ai la certitude *qu'il a tort*.

Il a longtemps eu l'espoir *que tout s'arrange*.

6. Adverbs and adverbial phrases

As well as the subject, verb, direct object and indirect object, many sentences contain other information about *when* the action of the verb took place, *where* it took place, *how* it was carried out and so forth. This information can be provided by adverbs – for example **yesterday**, **here** or **well** – or it can be provided by phrases which function in the same way as adverbs – **the last week in December** (= when), **in a village in the south of France** (= where), **with a great deal of success** (= how). As well as time, place and manner, such adverbial phrases can also express cause, purpose and so on.

■ When they are based on nouns, adverbial phrases can begin with a preposition such as **à**, **de**, **avant**, **après** and so on (*see* PREPOSITIONS, **2.**), or they can consist of the noun on its own or preceded by a definite or indefinite article. Such phrases can always be substituted by an adverb having roughly the same meaning, though generally providing less detail:

Je vis *à Paris*. (= Je vis *ici*.)
Il a habité Madrid *pendant des années*. (= Il a *longtemps* habité Madrid.)
Il travaille *la nuit* et dort *le jour*. (= Il travaille *tard* et dort *tard*.)
J'y vais *samedi*. (= J'y vais *bientôt*.)

■ The adverbial pronouns **en** and **y** can often stand for adverbial phrases of place, **en** standing for those introduced by **de**, usually meaning **from**, and **y** standing for those introduced by **à**, usually meaning **at**, **in** or **to** (*see* PRONOUNS, **3.**):

Ils sont arrivés *de New York* hier. → **Ils *en* sont arrivés hier.** (they arrived from there)
Elle habite *à Montréal* depuis longtemps. → **Elle *y* habite depuis longtemps.** (she has lived there.)

> NOTE: Adverbial phrases can appear at different points in the sentence if they apply to the sentence as a whole, although the emphasis may change as a result:
>
> **D'ici, on ne voit rien.** → **On ne voit rien *d'ici*.**
>
> In this case, the phrase **d'ici** applies not to the verb **voit**, but to **on ne voit rien**.
> However, if an adverbial phrase applies only to the verb, it must be placed after it:
>
> **Je vais *à Paris*.**
> **Il part *pour l'étranger*.**

CENT QUATRE-VINGT-CINQ   185

DIFFERENT KINDS OF SENTENCE

1. **Statements**
   il fait froid
2. **Commands**
   viens vite ▲ n'approchez pas ▲ je préfère que tu le fasses
3. **Exclamations**
   quelle chaleur ! ▲ que tu es bête !
4. **Questions**
   viendra-t-il ? ▲ je me demande s'il viendra

All sentences can be classified as either statements, commands, exclamations or questions. All four types of sentence can also be put into the negative.

1. Statements

A sentence is called a statement when it states something as a fact:

Il fait froid ce matin.

2. Commands

A sentence is called a command when it gives an order.
■ The order can be expressed by a verb in the imperative (*see* VERBS, **8.**5):

Viens vite.
Dépêche-toi !
Tais-toi !

In the negative, the imperative expresses a command *not* to do something:

N'approchez pas.
Ne lui dites rien.

■ Both commands to do things and commands not to do things can also be expressed by a verb of wishing followed by a clause whose verb is in the subjunctive (*see* VERBS, **8.**4). Such clauses are normally (though not always) translated into English by an infinitive. However, it is important to realize that in French an infinitive can be used in such situations only after a very small number of verbs. In most cases a clause will be required:

Je ne veux pas **qu'il** *intervienne*. (I don't want him to get involved.)
Je préfère **que** tu le *fasses*. (I prefer you to do it.)
J'exige **qu'il** *fasse* **des excuses tout de suite.** (I demand that he apologize immediately.)

Here are two examples of a verb of wishing followed by an infinitive:

Je te défends **de lui** *répondre*. (I forbid you to answer him.)
Il m'a dit **de venir.** (He told me to come.)

■ Commands may also be expressed by the use of a sentence with a verb in the subjunctive preceded by **que**. This construction is only used for 3rd persons singular and plural. It is usually translated into English as **let**, or **do not let** if negative:

Surtout que les enfants *ne sortent pas*. **Qu'ils m'**attendent. (Don't let the children go out. Let them wait for me.)

■ **Let's** or **let us** is expressed in French by the first person plural form of the the verb without the subject pronoun **nous**:

Sortons **d'ici.** (Let's get out of here.)
Allons **voir ce film.** (Let's go and see this film.)

■ The infinitive form can be used to give instructions (*see* VERBS, **8.6**).

■ The imperative can also be used to express a request rather than an order, or to give advice:

Si tu n'es pas sûr, *demande* **à Paul ce qu'il en pense.**
Essaie **donc avec une autre clé, ça ne marchera jamais avec celle-ci.**

> NOTE: A polite order can be given by using the conditional of a verb such as **aimer**, or **vouloir**, followed by a clause whose verb is in the subjunctive:
>
> *Je voudrais* **que tu** *fasses* **un effort.** (I would like you to make an effort.)
> *J'aimerais bien* **que tu te** *dépêches* **un peu.** (I'd like you to get a move on.)

3. Exclamations

Exclamations express feelings and emotions of various kinds (wishes, regrets, surprise, admiration, indignation and so on):

Pourvu qu'il ne pleuve pas ! (I hope it doesn't rain!)
Comme c'est dommage ! (What a pity!)
Ça alors ! (You don't say!)
Encore lui ! (Him again!)
Qu'est-ce que c'est beau ! (How beautiful!)
Quelle chaleur ! (How hot it is!)
Quel culot ! (What a nerve!)

■ In exclamations introduced by **que** or **comme**, the adjective or adverb is placed *after* the verb in French:

Que tu es bête ! (How silly you are!)
Comme c'est difficile ! (How difficult it is!)
Comme il chante mal ! (How badly he sings!)

■ Commands are often expressed in the form of exclamations with a verb in the imperative:

Viens **ici tout de suite !**

4. Questions

Questions can be asked directly in sentences on their own, or they can be asked indirectly in a subordinate clause.

■ The question can relate to the whole of the sentence. Such questions allow only **yes** or **no** as an answer.

COMPARE

There are two words for **yes** in French: **oui** in the case of an ordinary question, but **si** if the question itself is in the negative:

'Tu viens ?' '*Oui.*'
'Vous ne voulez pas vous joindre à nous ?' '*Si.*'(Don't you want to join us? Yes.)

■ If the question relates not to the whole of the sentence, but only to part of the sentence – the subject, the object and so on – the question will begin with:
- an interrogative pronoun if the information requested relates to a person or thing
- an interrogative adverb if the information requested relates to place or time and so on
- the interrogative adjective quel if a particular item or set of items is to be singled out from a group:

> '*Qui* l'a mis au courant ?' 'Marianne.'
> '*Quand* revient-il ?' 'Ce soir, je crois.'
> *Quels documents* avez-vous déjà lus ?

> NOTE: In English, we often add a little phrase such as **isn't he**, or **didn't they** at the end of a question to give it extra emphasis. The verb in the phrase, as well as its subject and the tense it is in, all depend on the actual question asked. In French, it is only ever the phrase **n'est-ce pas** which is used:
>
> **Ils sont arrivés hier, n'est-ce pas ?** (They arrived yesterday, didn't they?)
> **Je t'en ai déjà parlé, n'est-ce pas ?** (I spoke to you about it already, didn't I?)
> **Il ne fait pas beau aujourd'hui, n'est-ce pas ?** (It's not very nice today, is it?)

4.1 Direct questions

■ Direct questions are often asked by using an interrogative word such as qui or où. In such cases the order is:

INTERROGATIVE + VERB + SUBJECT
Combien sommes-nous ?
Laquelle préfères-tu ?
Quand arrivent-ils ?
À quelle heure prend-elle le train ?

This is quite a formal way of asking a question.
■ If the subject is a pronoun, a direct question can also be indicated by

simply changing the order of subject and verb. This way of asking a question is found most frequently in rather formal French:

VERB + SUBJECT PRONOUN
Viendront-ils **tous ?**

If the subject is a noun, it is placed in front of the verb as usual, but the pronoun corresponding to the subject must also be used. The pronoun is placed *after* the noun, giving the order:

SUBJECT + VERB + PRONOUN
Les enfants viendront-ils **tous ?**

■ In everyday spoken language a direct question can be asked without placing the subject after the verb, as long as the sentence is said in such a way that it sounds like a question, the voice rising at the end:

Ils viendront **tous ?**

If there is an interrogative word or phrase in such cases, it is placed at the *end* of the sentence:

Ils viendront **quand ?**
Leur train arrive **à quelle heure ?**

■ Questions in French can often contain est-ce que, indeed this is very common in spoken French. In these cases the order remains SUBJECT + VERB:

Combien *est-ce que* **nous sommes ?**
Laquelle *est-ce que* **tu préfères ?**
Quand *est-ce que* **leur train arrive ?**
*Est-ce qu'***ils viendront tous ?**
Est-ce que **les enfants viendront tous ?**

Est-ce que is used in questions which begin with an interrogative adverb or the pronouns qui and que if they are the *object* of the verb:

Pourquoi est-ce que **tu te fâches ?**
Qui est-ce que **tu as vu ?**

However, if qui and que are the *subject* of the verb, est-ce qui is used instead:

Qui est-ce qui **les a prévenus ?**
Qu'est-ce qui **se passe ?**

> *NOTE:* Remember that, although it is quite possible to put a preposition at the end of a question in English, this is *never* possible in French. In French, the preposition must always be at the *beginning* of the question:
>
> **De qui est-ce que vous parlez ?** (Who are you talking about?)
> **Avec quoi est-ce que tu l'as fait ?** (What did you do it with?)

4.2 Indirect questions

An indirect question always takes the form of a subordinate clause (*see* CLAUSES, **1**.2) introduced by an interrogative word. This subordinate clause will always follow a main clause containing a verb which means to ask, to wonder, to know and so on. The order of words in the indirect question is always SUBJECT + VERB as it is in English. There is never a question mark at the end of an indirect question:

Direct	*Indirect*
Viendra-t-il ? →	**Je me demande *s'il viendra*.** (I wonder if he'll come.)
Où va-t-il ? →	**Je ne sais pas *où il va*.** (I don't know where he's going.)

Note that a direct question which begins with que or qu'est-ce que will begin with ce que when it is changed into an indirect question, and a direct question which begins with qu'est-ce qui will begin with ce qui as an indirect question:

Qu'est-ce que tu veux ?	→	**Je lui ai demandé ce qu'il voulait.**
Qu'est-ce qui se passe ?	→	**Je voulais savoir ce qui se passait.**

> *NOTE:* As in the case of direct questions, a preposition can *never* appear at the end of an indirect question. It must always be placed at the beginning:
>
> **Je me demande *de qui* ils parlent.** (I wonder who they're talking about.)
> **Je ne sais pas *avec quoi* il l'a fait.** (I don't know what he did it with.)

■ As in English, indirect questions can sometimes be asked using the infinitive of the verb:

> **Je ne sais pas** *quoi faire.* (I don't know what to do.)
> **Je me demande** *qui inviter.* (I'm wondering who to invite.)

4.3 Different types of interrogative word

Interrogative adverbs and pronouns are described in PRONOUNS, **8.**

> *NOTE:* The same interrogative words are used for both direct and indirect questions.

■ Qui, à qui, de qui, quel and lequel (as well as forms of lequel such as auquel and duquel) are used to establish the identity of a person:

> **Je me demande** *qui* **vient de sonner.**
> *Quel* **est le coupable ?**
> *Lequel* **d'entre vous pourrait m'aider ?**

■ Que, quel, lequel, à quoi and de quoi are used to identify a particular object or thing:

> *Qu'est-ce que* **c'est ?**
> **Est-ce que tu sais** *quelle* **heure il est ?**
> *Quelle* **décision avez-vous finalement prise ?**
> **Dis-moi** *lequel* **tu as acheté.**
> *À quoi* **penses-tu ?**
> **Je me demande** *de quoi* **vous parliez.**

■ If the question has to do with the circumstances in which the action took place:

– Quand (when) is used to ask about time:

> *Quand* **aurez-vous fini ?**
> **Dites-moi** *quand* **vous aurez fini.**

– Où (where) is used to ask about place:

> *Où* **sont mes lunettes ?**
> **Je me demande** *où* **sont passées mes lunettes.**

– Comment (how) is used to ask questions about the way something was done, or the means used to do it:

Comment avez-vous fait pour entrer ?
On ne sait pas *comment* ils ont fait pour entrer.

Comment can also be used with the verb être to ask for a description of someone or something, in which case it usually translates into English as what ... like?

Comment est ton frère ? Il est grand et blond. (What is your brother like?)
Je lui ai demandé *comment* était son frère.

– Pourquoi (why) is used to ask about cause or reason:

Pourquoi est-ce qu'il a l'air aussi mécontent ?
Je me demande *pourquoi* il a l'air aussi mécontent.

– Combien (how much, how many) is used to ask questions about amount or number. The preposition de is always placed between combien and any noun which comes after it:

Combien d'enfants ont-ils eus ?
Je me demande *combien* d'enfants ils ont eus.

Combien is also used to enquire about prices:

Combien coûte cette voiture ?
Dites-moi *combien* coûte cette voiture.

4.4 Negative and rhetorical questions

■ As in English, negative questions are often used in French to check whether something is or is not the case. The answer is either si (yes) or non (no), but never oui!

'Il ne vient pas, alors ?' '*Si*.'
'Est-ce que vous n'en reprendriez pas un peu ?' '*Non*, merci.'
(Wouldn't you like a little more? No thanks.)

■ Rhetorical questions are questions to which the speaker already knows the answer:

Est-ce qu'il ne devait pas nous rejoindre à onze heures ?

MAKING VERBS NEGATIVE

> **1. Different Types of Negative**
> ne ... pas ▲ ne ... jamais ▲ ne ... personne
> **2. Using more than one Negative**
> **3. Expressing *Only* or *Just***
> **4. Expressing *Neither do I, Neither does he* etc.**
> moi non plus ▲ lui non plus

1. Different types of negative

■ Verbs can be made negative by combining them with any of the following:

> **ne ... pas** (not) ▲ **ne ... plus** (no ... longer) ▲ **ne ... jamais** or **jamais ... ne** (never) ▲ **ne ... rien** or **rien ... ne** (nothing) ▲ **ne ... aucun** or **aucun ... ne** (no) ▲ **ne ... personne** or **personne ... ne** (no-one, nobody) ▲ **ne ... nulle part** (nowhere).

> *NOTE:*
> * In English, we often use the verb **to do** when we make a verb negative. For example, we say **I know** but **I do not know**, **I went** but **I did not go**. This *never* happens in French, where the negative is simply used with the normal verb: **je sais** → **je ne sais pas; je suis allé** → **je ne suis pas allé**.
>
> * Remember also that most of these negatives have two possible forms in English. For example, we can say **he knows nothing** or **he doesn't know anything**, **I spoke to no-one** or **I didn't speak to anyone**. Normally the shorter form – **no-one, nothing** etc. – is more emphatic than the longer one – **not ... anyone, not ... anything** and the like. The exception is **not ... ever**, which is more emphatic than **never**.

■ Ne is *always* placed before the verb. As regards the second part of the negative, its position can vary.

– In the case of **pas, rien, aucun** and **personne**, the second part of the negative will normally come after the verb if it is part of the object, and it will normally come before the verb if it is part of the subject.

> **Je** *ne* **sais** *pas.* (I don't know.)
> *Pas* un seul *n'*est venu. (Not a single one came.)
> **Je** *n'*en sais *rien.* (I don't know anything about it.)
> *Rien ne* presse. (There's no hurry.)
> *Aucune* menace *n'*a eu d'effet sur lui. (No threat had any effect on him.)
> **Je** *ne* connais *aucun* d'eux. (I don't know either <u>OR</u> any of them.)
> **Je** *n'*ai vu *personne.* (I didn't see anyone.)
> *Personne ne* voulait le faire. (No-one wanted to do it.)

– In the case of **plus, jamais** and **nulle part**, the second part of the negative is normally placed after the verb, though it may sometimes be placed before the verb for emphasis.

> **Ils** *ne* **sont** *jamais* **venus ici.** (They never came here.)
> *Jamais* ils *ne* sont venus ici. (They didn't ever come here.)
> **Je** *ne* les vois *nulle part.* (I can't see them anywhere.)

NOTE: **Ne ... pas** can be made stronger by replacing it with **ne ... pas du tout** (not at all), or it can be softened by using **ne ... pas trop** (not so much), **ne ... pas vraiment** (not really) or **ne ... pas tellement** (not so much):

> Elle *n'*a *pas du tout* compris. (She did not understand at all.)
> Je *n'*aime *pas trop* les haricots verts. (I'm not too keen on green beans.)
> Je *n'*ai *pas tellement* envie de sortir ce soir. (I'm not too keen on going out tonight.)

■ Ne ... **guère** (scarcely) and ne ... **point** (not at all) are only used in literary French:

> Il *n'*avait *guère* envie d'être mêlé à cette affaire.

■ If the verb is in the infinitive, both parts of **ne pas, ne plus** or **ne jamais** are placed *before* the infinitive:

> Il est préférable de *ne pas* s'exposer au soleil en plein midi.

■ In very formal French **ne** is sometimes used on its own with a verb *without* making it negative:

– after verbs expressing doubt or fear. The verb which follows **ne** is in the subjunctive:

Je crains qu'il *ne* vienne. (= je crains qu'il vienne: I'm afraid he will come.)

– after plus, moins, meilleur, moindre, pire and autre. The verb which follows ne is in the subjunctive:

Ça coûte moins cher que je ne pensais.
La situation est pire qu'elle ne l'a jamais été.

– in subordinate clauses introduced by avant que (before), à moins que (unless) or de peur que (lest). The verb which follows ne is in the subjunctive:

Pars avant qu'il *ne* soit trop tard. (= avant qu'il soit trop tard: before it's too late)
Ils fermèrent la fenêtre de peur que l'orage *n'*éclate. (= de peur que l'orage éclate: lest the storm should break)

■ In literary French, ne is often used on its own with the verbs oser, pouvoir and savoir, which are then made negative, even though pas is not used:

Elle *n'*osait s'adresser à eux. (She did not dare speak to them.)
Je *ne* sais que faire. (I don't know what to do.)

■ Note that in everyday spoken French ne is often left out when the verb is made negative. This usage is not considered to be correct:

J'en sais rien.
Je sais pas.

■ Ne is omitted before other negatives when they are used without a verb. This happens most often when they are used to answer a question:

Qui est venu ? Personne. (Who came? No-one.)
Qu'est-ce que tu as fait ? Rien. (What have you done? Nothing.)
Tu es prêt ? Pas encore. (Are you ready? Not yet.)
Il est parti ? Pas que je sache. (Has he gone? Not so far as I know.)

2. Using more than one negative

English seldom uses two negatives together. To join two sentences such as He never knows and He knows nothing, we would say He never knows *anything* – in other words, the second negative (nothing) is replaced by anything. Other examples are He never speaks to anyone, We no longer go anywhere and so on. In French, however, it is quite correct to have two negatives after ne without having to change the form of either of them:

Il *ne* dit *jamais rien.*

Elle *ne* parle *jamais à personne*.
Il *ne* va *plus nulle part*.

■ Double negatives of this kind can also be found when an infinitive is preceded by sans:

Il s'en va *sans jamais parler à personne*. (He leaves without ever speaking to anyone.)

3. Expressing *only* or *just*

■ The idea of only or just can be expressed using ne … que or ne … plus que:

Il *ne* reste *que* trois yaourts. (There are only three yoghurts left.)
Il *ne* reste *plus que* trois yaourts. (There are only three yoghurts left.)
Je *n'*ai eu *que* le temps de sauter dans un train. (I just had time to jump on a train.)

■ Note that ne … que and ne … plus can only be used if the idea of only or just applies to the object of the verb. If it applies to the verb itself, an adverb such as simplement would be used:

Je voulais *simplement* demander. (I only wanted to ask.)

For just relating to time – he has just arrived – *see* VERBS, **3**.4.

> *NOTE:* **Ne** and **que** can in fact be some distance apart – in some cases even several lines away from each other:
>
> **Le P.D.-G. avait dit qu'il *n'*était prêt à augmenter les salaires des travailleurs qui occupaient l'usine de Metz *que* s'ils parvenaient à augmenter la productivité.**

■ The same idea can also be expressed by the adverb seulement:

Il reste *seulement* trois yaourts.
J'ai *seulement* eu le temps de sauter dans un train.

4. Expressing *neither do I*, *neither does he* etc.

The idea neither do I, neither does he and so on is expressed in French by the appropriate form of the stressed subject pronoun (*see* PRONOUNS, **1**.) followed by non plus. The verb used in English changes according to the sentence, but no verb is used in the French construction:

'Je n'aime pas les épinards.' 'Moi non plus.' (Neither do I.)
Je ne suis pas d'accord et *lui non plus*. (I don't agree and neither does he.)
'Je n'y suis jamais allée.' 'Moi non plus.' (Neither have I.)

CLAUSES

> 1. **Different Types of Clause**
> 2. **Adjectival Clauses**
> 3. **Noun Clauses**
> 4. **Adverbial Clauses**
>
> All sentences contain at least one clause, and many sentences contain more than one clause. A clause is a group of words which together make sense, either on their own or with other clauses. One of the words in a clause *must* be a verb in a form other than the infinitive or the present participle. The number of clauses in a sentence is always the same as the number of such verbs in that sentence.
>
> For example, **I will go to France next year** contains one clause, since it contains one verb: **go. I will go to France next year to learn French** still contains only one clause since the second verb is in the infinitive: **to learn.** However, **I will go to France next year if I have enough money** has two clauses since it contains the two verbs **go** and **have.** The two clauses are **I will go to France next year** and **if I have enough money.**

1. Different types of clause

1.1 Sentences which consist of only one clause

Many sentences consist of only one clause. These sentences have only one verb, and make perfect sense on their own without the need to add anything else:

Il fait jour. (It is daylight.)
Faites attention à la marche. (Mind the step.)

1.2 Main and subordinate clauses

■ A clause which could form a sentence on its own is called a main clause, while a clause which could not stand on its own is called a subordinate clause. To take as an example: If it rains, I'll go to the cinema, I'll go to the cinema would make sense on its own and is therefore a main clause. If it rains would not make sense on its own, however. It either needs another clause to tell you what will happen if it rains, or it needs to be functioning as the answer to a question such as Are you going to the cinema? Since it could not form a sentence on its own, it is a subordinate clause.

Je pense qu'il a raison. (*Je pense* is the main clause, and *qu'il a raison* is the subordinate clause.)

■ A subordinate clause can be linked to a main clause by:
– a relative pronoun (qui, que, quoi, dont, où or lequel), used to introduce an adjectival clause (*see* **2.** below and PRONOUNS, **7.**)

J'aime le quartier *où j'habite*. (I like the district I live in.)

– the conjunction **que** (that), used to introduce a noun clause. Remember that while in English that can often be left out before a noun clause, **que** can *never* be omitted in French (*see* **3.** below and CONJUNCTIONS, **2.1**):

Je pense *que tu as raison*.

– a subordinating conjunction other than **que** indicating time (quand, avant que etc.), purpose (pour que, afin que), condition (si, pourvu que) and so on:

Je ne sors pas *parce qu*'il pleut.

2. Adjectival clauses

■ Adjectival clauses are *always* linked to the main clause by one of the relative pronouns qui, que, quoi, dont, où or lequel (*see* PRONOUNS, **7.**). Remember that while certain relative pronouns can be left out in English, they can *never* be left out in French.

■ Adjectival clauses function like an adjective, and they describe a person or object, or group of persons or objects, mentioned earlier in the sentence. This or these person(s) or object(s) are called the *antecedent* of the adjectival clause. The adjectival clause could be replaced by an adjective and the sentence would still make sense:

Elle m'a montré les photos *qu'ils ont prises en Sicile*. (= Elle m'a montré les nouvelles photos.)

■ The antecedent of an adjectival clause can also be one of the pronouns ce, celui, celle, celles or ceux (*see* PRONOUNS, **6.**):

Sa grand-mère lui achète tout *ce qu'elle demande*. (Her grandmother buys her everything she asks for.)

■ As in English, there are two types of adjectival clause in French:

– *Defining* adjectival clauses single out the antecedent from other persons or objects of its kind. If these clauses are removed the meaning of the sentence changes:

Les élèves *qui étaient en retard* se sont fait gronder. (= Only those pupils who were late were told off.)

Il apprécie les gens *qui savent ce qu'ils veulent*. (= He only appreciates people who know what they want.)

– *Non-defining* adjectival clauses merely provide additional information about the antecedent without singling it out in any way. As in English, they are separated off from the rest of the sentence by commas. If they are left out the meaning of the sentence remains basically unchanged. They can sometimes provide information as to *why* the action of the sentence has taken place:

Les élèves, *qui étaient en retard*, se sont fait gronder. (= All the pupils were told off because they were all late.)

■ The verb in the adjectival clause can be in the indicative or in the subjunctive (*see* VERBS, **8.**):

– It is in the indicative if it refers to something clearly identified which is known to exist. Most adjectival clauses fall into this category:

Ils ont acheté une maison qui *a* deux étages.

– It is in the subjunctive:

– if the antecedent refers to someone or something indefinite which will only become definite in the future or may never become definite:

Nous cherchons quelqu'un qui *comprenne* le français. (*quelqu'un* does not refer here to a specific person, but to someone who has yet to be found)

BUT

Nous avons trouvé quelqu'un qui *comprend* le français. (now *quelqu'un* does refer to a specific person, so the verb is in the indicative)

– if the antecedent is negative:

Il n'y a personne qui *soit* **capable de faire cela.** (There is no-one who is able to do that.)
Il n'y a rien qu'on *puisse* **faire.** (There's nothing we can do.)

– if the antecedent is preceded by **seul** or **ne … que**, both of which mean **only**:

Tu es le seul qui *puisse* **l'aider.** (You are the only one who can help him.)
Il n'y a que lui qui s'y *connaisse.* (He's the only one who is familiar with it.)

– if the antecedent is described by an adjective which is in the superlative (*see* ADJECTIVES, **5.**2):

C'est le meilleur film que j'*aie* **jamais vu.**
Elle est la personne la plus intelligente que je *connaisse.*

■ Occasionally the verb in the adjectival clause is not expressed, so that the clause appears to contain only an infinitive:

Ils ont trouvé quelqu'un à qui *vendre* **leur appartement.** (= à qui *ils peuvent* vendre leur appartement)

3. Noun clauses

Noun clauses are so called because if you replaced them with a noun the sentence would still make sense (though it might mean something different). For example, if you say I believe **that he is telling the truth**, you could replace the noun clause **that he is telling the truth** with the noun **his story** – I believe **his story** – and the sentence would still be perfectly meaningful.

■ Noun clauses are always linked to the main clause by **que** (**that**), and they can be the subject, object or complement of the verb in the main clause (*see* BUILDING SENTENCES). Remember that while the word **that** can often be left out before a noun clause in English, **que** can *never* be left out in French.

Je pense *qu'il va faire froid demain.* (I think it will be cold tomorrow.)
Elle est sûre *qu'il a tort.* (She is sure he is wrong.)
J'ai la certitude *qu'il a raison.* (I am sure he is right.)

CLAUSES

■ Noun clauses follow verbs of opinion such as **penser**, **croire**, **estimer**, **savoir**, **considérer** or **supposer**; phrases which have similar meanings, such as **être sûr que**, **avoir la certitude que** or **être certain que**; or verbs such as **dire**, **expliquer** or **affirmer** which are used to make statements. They can also follow verbs expressing doubt, wishes or fear.

■ Noun clauses can fulfil the following functions:

– They can act as the direct object of the verb. The noun clause could be replaced by a noun or pronoun as the object of the verb in the main clause:

> **Je vois *que tu es pressé*.** (= Je vois ceci.)

– They can act as the subject. The noun clause could be replaced by a noun which is the subject of the verb in the main clause:

> ***Qu'il soit là* me rassure.** (= Sa présence me rassure.)

– They can act as the complement:

> **L'essentiel est *que tu arrives à l'heure*.**

■ The verb in the noun clause can be in the indicative or the subjunctive (*see* VERBS, **8.**):

– It is in the indicative after verbs, nouns and adjectives which express an opinion, a judgment or a certainty:

> **Je sais qu'il *a* dit la vérité.**
> **J'ai la certitude qu'il nous *cache* quelque chose.**
> **Je suis sûr que vous vous *trompez*.**

– It is in the subjunctive after verbs, nouns and adjectives which express a wish, fear or doubt, or another feeling such as joy or regret:

> **J'ai bien peur qu'il n'*ait* raison.**
> **Elle a peur qu'il *fasse* trop froid en montagne.**
> **On peut craindre qu'il ne se *soit* découragé.**
> **Je ne suis pas sûr qu'il y *parvienne*.**
> **Je ne pense pas qu'il *ait* raison.**
> **Je suis heureuse que tu *sois* venu.**

– When the noun clause comes first in the sentence, its verb is in the subjunctive:

> **Qu'ils *veuillent* le faire est très peu probable.**

4. Adverbial clauses

Adverbial clauses are introduced by a conjunction other than **que**, or by a compound conjunction which combines another word with **que**. They provide additional information which brings greater precision to the meaning of the main clause. In this sense, they function in exactly the same way as adverbs.

4.1 Adverbial clauses of time

■ Adverbial clauses of time are introduced by conjunctions or phrases relating to time:

J'ai ouvert la porte *dès qu'il a sonné*. (as soon as he rang)

■ The verb in the clause of time can be in the indicative or the subjunctive:

– It is in the subjunctive after the conjunctions **avant que** (before), **jusqu'à ce que** (until), and **en attendant que** (until):

J'aurai fini mon travail *avant qu'il arrive*.

– It is in the indicative with all other conjunctions, for example **quand**, **lorsque**, **dès que**, **après que** and **au moment où**:

Elle se lève *dès qu'il fait jour*.

> NOTE:
> * Whereas English uses a present tense in a clause of time to refer to an event which will take place in the future, in French the verb in the clause of time is always put into the *future* tense:
>
>   **Je lui en parlerai quand il *arrivera*.** (I'll speak to him about it when he arrives.)
>   **Je le ferai quand tu *rentreras*.** (I'll do it when you get back.)
>
> * Where English uses a perfect tense, French uses a future perfect:
>
>   **Je sortirai quand j'*aurai fini* mes devoirs.** (I'll go out when I have finished my homework.)
>
> * Where English uses an imperfect tense in indirect speech, French uses a conditional:
>
>   **Il m'avait dit qu'il le ferait dès qu'il *pourrait*.** (He told me he would do it as soon as he could.)

■ Sometimes the clause can be replaced by a verb in the infinitive:

Je recommencerai à travailler *après avoir fait la sieste.* (I'll start work again after having a nap.)

4.2 Adverbial clauses of purpose

■ Adverbial clauses of purpose are introduced by conjunctions or phrases which allow the subordinate clause to express a purpose or goal in relation to the main clause. The conjunctions most often used are **pour que** and (less frequently) **afin que**, both of which mean **so that**.

■ The verb in a clause of purpose is always in the subjunctive:

J'ai laissé le portail ouvert *pour que vous puissiez garer votre voiture à l'intérieur.* (so that you could park your car inside)

Elle t'a tout dit *pour que tu saches à quoi t'en tenir.* (so that you would know where you stand)

NOTE: In English, purpose can often be expressed simply by using the infinitive. This is also possible in French provided there is only one subject involved in the sentence. In such cases, the infinitive is preceded by the preposition **pour**:

Téléphonez *pour fixer un rendez-vous.* (= *You* will phone and *you* will get the appointment.)

Elle travaille *pour gagner un peu d'argent.* (= *She* is working and *she* is earning the money.)

However, if more than one subject is involved, a clause with its verb in the subjunctive *must* be used in French, even though an infinitive may still be possible in English:

Je le ferai pour que tu *puisses* **y aller.** (= *I* will do it, but *you* will go there.)

Il a acheté le livre pour que tu le *lises.* (= *He* bought the book, but *you* will read it: in English, He bought the book for you to read.)

4.3 Adverbial clauses of reason

■ Adverbial clauses of reason are introduced by a conjunction which allows them to express the reason(s) for the action expressed by the verb in the main clause. By far the most common conjunction used in such clauses is **parce que** (because):

Il est arrivé en retard *parce qu'il a raté son bus.*

■ The verb in adverbial clauses of reason can be in the indicative or the subjunctive:

– It is in the subjunctive after the conjunctions **non que** (not because) and **soit que ... soit que ...** (whether ... or ...):

> **Je ne *pourrai* pas venir, *non que je n'en aie pas envie*, mais parce que je n'aurai pas le temps.** (not because I don't want to)

– It is in the indicative after all other conjunctions – **parce que, puisque** etc.:

> **Couvrez-vous bien *parce qu'il fait froid*.** (Wrap yourself up well because it is cold.)

– An infinitive can also be used:

> **Il s'est fait gronder *pour avoir menti*.**

4.4 Adverbial clauses of result

■ Adverbial clauses of result are introduced by conjunctions or phrases which allow them to indicate the result or consequences of the action expressed by the verb in the main clause. These conjunctions usually translate into English as so that, or so ... that:

> **Les bureaux étaient fermés, *si bien que j'ai dû revenir le lendemain*.** (so that I had to go back the following day)
> **Il est *tellement* petit *que je n'arrive pas à le voir*.** (It is so small that I can't see it.)
> **Elle est *tellement* forte à ce jeu *que nous avons perdu*.** (She's so good at this game that we lost.)
> **Il fait *si* chaud *qu'elle s'endort tout le temps*.** (It's so hot that she keeps dozing off.)

■ The verb in an adverbial clause of result can be in the indicative or the subjunctive:

– It is in the subjunctive after the conjunctions **trop ... pour que** and **au point que**:

> **Il est *trop* tôt après son accident *pour qu'il puisse* remarcher.**

After **trop ... pour que**, the most usual way of translating an adverbial clause into English is simply to replace the verb in that clause by an infinitive:

> **Il est trop tard *pour que* nous puissions faire quoi que ce soit.** (It is too late for us to do anything.)

Ce problème est trop compliqué *pour que* vous puissiez le résoudre tout seul. (This problem is too complicated for you to solve all by yourself.)

– It is in the indicative after all other conjunctions – si bien que, de telle sorte que, tellement … que etc.:

Il a fait *tellement* chaud *que* les arbres *ont* déjà des bourgeons. (It has been so hot that the trees are already budding.)

4.5 Adverbial clauses of concession

■ Adverbial clauses of concession are introduced by conjunctions or phrases which indicate some kind of obstacle to the action of the verb in the main clause taking place. The most common conjunctions are quoique and bien que, both of which mean although:

Elle est sortie *bien que le médecin le lui ait formellement interdit*. (although the doctor strictly forbade her to)

■ The verb in a clause of concession can be in the indicative or the subjunctive:

– It is in the subjunctive after bien que and quoique:

Elle vous rappellera *bien qu'elle ait beaucoup de travail en ce moment*.

– It is in the indicative after même si, meaning even if:

Même si elle *avait été* au courant, elle n'aurait rien pu faire. (even if she had known)

– The verb is put into the conditional after quand bien même, which also means even if. The expression is quite formal:

Quand bien même elle *aurait été mise* au courant, elle n'aurait rien pu faire.

– Most other kinds of concessive clause in French require their verb to be put into the subjunctive:

Qui que vous *soyez*, vous ne pouvez pas entrer. (whoever you are)
Si intelligent qu'il *soit*, il ne peut pas résoudre le problème.
(however intelligent he might be)
Où que vous *alliez*, vous ne le trouverez pas. (wherever you go)

4.6 Conditional clauses

■ Conditional clauses are introduced by conjunctions or phrases which allow them to indicate a condition on which the action expressed by the verb of the main clause depends. By far the most common conjunction is si, meaning if:

Je viendrai t'aider *si j'ai le temps*.

■ The verb in the conditional clause can be in the indicative or the subjunctive:

– It is in the indicative after si, sauf que, suivant que and selon que. The tense of the verb in a clause introduced by si is always the same as it would be in English:

Je le ferai *si j'ai le temps*. (if I have time)
Je te le dirais *si je le savais*. (if I knew)
Il serait venu *s'il l'avait su*. (if he had known)

However, after suivant que and selon que, both of which mean depending on whether, the verb in the conditional clause is in the same tense as the verb in the main clause:

***Suivant que les gens seront plus ou moins nombreux*, il faudra ou non rajouter des chaises.** (depending on whether lots of people come or not)

– It is in the subjunctive after à condition que (on condition that), à moins que (unless) and pourvu que (provided that, so long as):

Faites comme bon vous semblera pourvu que le résultat *soit* valable. (Do as you see fit provided the result is valid.)
Je te le prête à condition que tu me le *rendes* vite. (I'll lend it to you on condition you give me it back soon.)

> NOTE: When two conditions are joined in French, the second is introduced by **que** (not si) and its verb is put into the subjunctive:
>
> **S'il accepte, et que les autres *soient* prêts à l'accepter aussi, nous le ferons.**

– It is in the conditional after au cas où (in case):

Rappelez-le-lui *au cas où il l'aurait oublié*. (Remind him, in case he has forgotten.)

(*See* AGREEMENT OF TENSES, **1.** for more information.)

4.7 Clauses of comparison

Clauses of comparison indicate a relationship between two things, expressing how they compare with each other in terms of size, amount, degree and so on. They are introduced by conjunctions or phrases which allow the clause to indicate this comparison with some element of the main clause (*see* EXPRESSING COMPARISON, **2.**):

Elle a réagi *comme on pouvait s'y attendre*. (as you might expect)
Elles ont travaillé *autant qu'il est possible*. (as much as possible)
Il est *moins* travailleur *que je ne pensais*. (He is less hard-working than I thought.)

▪ Verbs used in comparative clauses are always in the indicative.

▪ The conjunctions which indicate comparisons are as follows:
– *comme* (as)

J'ai fait tout *comme* tu m'avais dit de le faire.
Il nous parle *comme* si nous n'y connaissions rien.

– *que* preceded by tel, de même, autant, plus, moins, aussi, ainsi or autre. The translation of que varies considerably depending on what it is combined with:

Elle est *telle que* nous l'imaginions. (just as)
De même que ses parents l'ont été, il est très influent. (just as)
Elle a gagné à ce jeu *autant qu'elle* a perdu. (as much as)
Il est *plus* grand *que* sa sœur ne l'était au même âge. (taller than)
Je suis *moins* fatiguée *que* je ne l'ai été. (not as … as)
Il est *aussi* gentil *qu'*on puisse l'être. (as … as)
Ils ont acheté une *autre* voiture *que* celle que j'avais vue. (different … from)

> NOTE: Very often the verb in a comparative clause is not actually expressed:
>
> **Elle nage *comme un poisson*.** (= comme un poisson nage)
> **C'est moins grave *que gênant*.** (= que ce n'est gênant)
> **Je suis moins pressé *que prévu*.** (= que je ne l'avais prévu)
> **Il parle d'elle *comme s'il l'avait toujours connue*.** (= comme il ferait s'il l'avait toujours connue)
> **Elle est rouge *comme une tomate*.** (= comme une tomate est rouge)

EXPRESSING COMPARISON

> ## 1. Comparative Sentences
>
> ## 2. Conjunctions and Adverbs used to Introduce Comparisons
> comme ▲ tel que ▲ si que ▲ de même que ▲ plus/moins que
> autant … autant ▲ plus … plus ▲ moins … moins
>
> There are many ways of expressing comparisons in French. In a comparison, the two items being compared are linked to each other by means of adverbs (**plus**, **moins**, **aussi**) and conjunctions (**que**, **comme**):
>
> **Elle est *plus* souvent chez elle *que* nulle part ailleurs.**
> (She is more often at home than anywhere else.)
> **Il fait beaucoup *plus* de choses *qu*'il en a l'air.** (He does a lot more than you'd think.)
>
> In a comparison two items can be presented as being equal or equivalent, or they can be presented as being different, these differences relating to quality, quantity or degree. This can be done by using the various kinds of comparative construction (equality, superiority or inferiority), as well as by using the superlative:
>
> **Il fait *aussi* chaud *qu*'hier.** (It is as hot as yesterday.)
> **Il est *plus* âgé *qu*'elle.** (He is older than her.)
> **Le temps est *moins* beau *qu*'hier.** (The weather is not so nice as yesterday.)
> **C'est *le plus* intelligent *de tous*.** (He is the most intelligent of all.)
> **C'est *le moins* cher *que j'ai trouvé*.** (It is the cheapest I could find.)

1. Comparative sentences

Comparative sentences can take many different forms:

■ Sentences expressing comparisons can contain two full clauses, one for each element of the comparison (*see* CLAUSES, **4.7**):

Je fais la cuisine comme j'ai appris à le faire.
Ils s'entendent aussi bien qu'il est possible.

When the first clause contains plus or moins, ne may be written before the verb in the second clause. This ne does *not* make the second verb negative.

Elle est beaucoup *plus douce* que ne l'est son amie. (She is much more gentle than her friend is.)

Ils sont *plus heureux* qu'on ne pense. (They are happier than people think.)

Il est *plus malin* qu'on ne croit. (He's smarter than people think.)

This ne is often omitted in informal French.

Note in particular the phrase **d'autant plus** + ADJECTIVE or ADVERB + **que**, which translates into English as **all the more** + ADJECTIVE or ADVERB + **because**:

C'est *d'autant plus agréable* qu'il fait très beau. (It is all the more pleasant because the weather is very nice.)

When there is no adjective or adverb, it translates as **all the more so because**:

C'est étonnant, *d'autant plus* qu'il l'a fait lui-même. (It's astonishing, all the more so because he did it himself.)

■ However, in many comparisons part of the second clause is not expressed and only those elements are kept which are necessary for the sentence to make sense.

– In some cases one of the elements of the comparison is expressed simply by a pronoun placed before the verb in the comparative clause. In these cases the pronoun is not translated into English:

Reprenez-en autant que vous *le* voulez. (= autant que vous voulez en reprendre – as much as you want)

Nous nous débrouillerons comme nous *le* pourrons. (= comme nous pourrons nous débrouiller – as best we can)

Elle en sait plus qu'il ne *le* faudrait. (= plus qu'il ne faudrait qu'elle en sache – more than she should)

In spoken French, le is omitted.

– Alternatively, the second element of the comparison can be reduced to just one part of the clause:

Elle est gaie comme *un pinson*. (= comme un pinson est gai)
Elle est légère comme *un papillon*. (= comme l'est un papillon)
Il est plus grand que *son frère*. (= que ne l'est son frère)

In such cases the second part of the comparison can be:

– a noun (someone's name or an ordinary noun), or a group of words which behave like a noun:

Il a fait aussi froid cette nuit que *dans la journée d'hier*.

– a pronoun on its own:

Elle est un peu plus âgée que *moi*.
Il chante mieux que *toi*.
Leur voiture est plus neuve que *la nôtre*.

NOTE: When a pronoun referring to a person appears in the second part of a comparison, it appears in its *stressed* form (*see* PRONOUNS, **1.**).

– an adjective:

Il est plus paresseux que *travailleur*.
Elle est plus souvent gaie que *triste*.
Elle est aussi cultivée qu'intelligente*.

– an adverb:

C'est beaucoup mieux qu'avant*.
Cette ville est restée aussi jolie qu'autrefois*.
Il fait moins beau qu'hier*.

NOTE: Traditional comparisons exist in French as in English – **as deaf as a post, as dull as ditchwater** and so on – as set phrases:

Il est *heureux comme un roi*. (as happy as Larry)
Elle est *belle comme le jour*. (as pretty as a picture)
Il est *comme un coq en pâte*. (He leads the life of Riley.)
Elle est *légère comme une plume*. (as light as a feather)

2. Conjonctions and adverbs used to introduce comparisons

2.1 Conjunctions

Usual conjunctions are comme, and que preceded by an adjective or adverb (ainsi, aussi, autant, autre, tel, de même, plus or moins) (*see* CLAUSES, **4.7**):

Tout s'est passé *comme* **prévu.**
C'était très bien *tel que* **c'était.**
C'était *moins* **difficile** *que* **ce que tu m'avais dit.**

2.2 Pairs of adverbs

Certain adverbs are used in pairs to establish a comparison between two different parts of the sentence. They are **autant**, **plus** and **moins**.

■ *Autant … autant* (as … as)

This construction introduces a contrast between the two different parts of the sentence. In English, the *second* part of the sentence is usually placed first:

Autant **il peut être charmant,** *autant* **aujourd'hui il est désagréable.**
(He is as unpleasant today as he is normally charming.)
Autant **j'apprécie ses idées,** *autant* **je déteste son caractère.**
(I dislike his personality as much as I appreciate his ideas.)

Sometimes the best translation is to use **although**, in which case the order of the French sentence is retained:

Autant **d'habitude j'aime ce que je fais,** *autant* **parfois cela me pèse.**
(Although I usually enjoy what I do, it gets me down sometimes.)

■ *Plus … plus* (the more … the more)

Plus **certains vins vieillissent,** *plus* **ils sont bons.** (The more certain wines age, the better they become.)
Plus **le soleil est chaud,** *plus* **il peut être dangereux.** (The hotter the sun, the more dangerous it is.)
Plus **on lit,** *plus* **on aime lire.** (The more you read, the more you enjoy reading.)

■ *Moins … moins* (the less … the less)

Moins **on fume,** *moins* **on a envie de fumer.** (The less you smoke, the less you feel like smoking.)
Moins **tu t'énerveras,** *moins* **tu risqueras de faire des erreurs.** (The less edgy you are, the less likely you are to make mistakes.)

■ *Plus … moins* (the more … the less)

Plus **le temps est gris,** *moins* **j'ai envie de partir.** (The greyer the weather is, the less I feel like leaving.)
Plus **l'été avance,** *moins* **les jours rallongent.** (The further on the summer gets, the shorter the days become.)

■ *Moins … plus* (the less … the more)

Moins **il y a de soleil,** *plus* **il fait froid.** (The less sun there is, the colder it gets.)
Moins **on dort,** *plus* **on est énervé.** (The less you sleep, the more edgy you become.)

EMPHASIZING DIFFERENT PARTS OF THE SENTENCE

1. **Using Pronouns**
2. **Using Phrases**

1. Using pronouns

■ A simple way of emphasizing one part of a sentence is to express it twice, once in the normal manner and once in the form of a stressed pronoun. The pronoun obviously has to be of the same kind as the part of the sentence being stressed. The part of the sentence being emphasized is then separated from the rest of the sentence by a comma.

This pronoun can be:

– a subject or object pronoun (*see* PRONOUNS, **1.**):

Paul, je l'ai appelé hier. (I called *Paul* yesterday.)
Moi, j'ai appelé Paul hier. (*I* called Paul yesterday.)
Moi, je l'ai appelé hier, *Paul*. (*I* called *Paul* yesterday.)
Je *lui* ai dit de se taire, *à Henri*. (I told *Henri* to be quiet.)

– one of the adverbial pronouns en and y (*see* PRONOUNS, **3.**):

À Londres, j'y vais très souvent. (I go to *London* very often.)
Des dessins animés, il *en* regarde beaucoup. (He watches a lot of *cartoons*.)

– a demonstrative pronoun (*see* PRONOUNS, **6.**):

Faire les courses, ça m'ennuie. (I hate *shopping*.)
Faire les magasins, c'est plus drôle. (*Going round the shops* is more fun.)

■ The item which is separated from the rest of the sentence can be placed before or after the verb:

Cette voiture, elle me plaît beaucoup.
Elle me plaît beaucoup, *cette voiture*.

■ A personal pronoun can also be emphasized by being expressed twice, once in its normal form and once in its stressed form. In this case, the *stressed* form of the pronoun is separated off from the rest of the sentence:

Toi, tu **ferais mieux de rester tranquille.**
Eux, ils **s'en sont bien tirés.**

2. Using phrases

■ Another way of emphasizing a part of a sentence (except for a verb) is to use one of the little phrases c'est … qui, c'est … que, voilà … qui, voilà … que, il y a … qui or il y a … que:

Ce n'est pas **lui** *qui* **te contredira.**
C'est **lui** *que* **je vois.**
C'est **à toi** *que* **je m'adresse.**
Voilà **quelqu'un** *qui* **s'y connaît.**
Voilà **des complications** *que* **personne n'avait prévues.**
Il y a **quelqu'un** *qui* **vous demande.**
Il y a **trois ans** *que* **je ne l'ai pas vue.**

■ The phrases can be combined with a stressed pronoun:

Paul, c'est lui que **je préfère.**

NOTE: **C'est** becomes **ce sont** when the item being emphasized is plural. The item must be the subject or direct object of the sentence for **ce sont** to be used:

Ce sont eux **qui vont être en retard.**

BUT

Ce n'est pas **à trois,** *c'est* **à huit qu'ils sont finalement arrivés.**
C'est **à eux que je m'adresse ?**

AGREEMENT OF TENSES

> ## 1. The Tenses of the Indicative and the Conditional
> ## 2. The Tenses of the Subjunctive
>
> *Agreement of tenses* is the name given to the rules governing the choice of tense in a subordinate clause, in relation to the tense which is used in the main clause. The action or the state expressed by the verb in the subordinate clause can be *before*, *at the same time as* or *after* the action or state expressed in the main clause. (*See* CLAUSES for an explanation of the difference between a main and a subordinate clause.)

1. The tenses of the indicative and the conditional

■ If the actions or states expressed in both main and subordinate clauses take place at the same time:

– the tenses of the verbs in both main and subordinate clauses can be the same:

PRESENT + PRESENT:
Je *trouve* qu'il *fait* trop chaud.
Je *suis* sûr qu'il *ment*.
Il *dit* qu'il *adore* ce genre de musique.

IMPERFECT + IMPERFECT:
Je *me disais* justement qu'il *faisait* trop chaud.
Je *croyais* qu'il *mentait*.
Il *prétendait* qu'il *adorait* ce genre de musique.

PERFECT + PERFECT:
J'*ai fait* ce que nous *avons décidé*.
Ils *ont* apparemment *oublié* ce qu'ils nous *ont promis*.
Il *a obtenu* ce qu'elle *a voulu*.

FUTURE + FUTURE
Elle *fera* ce qu'elle *pourra*.
Il vous *dira* ce qu'il *saura*.

> *NOTE*: Remember that in French a future tense is used in a clause of time which refers to a future action:
>
> **Elle vous *téléphonera* dès qu'elle *aura* une minute.** (as soon as she has a minute)

– the tenses of the verbs in both main and subordinate clauses can be different, in which case they can be combined as follows:

FUTURE + PRESENT:

Nous *mangerons* ce qui *reste*.
Vous *direz* ce que vous *savez*.

> *NOTE*: A future tense can never be used instead of a subjunctive after verbs of wishing, statements of necessity and the like (*see* VERBS, **8.**)
>
> **Il *voudra* qu'elle se *dépêche*.**
> **Il *faudra* qu'elle *parte*.**

PERFECT + IMPERFECT:

J'*ai pensé* qu'il *valait* mieux ne rien dire.
Tout le monde *a cru* qu'il *mentait*.
J'*ai fait* ce qu'on me *demandait* de faire.

PAST HISTORIC + IMPERFECT (only in written French):

Je *pensai* donc qu'il *valait* mieux ne rien dire.
Ils *écoutèrent* attentivement ce qu'il *avait* à leur dire.

IMPERFECT + PERFECT:

Je *travaillais* quand ils *sont arrivés*.
Tu *dormais* quand l'orage *a éclaté*.

■ The action or state expressed in the main clause can occur *before* that of the subordinate clause. In such cases the following combinations are possible:

PRESENT + FUTURE:

Je *pense* qu'elles *viendront*.
Je *crois* qu'il se *dépêchera*.
Il *dit* qu'elle *sera* là.

PRESENT + CONDITIONAL PRESENT:

Tu *crois* qu'il *serait* capable de s'en sortir tout seul ?

IMPERFECT + CONDITIONAL PRESENT:

Je *savais* bien que ce *serait* trop tard.

Je *croyais* qu'il ne *voudrait* pas.

PERFECT + CONDITIONAL PRESENT:

J'*ai pensé* qu'il le *ferait*.

J'*ai deviné* ce qui se *passerait*.

NOTE:

* If the verb in the main clause is in the present indicative, the fact that the action of the subordinate clause takes place later is shown by the use of the future tense:

Je *pense* que tout se *passera* bien.

Je *sais* qu'il le *fera*.

* If the verb in the main clause is in a past tense, the fact that the action of the subordinate clause takes place later is shown by the use of the conditional:

Je *pensais* que tout se *passerait* bien.

Je *savais* qu'il le *ferait*.

■ If the action or state expressed in the main clause occurs *after* that of the subordinate clause, the tense used in the subordinate clause can be:

– a simple tense (i.e. one which consists of only one word):

PRESENT + IMPERFECT:

Je *suis* sûre qu'il *disait* vrai.

Je *répète* ce qu'il me *racontait*.

FUTURE + IMPERFECT:

Je *ferai* ce qu'il m'*expliquait*.

J'*apprendrai* tout ça par cœur comme il me le *conseillait*.

– a compound tense (i.e. one which consists of more than one word):

PRESENT + PERFECT:

Je *crois* qu'il *a terminé*.

Elle *apprécie* ce qu'ils *ont fait*.

PRESENT + FUTURE PERFECT:

Je ne *sais* pas ce qu'elle *aura dit*.

J'*essaie* de deviner ce qu'il *aura découvert*.

PRESENT + CONDITIONAL PERFECT:

Je *pense* qu'il *aurait eu* peur.

Tu *crois* qu'il *aurait dû* en parler d'abord ?

FUTURE + FUTURE PERFECT:
Je vous *préviendrai* dès qu'elle *aura terminé*.
Je vous *transmettrai* fidèlement tout ce qu'il m'*aura dit*.

IMPERFECT + PLUPERFECT:
Tu *croyais* qu'elle *avait menti*.
Elle *était* toute pâle parce qu'elle *avait eu* peur.

IMPERFECT + CONDITIONAL PERFECT:
Je *pensais* qu'il *serait venu*.
J'*étais* pourtant certaine qu'il *aurait refusé*.

PERFECT + PLUPERFECT:
J'*ai cru* qu'il ne m'*avait pas vue*.
J'*ai perdu* ce qu'il m'*avait donné*.

PERFECT + CONDITIONAL PERFECT:
J'*ai cru* qu'il me l'*aurait pardonné*.
J'*ai entendu* dire qu'on l'*aurait volé*.

NOTE: The use of a compound tense indicates that the actions in question are seen as over and done with:

Je me demande ce que tu en *penses*. → **Je me demande ce que tu en *as pensé*.**
Je me suis demandé ce que tu en *pensais*. → **Je me suis demandé ce que tu en *avais pensé*.**

■ Si is used to introduce conditional subordinate clauses. The following combinations of tenses can be found:

PRESENT + PRESENT:
Nous *partons*, si tu *es* d'accord.
***Dis*-le-moi, si tu ne *comprends* pas.**

PRESENT + PERFECT:
S'il s'*est trompé*, il s'en *excuse*.

FUTURE + PRESENT:
Nous n'*aurons* pas à nous dépêcher, s'il *arrive* à l'heure.
Si tu *perds*, tu *seras* déçu.

CONDITIONAL PRESENT + IMPERFECT:

Nous ne *verrions* pas la fin, si nous *partions*.

Si tu *écoutais*, tu *comprendrais*.

FUTURE PERFECT + PERFECT:

Le match *aura eu* lieu, surtout s'il *a fait* beau.

S'il *a plu*, il *aura été* annulé.

CONDITIONAL PERFECT + PLUPERFECT:

Nous *serions venus* si on nous *avait prévenus*.

S'il nous l'*avait dit*, nous n'*aurions* pas *fait* d'erreur.

NOTE:

* If the verb in a conditional clause introduced by **si** is in the imperfect, the verb in the main clause is almost always in the conditional present:

Il *dormirait* s'il le *pouvait*.

S'il *voulait*, il *serait* plus gentil.

* If the verb in the conditional clause is in the pluperfect, the verb in the main clause is almost always in the conditional perfect:

Il *aurait dormi* s'il l'*avait pu*.

S'il l'*avait voulu*, il *aurait été* plus gentil.

2. The tenses of the subjunctive

■ The present subjunctive is used in the subordinate clause when the verb in the main clause is in the present or future indicative:

Je *redoute* qu'il *vienne*.

Je lui *dirai* qu'il ne *vienne* pas.

■ The perfect subjunctive is commonly used when the verb in the main clause is in a past tense:

Je *redoutais* qu'il ne *soit parti* sans moi.

Je *souhaitais* qu'il *ait réussi*.

This is only possible if the action in the subordinate clause takes place before that of the main clause, as in the examples above. Otherwise the present subjunctive is used, even when the verb in the main clause is in a past tense:

Il *voulait* que je le *fasse*. (He wanted me to do it.)

Je *craignais* qu'il ne *soit* pas d'accord. (I was afraid he wouldn't agree.)

In literary French, the imperfect subjunctive may still be found:

Je *craignais* qu'il ne *fût* pas d'accord.

REPORTED SPEECH

> **1. Direct Speech**
>
> **2. Indirect Speech**
>
> Reported speech is repeating what someone said in the past. There are two different kinds: *direct speech* and indirect speech.
>
> **Il m'a dit : 'Je te rappellerai demain.'** (= direct speech)
> **Il m'a dit qu'il me rappellerait demain.** (= indirect speech)

1. Direct speech

■ In direct speech the original words are repeated in exactly the same way as they were originally said:

Marie m'a dit : 'Tu n'as pas changé du tout !'

■ The person whose speech is being reported can be the same as the person speaking:

Je me suis demandé : 'Est-ce que c'est vrai ?'

However, it is most often other people whose words are being quoted:

Je ne me souviens plus de ce qu'il m'a dit, si c'était : 'Tu devrais lui en parler', ou bien : 'Je suis sûr que tu lui en as déjà parlé.'

■ In both French and English, direct speech is indicated by quotation marks around the words quoted.

■ In written French, the change from one speaker to another is indicated by a dash. The quotation marks are closed only at the end of an unbroken section of conversation, not at the end of each speaker's comments as in English:

'C'est bizarre !
- Pourquoi ?
- Je ne sais pas, je trouve ça surprenant.'

■ Sections of the conversation can be introduced or followed by verbs such as dire, demander, s'écrier etc.:

> **'Qu'en pensez-vous ?', demanda-t-elle.**
> **'Encore !', s'écria-t-il.**

> *NOTE:* Remember that the normal order of subject and verb is inverted when the verb follows direct speech.

2. Indirect speech

■ In indirect speech the words actually spoken are changed and appear in a subordinate clause which is introduced by a verb of saying of some kind:

> **Elle m'a annoncé qu'elle allait se marier.**
> **Il m'a dit à quel point il était déçu.**

■ Indirect speech is very common in story-telling:

> **Je n'ai pas dit qu'il ne se sentait pas bien, mais qu'il était un peu déprimé.**

ACCENTS, THE DIAERESIS AND THE CEDILLA

1. **Accents**
   é ▲ è ▲ ê
2. **The Diaeresis**
   ï ▲ ë
3. **The Cedilla**
   ç

1. Accents

■ Accents are placed on vowels to show how the vowel is to be pronounced.

■ There are three kinds of accent in French:

– the *acute*, as in é

– the *grave*, as in è

– the *circumflex*, as in ê.

■ The table below shows the possible combinations of accents and vowels:

	a	e	i	o	u
acute		é			
grave	à	è			ù
circumflex	â	ê	î	ô	û

1.1 The acute

The acute accent is found only on the vowel e. It indicates the sound [e]:

> **allongé** [alɔ̃ʒe]
> **été** [ete]
> **départ** [depar]

NOTE: In the following words the acute does not indicate a closed e [e], but an open e [ɛ]:

> **événement** [evenmã] (second é only)
> **réglementaire** [rɛɡləmãtɛr]

1.2 The grave

■ On an e, the grave accent indicates the sound [ɛ]:

   très [trɛ]
   près [prɛ]
   règle [rɛgl]

■ On an a or a u, it is used to differentiate between words which would otherwise be written the same:

– a and à

   Elle *a* voulu aller *à* la mer.

– la and là

   ***La* valise est *là*.**

– ou and où

   Tu viens *ou* non ?
   Va *où* tu veux.

The vowels à and ù are pronounced the same as a and u. The accent has no effect on pronunciation; it is there merely to distinguish the words in writing.

1.3 The circumflex

■ On an e, the circumflex accent indicates the sound [ɛ]:

   être [ɛtr]
   forêt [fɔrɛ]
   vêtu [vɛty]

■ On an a, it indicates a more open sound. The difference between â and a is rather slight and is not observed by all speakers.

   câble [kabl]
   grâce [gras]

■ On an o, it indicates the sound [o]:

   pôle [pol]
   côté [kote]

■ On an i, the circumflex does not alter pronunciation at all. The letters i and î – and ai and aî – are pronounced in exactly the same way:

   dîner [dine]
   naître [nɛtr]

■ On a u, it does not alter the pronunciation at all. The letters u and û are pronounced in exactly the same way:

   sûr [syr]
   goût [gu]

> *NOTE:*
> * Remember the spelling of the following word:
>
> **piqûre** [pikyr]
>
> * A circumflex is always found on the first and second persons plural of the past historic:
>
> **faire** → nous fîmes, vous fîtes
> **avoir** → nous eûmes, vous eûtes
>
> * The circumflex is also used to distinguish the possessive adjectives **notre** and **votre** from the corresponding possessive pronouns **le nôtre** and **le vôtre**.
>
> * Verbs in **-aître** and **-oître** take a circumflex in all those forms where an **i** comes before a **t**:
>
> **Il le connaît.**

2. The diaeresis

■ When it is placed above an i, the diaeresis indicates that the i and the preceding vowel have to be pronounced separately:

haïr ['air]
naïf [naif]
coïncidence [koɛ̃sidɑ̃s]

■ When it is placed on an e, the diaeresis indicates that the e of the feminine of words ending in -gu is not pronounced:

ambigu	→	ambiguë
aigu	→	aiguë
exigu	→	exiguë

3. The cedilla

■ A cedilla is placed under the letter c in front of the vowels a, u and o to indicate that the c is to be pronounced [s] and not [k]:

leçon [ləsɔ̃]
façade [fasad]
déçu [desy]

■ In front of e and i, c is pronounced [s] and the cedilla is not required:

face [fas]
ceci [səsi]

GUIDE TO SPELLING AND PRONUNCIATION

> 1. The International Phonetic Alphabet
> 2. The French Alphabet

1. The International Phonetic Alphabet

The symbols given in square brackets below come from the International Phonetic Alphabet (IPA). This is a special alphabet which indicates sounds rather than how words are spelt. Many consonant sounds in IPA are the same as they are in the English alphabet, as the following examples will show:

English	*French*
pat [pæt]	**patte** [pat]
set [sɛt]	**cette** [sɛt]
feel [fiːl]	**file** [fil]

However, there are a few special symbols for consonants:

[ʒ] is the sound of s in **measure** (English) or the j in **jaune** (French).
[ʃ] is the sound of sh in **shoe** (English) or the ch in **choux** (French).
[j] is the sound of y in **yes** (English) or in **payer** (French).
[ɲ] is similar to the sound of ni in **onion** (English) but is pronounced more as a single sound. It is the sound of gn in words such as **agneau**, **magnifique** in French.

The symbols for vowels are a little more complex.

[a] is a short sound, like the a in **lac** and **papillon**.
[ɑ] is slightly longer, like the a in **tas**, **âme**.
[ɛ] is the sound of e in **être** and **dette** (French).
[e] is the sound of e in the French words **des**, **aller** and **année**.
[ɔ] is similar to the sound of o in **pompom** (English). It is found in French words like **gomme** and **pomme**.
[o] is the vowel sound in such French words as **eau**, **beau** and a**u**tre.
[u] is the sound of oo in **cool** (English) and the **ou** of **coule** (French).

[ɥ] is a very light [w] sound with no equivalent in English. It is found with [i] in French words like **fuite** and **bruit**.

[y] This sound does not exist in Standard English. It is the sound of **u** in French words such as **sur**, **dur** and so on.

[i] is the sound of ea in **meal** (English) and i in **mille** (French).

[ø] is not unlike the vowel sound of the English word **heard**. It is the sound of eu in French **eux** and **jeu**.

[œ] is a slightly more open version of [ø], as in French **heure** and **œuf**.

[ə] is the sound of the e in **father** (English) and **de**, **le** etc. in French.

A tilde (~) placed over a vowel indicates that it is a nasal vowel. For example, the pronunciation of **blanc** is indicated as [blɑ̃] in the IPA.

An apostrophe appearing at the beginning of the IPA symbols for a word means that an s at the end of the previous word would not be pronounced, even though the word in question begins with a vowel. For example, the word **héros** is pronounced ['ero]. This means that in **les héros**, the s at the end of **les** is not pronounced. In fact, [lezero] is the correct pronunciation for **les zéros** (the zeroes).

2. The French alphabet

A

a indicates the sound [a]: **ballon**.

It also indicates the sound [ɑ], often, but not always, shown by the addition of a circumflex: **pâte**, **bas**.

Before the nasal consonant n, a can be pronounced [ɑ̃]: **ancien**.

If a is followed by a double n, it is pronounced [a]: **année**.

ai is pronounced [e]: **aimer**.

aï is pronounced [ai]: **naïve**.

ain is pronounced [ɛ̃]: **châtain**.

B

b indicates the sound [b]: **bac**, **bébé**, **bouche**.

> *NOTE:* **B** is not pronounced at the end of **plomb** but *is* pronounced at the end of **snob**, **nabab**, **baobab**.

C

c indicates the sound [k] before the vowels a, o and u: carrefour, coin, curieux.

c indicates the sound [s] before the vowels e and i and also before y: ceinture, cintre, cyprès.

Before a, o and u the sound [s] is written ç (c cédille): ça, façon, il a reçu.

ch is almost always pronounced [ʃ]: chaud, cheval.

> NOTE: In the words **chaos**, **chloroforme**, **chœur**, **chrétien**, **chrome** and **chronique**, **ch** is pronounced [k].

D

d indicates the sound [d]: grandir.

d is always pronounced, unless it constitutes the last letter of a word: grand, bond.

d at the end of a word is pronounced [t] when it is in liaison with the following vowel:

Qu'attend-elle ? [katɑ̃tɛl]
un grand écrivain [œ̃grɑ̃tekrivɛ̃]

E

The letter e is the most commonly used letter in French.

1. Unaccented E

e indicates the sound [ə], known as **mute e**: je, revenir.

e is pronounced [e] before final r: chanter, léger.

e is pronounced [e] before final z: chez, aimez.

e is pronounced [e] before final s: les, des.

e is pronounced [ɛ] before a double consonant: elle, benne.

unless this double consonant is a double s or m inside a word: ressembler [rəsɑ̃ble], emmener [ɑ̃mne].

e is pronounced [ɛ] before a final voiced consonant (in other words, a consonant which is actually pronounced): sel, fer.

e is pronounced [a] before -mme and -mment: femme, violemment.

en at the beginning of certain words is pronounced [ã]: s'ennuyer.

en is pronounced [ɛ̃] unless the n is followed by another consonant: examen.

emb, emp or emm is pronounced [ã]: embarrasser, emporter, emmener.

ei is pronounced [ɛ]: peine, neige.

eu is pronounced [œ]: heure, or [ø]: feu, jeu.

œ is pronounced [œ]: œil.

œu is pronounced [œ]: œuvre, sœur, œuf or [ø]: œufs.

> NOTE: E has no effect at all on the pronunciation of the other vowel in eu [y], dévouement [devumã], il nie [ni], scie [si].

2. E acute (é)

é indicates the sound [e]: été.

(*See* Accents.)

3. E grave (è) and e circumflex (ê)

è and ê indicate the sound [ɛ]: très, être.

(*See* Accents.)

F

f indicates the sound [f]: faire, finir.

> NOTE:
> * F is not pronounced at the end of certain words such as clef [kle], nerf [nɛr], œufs [ø], bœufs [bø].
> * F is pronounced [v] in certain cases of liaison:
>
>   Il a neuf ans. [nœvã]
>   Il est neuf heures. [nœvœr]

G

The letter g corresponds to the sound [g] before a, o, u: gare, gomme, guttural.

It indicates the sound [ʒ] before e and i: gentil, girouette.

To indicate the sound [g] before e and i, a u is inserted between the g and the vowel: **guérir, guitare**.

To indicate the sound [ʒ] before a, o and u, an e is inserted between the g and the vowel: **il neigeait, nous mangeons**.

gn corresponds to the sound [ɲ]: **oignon, règne, peigne**.

g is not pronounced at the end of certain words: **sang, poing**.

> *NOTE:*
> * In **second** [səgɔ̃], and **seconde** [səgɔ̃d], the c corresponds to a **g**.
> * In **vingt** and **doigt**, neither the **g** nor the **t** is pronounced.

H

The letter h is never pronounced in French.

The h known as *aspirate h* indicates that a word beginning with this type of h will not form a liaison with the preceding word. If the preceding word is an article, it will not be elided either, i.e. **le** and **la** will not become **l'**. The fact that an h is aspirate is indicated by ['] in phonetics:

un haricot [œ̃ 'ariko] ▲ **le hérisson** [lə 'erisɔ̃]

The h known as *mute h* indicates that a word beginning with this type of h does form a liaison with the preceding word. If this word is an article, it will be elided:

une hésitation [yn ezitasjɔ̃] ▲ **l'hésitation** [lezitasjɔ̃]

For the pronunciation of ch, see **C** above.

I

i indicates the sound [i].

(*See* **Accents**.)

i diaeresis (ï) is pronounced separately from the vowel preceding it: **naïf, coïncidence**.

(*See* **A** and ACCENTS, THE DIAERESIS AND THE CEDILLA, **2**.)

J

j indicates the sound [ʒ]: **jeune**.

K

k indicates the sound [k]: képi, kangourou.

L

l indicates the sound [l]: laver, voile, île.
ll indicates the sound [l]: ville, and the sound [j]: fille.
eill indicates the sound [ɛj]: veille.
ieill indicates the sound [jɛj]: vieille.

M

m indicates the sound [m]: même, maman.
mm also indicates the sound [m]: emmener.
em corresponds to the sound [ãm] when followed by a consonant: emmener, emporter, embrouiller.
(*See* E.)

N

n indicates the sound [n]: nager.
When combined with a preceding a, e, i, o or u, n indicates the sounds:
– [ã]: fantaisie
– [ã]: envie
– [ɛ̃]: brin, fin
– [ɔ̃]: son
– [œ̃]: brun.
(*See* G.)

O

o can be pronounced [ɔ]: soleil.
o can also be pronounced [o]: pôle.
Before the nasal consonants n and m (but not nn or mm), o is pronounced [ɔ̃]: non, nom.
oi is pronounced [wa]: croire
ou is pronounced [u]: nous
oy is pronounced [waj]: noyer

œ is pronounced [œ]: œil

œu is pronounced [œ]: œuvre, sœur, œuf or [ø]: œufs.

P

p indicates the sound [p]: apercevoir, apte.

pp is pronounced in the same way as p: apporter.

In the middle or at the end of a word, p can sometimes be unpronounced: compter [kɔ̃te], champ [ʃɑ̃].

Q

The letter q is always followed by the vowel u.

qu indicates the sound [k]: quoi, quartier.

R

r indicates the sound [r]: revenir, sortir.

rr also indicates the sound [r]: guerre.

When it is preceded by an e at the end of a word, r is not pronounced but indicates that the e *is* pronounced [e]: aimer.

> *NOTE:* When **er** appears at the end of a word of foreign origin, it *is* pronounced:
>
> **le leader** [lidœr] ▲ **le speaker** [spikœr]

S

s indicates the sound [s]: soir, semblable.

s between two vowels indicates the sound [z]: ciseaux.

ss between two vowels indicates the sound [s]: ressembler, casser.

s is not pronounced at the end of a word: pas, aimais, les (<u>BUT</u> hélas [elas], jadis [ʒadis] and cassis [kasis]).

> *NOTE:* The **s** at the end of **os** [ɔs] is pronounced when the noun is singular. In the plural it is pronounced [o]

T

t indicates the sound [t]: tenir, apte.

tt also indicates the sound [t]: attacher.

t is not pronounced at the end of a word: lait, faisait, forêt (BUT sept [sɛt], mat [mat] and zut [zyt]).

U

u indicates the sound [y]: unique.

un is pronounced [œ̃] when it is not followed by a vowel: brun. (*See* **Accents.**)

ou is pronounced [u]: nous.

ui is pronounced [ɥi]: aujourd'hui.

eu is pronounced [ø]: eux.

V

v indicates the sound [v]: venir.

W

w indicates the sound [v]: wagon.

X

x indicates the sound [gz]: exercice.

x also indicates the sounds [ks]: excuse, explication, and [z]: deuxième, sixième.

Y

y indicates the sound [i]: hydrater.

oy is pronounced [waj]: noyer.

ay is pronounced [ej]: ayez.

If it is followed by a consonant, ay is pronounced [ei]: pays, paysage.

uy is pronounced [ɥij]: bruyant.

Z

z indicates the sound [z]: zèbre.

z after e is not pronounced at the end of a word: laissez, assez.

GLOSSARY

Words in *italics* are defined in their alphabetical position in this glossary.

Active (voice)

The active voice is the form in which *verbs* most often appear. In the active voice the *subject* of the verb carries out the action of the verb, or is in the state expressed by the verb; in the *passive* voice the action of the verb is carried out on the subject:

> *Il a acheté* un journal.
> *Elle n'aime pas* le bruit.

Adjectival clauses

Adjectival clauses are *subordinate clauses* introduced by a relative *pronoun* (in English who, which and so on; in French qui, que and complex forms such as lequel). Like adjectives, they describe a *noun*. This noun is called the *antecedent*:

> Le pont *que tu vois là-bas* est le plus ancien de Paris.
> Le plat *qui est dans le four* brûle.
> Cette personne, *que je ne connaissais pas,* m'a arrêtée dans la rue.
> Leurs amis, *qui habitaient à côté,* n'étaient pas là.

Adjectives

Adjectives are words which are used to describe a *noun*, or alternatively to define it in some way (as in the case of *possessives*, *demonstratives*, numerals or indefinite adjectives like quelque, plusieurs etc.).

Adjectives can be linked to the noun in one of two ways:

– they appear immediately before or after the noun:

> un ciel *bleu* ▲ une pêche *mûre* ▲ un *ancien* ami

– they are linked to the noun by the verb être or verbs such as sembler or paraître:

> Les nuages sont *menaçants.*
> Elles sont *pressées.*

Adverbial phrases and clauses

Adverbial phrases can be of time, place, manner, cause, purpose, consequence, amount or means. They have the same function as *adverbs* in that they provide additional information regarding the circumstances in which the action of the main *clause* is carried out:

> **Ils se sont levés *de bonne heure*.**
> **Je dois être *à la gare vers six heures*.**

Adverbial clauses also provide additional information regarding the circumstances in which the action of the main clause is carried out:

> **Je lui parlerai *quand il arrivera*.**

Adverbs

Adverbs provide additional information about the way in which the action of a *verb* is carried out, or the broader circumstances in which it takes place. Adverbs are always *invariable* and can affect the meaning of:

– the entire sentence:

> **Heureusement, il a fait beau.**
> **J'ai lu ce livre *aujourd'hui*.**

– the verb:

> **Il a parlé *machinalement*.**
> **Elle court *vite*.**

– an *adjective* or another adverb:

> **C'est *vraiment* facile.**
> **Ils ont *vraiment* bien réussi.**

When an adverb relates to an entire sentence it can appear at various points in the sentence, although its position changes the emphasis somewhat:

> **Il fait chaud *aujourd'hui*.** → **Aujourd'hui, il fait chaud.**

Agent

In the *passive* voice, the agent is the person or thing which carries out the action of the *verb*. In English it is introduced by the word **by**, and in French by **par** or, less frequently, by **de**:

> **Cette maison a été conçue *par* un grand architecte.**
> **Il est apprécié *de* ses amis.**

Animate nouns

An animate *noun* refers to a human being or an animal, in other words to living things.
⇨ **Inanimate nouns**

Antecedents

The antecedent is the *noun* or *pronoun* described by an *adjectival clause*:

> *La personne* **qui devait vous recevoir vous attend.**

Apposition

An *adjective*, *noun* or noun group is in apposition if it is placed after another noun or noun group in order to provide more information about it. Words or phrases in apposition are always separated off from the rest of the sentence by commas:

> **Pierre,** *méfiant*, **n'a pas accepté.**
> **M. Durand,** *le directeur des ventes*, **assistera à la réunion.**

Articles

Articles belong to the class of *determiners*. There are three types of article in French: the definite article, **le, la, l', les** (the in English); the indefinite article, **un, une, des** (a, an in English); and the partitive article, **du, de la, de l', des** (which corresponds roughly to some in English, though it is not always translated).

Aspect

The aspect of a *verb* determines whether the action or state expressed by the verb is seen as completed or not. Strictly speaking there are no formal indications of aspect in French. Aspect is expressed mostly by the use of:
– the compound form of verbs, which indicates that the action has been completed:

> **Ils** *ont dîné*.
> **Elle** *aura compris*.

– phrases such as **aller** + INFINITIVE or **être sur le point de** + INFINITIVE, which indicate that the action has not yet started:

> **Nous** *allons commencer*.

Il *est sur le point de s'endormir.*

– the phrase être en train de + INFINITIVE, which indicates that the action is currently taking place. This is the French form of the *progressive* in English (we are coming, they were singing):

Nous *sommes en train de nous préparer.*
Ils *sont en train de jouer.*

Aspirate h

An aspirate h is an h at the beginning of a word which prevents *liaison* from occurring.

Auxiliaries

The auxiliaries are *verbs* which, as well as having their normal meanings, can also be used to form other compound verbs (i.e. verbs consisting of more than one word). They can have a different meaning depending on whether they are used as auxiliaries or as normal verbs:

Faire as a normal verb:

Ils *ont fait* des gâteaux. (faire = to make)

Faire as an auxiliary:

Le bébé *a fait tomber* son jouet. (faire tomber = to knock over)

The main auxiliaries, used to form all the compound *tenses* and also the *passive voice*, are avoir and être. They are followed by a past *participle*:

Ils *sont* tombés.
Elles *ont* joué.
Tu t'*es* trompé.
Je me *suis* bien amusée.

Faire, laisser, devoir, savoir, falloir and pouvoir can also function as auxiliaries. The verb following them is always in the *infinitive*:

J'ai *fait repeindre* ma chambre.
Elle *doit se coucher*.
Tu *peux sortir*.

Clauses

A clause is a group of words which makes sense; one of the group is always a *verb*. In a complex sentence there can be two or more clauses, linked either by coordinating or by subordinating *conjunctions*.

Complements

There are two types of complement: *subject* and direct *object*.

When it appears as the subject, the complement is found after the *verb* être or after verbs of state. It is usually a *noun* or an *adjective*:

Il est *professeur*.
Ses joues sont *rouges*.

When it appears as an object, the complement is found after verbs expressing an opinion or judgment. It then describes the object of those verbs:

Je *le* crois *honnête*.
Il *l'*a trouvée *gentille*.

Compound nouns

A compound *noun* is a noun which consists of more than one word. Sometimes the different words are linked by *prepositions*:

une tasse à thé (a tea cup)
une cuillère en bois (a wooden spoon)

Sometimes the two words are simply placed side by side:

un facteur clé (a key factor)

Conditional

The conditional is the equivalent of the *tense* formed in English with would (I would go, you would think and so on). Its two main uses are in conditional sentences and in *indirect speech*:

Je l'*achèterais* si j'avais assez d'argent.
Il m'avait dit qu'il *irait* le lendemain.

Conjugations

The conjugation of a *verb* comprises all the forms of all the *tenses*, *moods*, voices (see *Active (voice)* and *Passive (voice)*) and *participles* of that verb. There are three main conjugations in French, though the conjugation of some verbs can be irregular in a number of ways. For more information on the conjugation of specific verbs, consult the verb tables (VERBS, **10.**).

Conjunctions

Conjunctions are used to link two words, two phrases or two *clauses*. There are two kinds of conjunction:

– coordinating conjunctions, which link two elements of the same kind (two *nouns*, two *adjectives*, two main *clauses*, two *subordinate clauses*):

> la faune *et* la flore ▲ fromage *ou* dessert
> Elle est jeune *et* jolie.
> Ces gens sont aimables *et* leurs enfants très gentils.
> La personne que j'ai rencontrée *et* qui m'a dit que vous étiez là est sympathique.

– subordinating conjunctions which link a subordinate clause to a main clause:

> Il nous rappelle sans cesse *qu'*il ne faut rien oublier.
> Je crois *qu'*il est rentré.

Contraction

Contraction is a process whereby two words join together to form one. It takes place in the masculine singular and plural and the feminine plural of the partitive *article*: de le and de les are replaced by du and des. It is also found in the masculine singular and masculine and feminine plural of the definite article used with the *preposition* à: à le and à les are always replaced by au or aux:

> *du* pain ▲ *du* lait ▲ *des* gâteaux ▲ *des* fraises
> *au* travail ▲ *aux* champs ▲ *aux* courses de chevaux

Note, however, that contraction takes place only when le or les are definite articles. If they are used as object *pronouns*, then contraction never takes place:

> J'ai oublié *de le* nettoyer. (I forgot to clean it.)
> Il n'est pas arrivé *à le* faire. (He did not manage to do it.)

Countable nouns

Countable *nouns* refer, as the name suggests, to items which can be counted one by one. They can be preceded by a numeral:

deux *arbres* ▲ **une** *table* ▲ **mille** *personnes*

⇨ Uncountable nouns

Demonstratives

The demonstrative *adjectives* in English are this, that, those and these, while the demonstrative *pronouns* are this one, that one and so on. In French there are also demonstrative adjectives and pronouns. Demonstrative adjectives belong to the category of *determiners*. Demonstrative adjectives and pronouns single out the item they describe or stand for from all other items of its kind:

ce **tableau** ▲ *cet* **appartement**
celui-ci ▲ *celui-là*

Determiners

Determiners are usually placed in front of the *noun*, and indicate its *gender* as well as whether it is singular or plural. They include various kinds of word, most notably *articles, demonstrative adjectives, possessive adjectives* and numerals:

les **personnes** ▲ *les autres* **personnes** ▲ *ces* **arbres** ▲ *ses* **jouets** ▲
quatre **couleurs**

Nouns rarely appear without a determiner of some kind. This can, however, happen when:

– the noun is a *complement* after the verb être:

Il est *dentiste*.
Elle est *chirurgien*.
Nous sommes *professeurs*.

– when the noun indicates what something is made of:

une chaise en *fer* ▲ **un tuyau en** *plastique* ▲ **un panier d'***osier*

– after the *preposition* sans:

Je m'en vais sans *inquiétude*.
Il est parti sans *crainte*.

Diaeresis

A diaeresis consists of two points written above a vowel. In French, it appears only above an i and an e. Above an i it indicates that this vowel is to be pronounced separately from the vowel in front of it (for example, haïr). It appears above an e only as part of the ending -guë at the end of a feminine *adjective*. It indicates that the preceding u is to be pronounced as a separate vowel. The e itself remains unpronounced.

Direct objects
⇨ Objects.

Direct speech

Direct speech is a form of reported speech in which the actual words originally spoken are reproduced literally. As in English, direct speech in French is enclosed within quotation marks:

'Venez tout de suite !', a-t-il dit.

⇨ Indirect speech

Endings

Endings, or inflection, are added to the stem of a *noun* to indicate *gender* and *number,* and to the stem of a *verb* to indicate person, number, *tense* and *mood*:

je déjeun*ais* ▲ il défendr*ait* ▲ elle interdir*a*

Feminines

All variable words have a masculine and a feminine form. The feminine is usually, but not always, indicated by the addition of an -e to the masculine form:

une jolie fille ▲ une pomme vert*e*
Elles ont l'air content*es*.

Function

The function of a word is the role it plays in the sentence. The main functions are *subject*, *verb*, *complement*, *object* and *adjective*.

Gender

In English, only *nouns* referring to people or animals can be masculine or feminine. All other nouns are neuter and are represented by the *pronoun* it. In French all nouns are either masculine or feminine, whether they refer to people, animals, objects, ideas or whatever. They must then be represented by the appropriate masculine or feminine pronoun.

There are, however, a small number of indefinite pronouns which can be neuter: ceci, cela etc.

Gerunds

The gerund consists of the *preposition* en followed by either the present or the perfect *participle*:

en courant ▲ en finissant ▲ en ayant pensé ▲ en étant resté

It can be the equivalent of on doing, while doing or by doing in English.
⇨ **Moods**

Imperative

The imperative is the *mood* which is used to give orders. It has very few forms (1st person plural, 2nd person singular and plural). It has a present and a perfect form:

va ▲ pars ▲ allons
sois arrivé ▲ aie terminé

Impersonal

Impersonal *verbs* only ever appear in the 3rd person singular. In English their subject is always it or there, and in French they always take the subject *pronoun* il. Some verbs such as falloir, and verbs relating to the weather such as pleuvoir, neiger and so on, only have impersonal forms.

Inanimate nouns

An inanimate *noun* refers to things and not to people or animals.
⇨ **Animate nouns**

Indicative

The indicative is used to present an action or a state as a fact. It is the most common *mood* of the *verb*, and is the one with the greatest number of *tenses*: present, past and future.

Indirect objects
⇨ **Objects.**

Indirect speech
Indirect speech is a form of reported speech in which the actual words originally spoken are not reproduced literally. They are changed to become a normal part of the sentence, and are not enclosed within quotation marks:

> **Il nous a demandé ce que nous voulions faire.**

His original words would have been Qu'est-ce que vous voulez faire ?
⇨ **Direct speech**

Infinitive
The infinitive is the equivalent of the to form of the *verb* in English (to do, to buy etc.). In French it ends in -er, -ir, -oir or -re. It can also be used as a *noun*:

> **Il me fait *rire*.**
> ***Nager* est bon pour la santé.**

⇨ **Moods**

Intransitive
An intransitive *verb* cannot take a direct *object*. It can also never appear in the *passive*:

> **Je reviens.**
> **Elle est partie.**
> **Elle est née le 10 juin.**

Invariable words
Invariable words are those such as certain nouns and adjectives (e.g. **chic**) which never change their form, and do not indicate masculine or feminine, singular or plural. *Adverbs, conjunctions* and *prepositions,* as well as *infinitives,* are also invariable.

Liaison

When a word in French begins with a vowel or a *mute h*, the final letter of a preceding word is sometimes pronounced as a result, even if it would not normally be pronounced otherwise. This process is known as liaison. For example, although the final **t** of **vingt** is not normally pronounced, it has to be pronounced in the phrase **vingt heures**. Likewise, the final **s** of **les** is pronounced in the phrase **les huîtres**. Remember that liaison never takes place if a word begins with an *aspirate h*: thus the **s** of **les** is not pronounced in the phrase **les héros**.

Main clauses

A main *clause* is a clause which makes sense on its own. For example, in the sentence **If I have enough money, I will go to France**, **I will go to France** is the main clause since it makes sense by itself.
⇨ **Subordinate clauses**

Moods

The moods are a part of the *conjugation* of a *verb*. There are seven moods in all (*indicative, conditional, subjunctive, imperative*, the *participles*, the *infinitive* and the *gerund*). Together with the *tenses*, they make up all the forms of a verb. While tenses refer primarily to time, moods relate more to whether the action of the verb is being presented as a fact at a given place and time, or whether it is presented as doubtful, hypothetical or unreal in some other way.

There are moods which can take different persons of the verb (indicative, conditional, subjunctive and imperative) and moods which do not take any person of the verb (the infinitive, the participles and the gerund). The indicative has the greatest number of tenses and allows the action of the verb to be placed with the greatest precision in the past, the present or the future. The imperative, the participles, the gerund and the infinitive have very limited conjugations which are unable to place actions precisely in time. It is only the context in which they find themselves which indicates whether they relate to the past, the present or the future.

Morphology

Morphology is the set of rules which govern the way words are formed.

Words can be formed in two different ways: by the addition of *prefixes* and *suffixes*, and by joining two words together to form a new word.

In the case of *nouns* and *verbs*, the part of the word which defines its meaning is called the stem. Prefixes, suffixes and endings are added to the stem to vary the noun or to conjugate a verb.

Mute e

A mute e is an e which is not in fact pronounced. A mute e appears at the end of a word, as in père, tranquille, fleuve and so on. Occasionally it can appear inside a word, as is the case of the second e in lendemain.

Mute h

A mute h is an h at the beginning of a word which allows *liaison*.

Negation

Negation is the process of making a *verb* or other word negative, and is carried out in English by words such as **not**, **never** and so on. In French it is carried out mainly by using ne ... pas and other similar forms (ne ... jamais, ne ... plus, ne ... rien, ne ... personne etc.):

> Elle *n'*est *pas* là.
> Il *ne* pleut *plus*.
> *Ne pas* fumer.

Nouns

Nouns are words which refer to persons or objects, and include names. There are also abstract nouns (which refer to concepts and ideas) and concrete nouns (which refer to tangible objects or persons). Nouns can appear as the *subject*, *object* or *complement* of a *verb*.

Number

Nouns, *adjectives*, *pronouns* and *verbs* in French can all appear in either the singular or the plural. It is important that adjectives agree in *number* with the noun they describe. In other words, if the noun is singular the adjective must be singular, and if the noun is plural the adjective must be plural. Likewise, a singular subject pronoun must be followed by a singular form of the verb.

Objects

The object of a *verb* is the person or thing on whom the action of the verb is carried out. The ability to take a direct object or not defines whether a verb is *transitive* or *intransitive*:

When it is direct, the object follows the verb without a preposition:

> **Elle lit *des livres*.**

When it is indirect, it is linked to the verb by à or de:

> **Il parle *au professeur*.**
> **Je me souviens bien *de* lui.**
> **On ne peut pas compter *sur* elle.**

Participles

In English the present participle is that part of the *verb* which ends in -ing (seeing, hearing etc.), while the past participle ends in -ed or -en (fixed, given), though there are in fact many irregular past participles in English. In French there are also two kinds of participle:

– the present participle ending in -ant, which is also used in forming the *gerund*:

> **(en) partant** ▲ **(en) hésitant** ▲ **(en) grossissant** ▲ **(en) commençant**

– the past participle ending in -é, -i or -u, which is used in forming the compound *tenses*:

> **j'ai *chanté*** ▲ **il aura *reçu*** ▲ **nous avions *aimé*** ▲ **en étant *resté***

There are also a number of irregular past participles in French.

Passive (voice)

The passive is formed in English with the *verb* to be and the past *participle*: the car was sold, the house was built and so on. In French, the passive voice is formed with the *auxiliary* être and the past participle. In the change from *active* to passive, the *object* of the active verb becomes the *subject* of the passive verb. The subject of the active verb becomes the *agent* of the passive verb, although the agent is not always expressed:

> **On a retrouvé sa carte d'identité.** → **Sa carte d'identité *a été* retrouvée.**

Only *transitive* verbs can be put into the passive.

Phrases

Phrases are groups of words which have the same function as a single word of a particular kind. There are:

– adverbial phrases which act as *adverbs*:

    tout de suite ▲ tout à coup ▲ dès que possible ▲ à la rigueur

– verbal phrases which act as *verbs*:

    avoir faim ▲ prendre peur ▲ tenir parole ▲ dire bonjour

– prepositional phrases which act as *prepositions*:

    en dépit de ▲ au devant de ▲ à côté de ▲ au-dessus de

– phrases which act as *conjunctions*:

    dès que ▲ alors que ▲ pendant que

Plurals

In most cases the plural of *nouns* is formed in French by adding an -s to the singular:

    les amis ▲ des tables ▲ ses habits

Sometimes -x is used instead, and it can be accompanied by a change in the root of the noun:

    des chevaux (un cheval) **▲ des choux**

Nouns, *adjectives*, *pronouns*, *verbs* and *participles* used as adjectives can all be put into the plural in French. *Adverbs* and *prepositions* are *invariable*, as are most cardinal numbers.

Possessives

Possessives can be either *pronouns* or *adjectives*. In English the possessive adjectives (sometimes called possessive *determiners*) are **my**, **your** etc., while the possessive pronouns are **mine**, **yours** and so on. In French, possessive adjectives agree in *gender* and *number* with the *noun* they are placed before:

    Ma voiture a été volée.
    Ses amis sont arrivés.
    Leurs enfants sont petits.

Prefixes

Prefixes are added to the beginning of a word to change its meaning.

However, they do not change the grammatical category of the word:

trouver	→	*retrouver*
tourner	→	*détourner*
faire	→	*défaire*
tour	→	*détour* ▲ *retour*

Once a prefix has been added, the meaning of the new word can be completely different from that of the original word:

rangement (= cupboard OR tidying up) → *dérangement* (= bother)

Prepositions

Prepositions and prepositional phrases are used to link groups of words. They can also be used to link a *verb* and its *object*:

Je viens *de* casser un des verres *à* pied.
Elle lui a offert un bouquet *de* roses *pour* son anniversaire.

Progressive

⇨ Aspect

Pronouns

Examples of pronouns in English are I, him, them and so on. Pronouns are used instead of *nouns* or to stand in for a person. They are very varied in form and can be the *subject*, *object* or *complement* of a *verb*. Pronouns are variable words, and agree in *gender* and *number* with the nouns they stand for:

Je vais repasser ma robe. → Je vais *la* repasser.
Il a remercié ses collègues. → Il *les* a remerciés.

Questions

A question can be formed:
– by inverting the order of *subject* and *verb*:

Viendra-t-il ?
Fera-t-il beau ?

– by using est-ce que:

> *Est-ce qu'*il viendra ?
> *Est-ce qu'*il fera beau ?

– by using an interrogative *pronoun*:

> *Qui* viendra ?
> *Que* devient-il ?
> *Quoi ?*

– by using rising intonation, i.e. the voice gets higher at the end of the sentence:

> **Tu viendras ?**
> **Tu me préviendras ?**

Questions can be:

– direct:

> **Est-ce qu'il sera là ?**
> **Que veux-tu ?**

– indirect:

> **Je me demande s'il viendra.**
> **Je ne sais pas s'il est réveillé.**

Reflexive verbs

Reflexive *verbs* are ones which are used with a reflexive *pronoun* (in English myself, yourself and so on). In French there are exclusively reflexive verbs which are only ever used with a reflexive pronoun, and other verbs which may be used with or without the reflexive pronoun but which change their meaning accordingly.

Sentences

A sentence is a group of words which makes sense, and which ends with a full stop. A sentence can be simple or complex. If it is simple it is the equivalent of a *main clause* on its own and will contain only one *verb*. In a complex sentence there are at least two clauses: one main clause and one or more *subordinate clauses*.

Subjects

The subject is the person or thing which carries out the action of the *verb* when the verb is in the *active voice*. All sentences, no matter how short, must contain a subject, even if it is not expressed, as in the case of *imperatives*. It is usually placed before the verb, though it can come after it in certain constructions (as, for example, questions which do not use the phrase est-ce que).

> *Quelqu'un* **chante.**
> *Il* **fait beau.**
> *Ces cerises* **sont très bonnes.**

Subjunctive

The subjunctive is one of the *moods* of the *verb*. It has fewer *tenses* than the *indicative*, lacking in particular a future tense. It is used primarily to express a subjective relationship between the speaker and what he or she is referring to (doubt, fear, possibility etc.), rather than simply presenting things as facts. Its use is also obligatory after certain subordinating *conjunctions*. It can also be used to give a command or to express a theory about something.

Subordinate clauses

A subordinate *clause* cannot stand on its own. It is linked to a *main clause* by a *conjunction*. It can:

– relate to the *verb* in the main clause:

> **Elle prétend** *qu'elle chante faux.*
> **Je ne dis rien** *parce que je suis en colère.*

– relate to the main clause as a whole:

> *Puisqu'il pleut,* **je reste à la maison.**
> *Quoiqu'il advienne,* **je serai là.**
> *S'il est au courant,* **c'est dommage.**

It can also appear as the *subject* of the verb in the main clause:

> *Qu'il vienne* **me paraît improbable.**
> *Qu'il dise cela* **m'étonne.**
> *Que je pense cela ou son contraire* **n'a pas d'importance.**

Suffixes

Suffixes are added to the end of a word. They can bring about a change in the grammatical category of the word:

direct (*adjective*)	→	**direct***ement* (*adverb*)
dessin (*noun*)	→	**dessin***er* (*verb*) ▲ **dessin***ateur* (*noun*)

Syntax

Syntax is the set of rules which govern how words are organized into sentences, the order they appear in and the relationships between them. It also deals with the function of different words. Traditionally it is contrasted with *morphology*, the study of the forms of words.

Tenses

The tenses of a *verb* set the action of that verb in different periods of time (past, present, future). Normally a tense has six forms, one for each person of the verb (three singular and three plural). Simple tenses consist of one word, compound tenses of more than one word. Tenses can appear in different *moods*.

Transitive

A transitive *verb* is a verb which can take a direct *object*.

Uncountable nouns

Uncountable *nouns* are ones which cannot normally be preceded by a numeral:

   l'eau ▲ **le courage** ▲ **la grandeur** ▲ **la farine**

Some words can be either *countable* or uncountable depending on their context and the meaning they carry in that context:

   les bœufs (animals) ≠ **du bœuf** (meat)
   une eau (a mineral water) ≠ **de l'eau** (= in general)

Variable words

⇨ **Invariable words**

Verbs

The verb is one of the main constituent parts of the sentence. It expresses either the action carried out by the *subject*, or the state the subject is in:

Le chat *dort*.
J'ai reçu des fleurs.
Il *a été* amusé.

Verbs fall into two main categories:

– *transitive* verbs, which can take a direct object:

J'ai vu ce film.
Vous *avez terminé* ce roman ?

– *intransitive* verbs, which cannot take a direct object:

Il *court* vite.
Nous *sommes partis* tout de suite.

⇨ **Auxiliaries**

INDEX

Achevé d'imprimer par
l'Imprimerie Hérissey - Évreux
Mai 1995 – N° d'éditeur : 18578
Dépôt légal : Mai 1995 – N° d'imprimeur : 69178
Imprimé en France - (Printed in France)